QUEENS AND EMPRESSES

By the same author

Wives of the Kings of England: From Normans to Stuarts
Wives of the Kings of England: From Hanover to Windsor
Prime Ministers' Wives
Oscar Wilde's Last Chance: The Dreyfus Connection
West Downs: A Portrait of an English Prep School
The Troubled Century: British and World History, 1914–93
The Inimitable P.G. Wodehouse

QUEENS AND EMPRESSES

From Cleopatra to Queen Victoria

Mark Hichens

Book Guild Publishing
Sussex, England

First published in Great Britain in 2010 by
The Book Guild Ltd
Pavilion View
19 New Road
Brighton, BN1 1UF

Typesetting in Times by
Keyboard Services, Luton, Bedfordshire

Printed and bound in Great Britain by
CPI Antony Rowe

A catalogue record for this book is available from
The British Library

ISBN 978 1 84624 533 6

CONTENTS

PREFACE

I swear again I would not be a Queen
For all the world.

So spoke Anne Boleyn in Shakespeare's *Henry VIII* (Act II, scene 3), and many queens must have re-echoed these words. For the lives of most of them have been tempestuous and tragic. Of those set forth in this book, two were executed, one committed suicide, one was divorced and one abdicated. Of those who married, all had unfaithful husbands save Queen Victoria, and she was a widow for twice as long as she was a wife.

Certainly they were a varied lot. Queen Elizabeth, classical scholar and able to speak six languages, was far removed from Catherine I of Russia, the ex-kitchen maid who could not read and write; and Christina the rough and ready hermaphrodite Queen of Sweden was very different from the graceful and beautiful Mary Queen of Scots; as was the tyrannical and lubricious Catherine the Great from the helpless and irresponsible Marie Antoinette; and the conscientious and forthright Maria Theresa bore little resemblance to the duplicitous Catherine de Medici; while a greater contrast between Queen Victoria, 'the Widow of Windsor', and Cleopatra, 'the Serpent of Old Nile', cannot be imagined.

Some queens left behind them great achievements. Queen Elizabeth saw England into a new era characterised by a flourishing of the arts and with peace and order displacing anarchy and civil war. Queen Victoria too changed the face of Britain from profligate and corrupt Regency to respectable and hard-working Victorian; and Catherine the Great left the land mass of Russia enlarged and a major power of Europe; and even Cleopatra, though renowned primarily for salacity, can claim to have warded off Roman suzerainty over Egypt.

As well as successes some queens have had to face up to great failures. Catherine de Medici failed to preserve the Valois dynasty in France. Maria Theresa, despite heroic efforts, failed to prevent the trimming down of her large sprawling empire; Mary Queen of Scots failed to become Queen of England; and Cleopatra failed to establish the Roman-Ptolemaic dynasty on which she had set her heart.

Some queens may have performed great acts of charity, but others have committed terrible crimes. Catherine de Medici was mainly (but not wholly) responsible for the massacre of St Bartholomew's Day, and Catherine the Great had a leading role in the partition of Poland. Queen Elizabeth, though she tried hard to disavow it, must bear the main responsibility for the illegal execution of Mary Queen of Scots, fellow Queen of a sovereign state; and Cleopatra must have been responsible for the murder of a sister and younger brother whom she regarded as rivals.

Domestic bliss was enjoyed by few: not by Catherine de Medici who bore her husband nine children but throughout her married life had to endure the overlordship of her husband's long-term mistress; nor by Catherine I of Russia who could never have supposed that Peter the Great would ever be monogamous. Maria Theresa, while bearing her husband 16 children, was always aware that she did not have his sole attention; and Marie Antoinette had to wait seven years for the consummation of her marriage to Louis XVI, and even then the evidence is that it was a painful and joyless affair. Napoleon and Josephine were certainly passionate at times but at others their marriage, punctuated by long separations and rancorous misunderstandings and blighted by the failure to conceive any children, was rarely on an even keel. Queen Victoria alone had 20 years of marital bliss, sharing her life devotedly with her husband and bearing him nine children.

It would seem then that the words of Anne Boleyn were not unjustified. The glittering clothes and jewellery, the superabundant luxury, the fawning courtiers and the exercise of power have not led to lasting happiness. This has, indeed, been a rare commodity among crowned heads.

1

CLEOPATRA VII, QUEEN OF EGYPT (69–30 BC)

No woman in history has achieved such notoriety as Cleopatra VII, Queen of Egypt and the so-called 'Serpent of Old Nile'. Her love affair with two great Romans, one of whom she brought to ruin, has set her up for all times as the archetypal *femme fatale* – sly, scheming and sex-mad. Over the ages this image has been much embellished in literature, the theatre and the cinema. But it is largely a fallacy. The contemporary evidence is that, although sexually potent, she was not a great beauty, nor was she unduly erotic. For much of her life she was celibate; two of her three marriages were to younger brothers hardly out of childhood and were unlikely to have been consummated; and, apart from Caesar and Antony, she was not known to have had any *grandes affaires*. Her only known children were one by Caesar and three by Antony.

Certainly she had an extraordinary life – adventurous, unstable and not without dark deeds. But there was another side to the coin: she was an adept and conscientious administrator and patriot, striving to keep Egypt clear of Roman domination. But history has been little interested in this.

The Ptolemaic dynasty in Egypt was founded in 323 BC on the death of Alexander the Great and the dissolution of his empire. The first Ptolemy, a Macedonian nobleman, was one of his ablest generals and saw that of all Alexander's provinces Egypt was the most desirable – fertile and easily defended. It was his intention to found a dynasty to take the place of the Pharaohs, and for this he and his successors would have to be invested with divinity, which meant that marriage to mere mortals was impossible, and so incest in the family was rife. The result of such inbreeding was that there had been some bizarre characters and desperate deeds, notably murder of near relatives who might be rivals to the throne.

Cleopatra's father, Ptolemy XII, was a pathetic figure. Weak and ineffective, his great wish was to be left in peace to eat and drink to excess and to play on his flute (hence his nickname 'Auletes' or 'flute player'). But little peace was to be given to him. At the time of his accession in 80 BC the Roman Empire was everywhere expanding, and eyes were being cast on Egypt, 'the jewel of the Mediterranean'. To preserve his throne it became necessary for him to have Roman support, and this was not freely available; it had to be bought. And so much of his reign was spent in Rome, canvassing favour and handing out bribes. But he was to discover that (like Ethelred the Redeless of England) the more he paid out the more was required of him. The only way this money could be found was by ever heavier taxation, which caused bitter discontent so that it became necessary for him once to flee the country. He was restored, however, by the intervention of a Roman army which included a dashing and ambitious young officer, Mark Antony, whose life in later years was to be fatally entangled with Cleopatra's in Egypt.

Ptolemy XII died in 51 BC. In his will he bequeathed his throne jointly to Cleopatra, then aged 18, and her brother Ptolemy XIII, eight years younger, who was also her husband. There was little likelihood that the two would coexist peacefully. Ptolemy had been left in the care of three guardians: Achillas a military commander, Theodotus a scholar-cum-lawyer, and Pothinus, a eunuch with a head for finance and a vicious temperament. It soon became evident to Cleopatra that they were out to eliminate her, and she fled to neighbouring Syria where she raised an army and returned to give battle to the forces of Ptolemy; but when in 48 BC the two armies were confronting each other in the Nile delta, there was a historic intervention in Egyptian affairs.

Civil war had been raging in the Roman Empire, but it came to an end in 48 BC with the defeat of Pompey by Caesar at Pharsalus in northern Greece. After the battle Pompey fled to Egypt where he should have found refuge as he had been a patron of Ptolemy XII, but to the guardians of Ptolemy XIII he was a fallen warrior on the losing side, and on landing he was treacherously murdered. If by so doing Ptolemy's guardians hoped to gain the favour of Caesar they were disappointed, for when he arrived in the country a few weeks later and was shown the severed head of Pompey he burst into tears and vented his disgust on the murderers, and ordered the release of Pompey's main supporters.

There was no pressing need for Caesar to stay on in Egypt any longer, as the main reason for his visit was to track down Pompey and prevent him raising another army, but he decided to remain. One reason for this was to raise money of which, as so often, he was desperately short; but he also felt impelled to settle the dispute between Cleopatra and Ptolemy. And so he settled into a royal palace and ordered the two of them to appear before him. Ptolemy and his guardians were the first to arrive, and in spite of their obsequiousness it soon became clear that they were plotting the same fate for Caesar as for Pompey; but he struck first. Pothinus, the eunuch, was despatched and the other two were sent fleeing and did not survive long. For the time being Ptolemy, then aged 13, was kept as a hostage.

For Cleopatra to obey Caesar's summons was difficult, as she would have to come through troops loyal to Ptolemy, but according to tradition (and there is no reason to disbelieve it) she made her way into the palace wrapped up in a bundle of carpets carried in by a merchant. It must, indeed, have been a dramatic moment when she emerged from the carpets and found herself in the presence of the most powerful man in the world. Caesar, then 52, was the greatest conqueror since Alexander with the Roman Empire at his feet. Cleopatra, 21, was youthful and inexperienced and hardly known outside Egypt.

The meeting was to be fateful. As well as a military genius Caesar was also a man of prodigious sexual potency. In his early life he had had homosexual tendencies, but later he had changed, married four times and become a multiple adulterer with liaisons all over the known world. It is doubtful if he was ever seriously in love with Cleopatra, but he was certainly intrigued by her; she was unlike any woman he had met before. For five months they were to live in proximity, during which Cleopatra became pregnant, almost certainly by Caesar although this was never acknowledged by him. For whatever reason Caesar dallied in Egypt and allowed himself for a time to be caught off guard, surrounded in his palace by a hostile Egyptian army, outnumbering his forces by five to one, as well as by a rampaging Alexandrian mob. A lesser commander might have pulled out, which he could have done, but Caesar stayed put, awaiting reinforcements, and when these arrived he gained a decisive victory.

It might be thought that the Alexandrine War, as it came to be

3

called, was just another of Caesar's victories, but there was a difference. He had stayed in Egypt much longer than he needed to have done when his presence was urgently required in Rome and other parts of the Empire. The popular explanation for this was his love for Cleopatra, but this must be doubtful. It is more likely that he had become entranced by Egypt's ancient civilisation.

When the fighting was over he and Cleopatra made a progress up the Nile in a magnificent barge– more of a floating palace (300 feet long, 45 feet wide, containing banqueting rooms, courtyards, grottos and shrines) past the great Pyramids and the Sphinx and temples of far greater antiquity than anything in Europe. And these could well have dazzled Caesar, as also did the gods and goddesses of the country.

Cleopatra was generally regarded as a reincarnation of the goddess Isis, while because of all his victories, there were those who looked on Caesar as a reincarnation of Amon, the greatest of their gods; and he may not have been entirely dismissive of this idea. Increasingly he was to show signs of a belief in his divinity, and in Rome, where republican feeling was still strong in some quarters, this would be dangerous. His Egyptian experience could have been fatal.

Before leaving Egypt it would have been possible for Caesar to have incorporated the country into the Roman Empire, but this he did not do. Instead he left Cleopatra enthroned with her husband, her younger brother Ptolemy XIV, aged 12, as co-regent (Ptolemy XIII having been drowned in the Nile during the war). He also left three legions to support them.

He then lost no time in reasserting his military genius, subduing revolts in Asia Minor, Africa and Italy before returning to Rome to celebrate a Triumph which was to be the most spectacular ever, although somewhat marred by the cruel and offensive parading of Cleopatra's younger sister and rival, Princess Arsinoe, in chains.

For the occasion Cleopatra was summoned from Egypt with her newborn son, Ptolemy Caesar or Caesarion as he was known. She arrived in state, accompanied by a large retinue of courtiers, eunuchs and slaves, and was housed suitably but at a distance from Caesar. As yet she was not well known; Queen of Egypt she might be and one of Caesar's mistresses, but she was not yet a notorious

4

character. If she and Caesar had visions that one day they would marry and be the founders of a great Julian–Ptolemaic dynasty, these had not yet come to the surface. Caesar was still married to Calpurnia and there were still wars to be fought. The sons of Pompey were mustering forces in Spain and becoming a serious menace. In 45 BC Caesar marched against them and in a close-fought battle, in which he was nearly killed, defeated them; although this was not the last to be heard of them.

He then returned to Rome where he celebrated another Triumph after which he set to work to put to rights the civil affairs of the city which had become chaotic – law and order were breaking down and the economy was out of control. The Republic was on its last legs and its leaders were manifestly incapable of dealing with the problems crowding in on them. A strong, firm autocrat was needed, and this could only be Caesar. Most people recognised this and extraordinary powers were vested in him – consul for ten years and dictator for life with the title Imperator. He was offered too the title of King but this he declined, sensing that kings were still repugnant to most Romans; although it must have been with reluctance as only thus could he have become the founder of a dynasty.

Caesar, by then 56 and beginning to show his age, lost no time in coming to grips with Rome's troubles, restoring order in the streets, settling grievances and formulating plans for great public works including temples, assembly rooms, theatres and canals. But then he was suddenly struck down. He was in effect master of an empire stretching from Britain to Mesopotamia which he had been instrumental in uniting, and he was becoming ever more convinced that he was not only of divine descent (he had long claimed to be descended from Venus) but was a god himself, and he tended to behave like one, which gave great offence to entrenched republicans. Led by Caius Cassius and Marcus Brutus (alleged to be Caesar's son), a group of them assassinated him as he entered the Senate at the foot of his old enemy, Pompey, on 15 March 44 BC.

To Cleopatra, who was still in Rome at the time, this was a lethal blow: it meant the end (for the present) of her dream of becoming Queen-Empress of the Roman Empire, and her position as queen of Egypt being threatened. And worse was to follow: when Caesar's will was made public there was no mention in it of herself or of Caesarion; they were markedly excluded. Most of his fortune was left to his great-nephew Octavian who was nominated his heir, thereby paving the way for a hereditary dynasty. There was then no reason for Cleopatra to remain in Rome, and she returned to Egypt soon after.

The assassins had hoped that by killing Caesar there would be general rejoicing; politics would be purged and a brighter future opened up. But this did not happen; at first there was paralysis and fear, then general lamentation which turned into blazing anger, so that the assassins had to leave the city for their country estates and then to seek refuge abroad. The dominant figure at first was Mark Antony, a brave, rough-hewn soldier who had been Caesar's right-hand man. As a military commander he was second only to his master but lacked his finesse and calm judgement, although during the critical period following Caesar's death he played his cards skilfully, and his funeral oration for Caesar, later embellished and made famous by Shakespeare, had had a vital part in thwarting the assassins. His main trial of strength, however, lay ahead in confrontation with Octavian, and in this he was to be less successful.

At the time of his great-uncle's death Octavian (the future Emperor Augustus) was a youth of 19 studying abroad. Shy, cold and unimpressive looking, there were few signs as yet of exceptional political acumen. On arrival in Rome he was astute enough for a time to lie low. He was not yet ready to take on Mark Antony, with whom he was never likely to coexist happily. They were very different human beings and their interests clashed, but in the aftermath of Caesar's death they needed each other, as Brutus and Cassius were raising forces in Greece for an invasion. And so they formed a Triumvirate with Marcus Lepidus, Master of the Horse, who had several legions at his command, to give battle to the anti-Caesareans.

With the imminence of a Roman civil war, the main concern of Cleopatra in Egypt was to back the winning side and to maintain her throne intact. As the mistress of Caesar and the mother of his son, she could expect short shrift from the assassins, nor was she likely to find sympathy from Octavian who would look on Caesarion as a rival. Her hopes then were pinned on Antony. Whether or not she had ideas then that he might replace Caesar as the co-founder of a Roman–Ptolemaic dynasty cannot be known. It was to be three years before this became a possibility.

Soon after her return from Rome the young Ptolemy XIV was

put to death, almost certainly at her instigation, so she was then the sole sovereign. In dealing with the internal affairs of Egypt she was to show some competence, giving the lie to the notion that she was no more than a scheming seducer. She proved an able administrator and tough negotiator, able to hold her own and to communicate in several languages including Egyptian, which she was said to be the first Ptolemy to speak fluently (rather than Greek). Tales of her lubricious practices were to become prevalent, and it may be that these were not groundless, but most were of later concoction and likely to have been extravagantly exaggerated.

Meanwhile in Rome Octavian was slowly gaining ground, spending money on well-placed bribes and popular festivals while Antony was dissipating his money on riotous living. Antony was, however, to be the hero in the decisive battles near Philippi in which Brutus and Cassius were defeated and committed suicide, and the anti-Caesarean faction overthrown. And afterwards when the Triumvirate divided the empire between them he was to have the lion's share – Transalpine Gaul, Greece and Asia Minor; Octavian being assigned Cisalpine Gaul, part of Italy and Spain, and Lepidus, a man of no great distinction, being relegated to north-west Africa.

Antony lost no time in asserting himself in his domains. Accompanied by a massive court of noblemen, sycophants, concubines and entertainers of various sorts, he made a triumphal tour of Greece and Asia Minor, hailed wherever he went as a mighty conqueror, a descendant of the god Hercules as well as, in view of his copious consumption of wine, 'the New Dionysus'. A great military commander he certainly was, but otherwise unsophisticated. He had dreams of uniting all the eastern Roman provinces into a separate empire headed by himself in magnificent estate. For this it would be essential to include Egypt, with its glittering capital of Alexandria. The country had been left independent by Caesar but it was heavily reliant on Rome for its security and economy. It was not long before Antony was casting longing eyes in its direction, and in 41 BC he summoned Cleopatra to meet him in Tarsus in Asia Minor.

Cleopatra was anxious to meet him, but was not prepared to come crawling like a vassal. She was after all a queen, and a descendant of many kings. She therefore came in the most splendid state possible – in a floating palace even grander than the one in which she and Caesar had sailed up the Nile. As described by Shakespeare:

> The barge she sat in, like a burnish'd throne,
> Burn'd on the water: the poop was beaten gold;
> Purple the sails, and so perfumed that
> The winds were love-sick with them; the oars were silver,
> Which to the tune of flutes kept stroke, and made
> The water which they beat to follow faster,
> As amorous of their own strokes.[1]

Nothing like it had been seen since some 900 years before when the Queen of Sheba had come to visit King Solomon in Jerusalem: 'And she came to Jerusalem with a very great train, with camels that bore spices, and very much gold, and precious stones; and when she was come to Solomon, she communed with him of all that was in her heart.'[2]

But Cleopatra outshone the Queen of Sheba. At the time she was 28, in her prime, and fully aware of her seductive powers. Antony must have seemed to her easy prey – then in his forties, burly, exuberant and infinitely susceptible. Their first meeting may have been 16 years before when he had been part of the Roman army which had restored her father to the Egyptian throne; but she must have met him on a number of occasions during the two years she was in Rome and was able to weigh him up. With her keen intelligence she would have seen that, though his physical charms were mighty, he had his weaknesses – basically he was a simple soul with few political skills, 'capable of conquering the world but incapable of resisting a pleasure'. No one would be more easily bedazzled by the opulence of the Orient.

And so she put on a fantastic show. At a banquet given on her barge no expense was spared. The walls of the chamber were lined with exquisite tapestries illuminated by myriad bright lights, the floor was knee-deep in rose petals, and the choicest foods and wines were served on solid gold plates and in solid gold goblets, all of which were presented to the guests on their departure. In the

---

[1] *Antony and Cleopatra*, Act II, scene 2.

[2] I Kings Chapter 10. It is recorded in Chapter 11 that at the time Solomon had 700 wives, princesses, and 300 concubines, which even Mark Antony could not match.

face of this Mark Antony was helpless – splendour beyond anything he could have imagined. He felt he had to reciprocate with a banquet of his own, but this was poor in comparison – 'of rustic awkwardness', as described by Plutarch.[3]

Predictably Cleopatra had no difficulty in luring Antony to come back with her to Alexandria where, during the winter months, she lavished on him all manner of delights. She realised she had on her hands a different man to Caesar, rugged and with simple tastes, and to these she pandered assiduously – gambling, drinking orgies, crude practical jokes, she went along with them all. And she was to find that he was much more pliant than Caesar: more could be gained from him, notably the island of Cyprus which was restored to Egyptian rule. He also saw to the death of her half-sister Arsinoe who, after her ordeal in Rome was living in harmless exile in Ephesus – but Cleopatra would tolerate no rivals.

Once again she was having dreams of becoming Queen-Empress of a Roman–Egyptian empire. Antony seemed to be within her grasp. He had a wife in Rome (his third) but, as with Caesar's wife, she did not consider this an impediment. But then came a setback. In the spring there arrived news of critical developments: in the east, Rome's most formidable enemy, the Parthians, were encroaching on Roman territory and the province of Judaea was under threat. And in Rome Octavian had been winning support, and Antony's wife Fulvia and his brother Lucius, who had been maintaining his interests there, had been forced to flee the city. Intoxicated as Antony might be with life in Alexandria, it was clearly time for him to emerge from depravity and reassert his authority; as Plutarch later wrote, 'like a man aroused from sleep after a deep debauch'. For Cleopatra his departure came as a shock. It was the end of her dreams. If she had hopes that he would soon be back, they were to be dashed. He was to be away for three and a half years. And worse was to follow.

Antony's reunion with Fulvia in Athens cannot have been amiable, partly because of his dalliance with Cleopatra and partly because of Fulvia's failure to contain Octavian. Soon afterwards, however, she died suddenly and the way might then have seemed to be clear for Antony to marry Cleopatra, but instead he made a 'political'

---

[3] A Greek philosopher and historian writing some 100 years later. Among his works was *Forty-six Parallel Lives* which included Mark Antony.

marriage to Octavian's sister, Octavia, in order to seal a compact he and Octavian had just made. Octavia was younger than Cleopatra and of great beauty and virtue, and Cleopatra's reaction must have been agonised, especially as she had just given birth to twins by Antony. For the present she was out in the cold, but the story was not yet over. Antony's rapprochement with Octavian was not likely to last. They were not natural allies, and Octavia, beautiful and virtuous though she might be, was not of the same ilk as Cleopatra.

The year 37 BC was to be crucial in Roman history. It started with the Triumvirate being renewed: Antony and Octavian came to terms; Lepidus as before was left largely unregarded in Africa. The basis of their agreement was that Octavian should combat Pompeius Sextus (son of Pompey the Great) who still held sway over part of the Mediterranean including Sicily, and whose ships constituted a serious threat to Rome's trade, particularly her corn supply; while Antony would restore order in Rome's eastern provinces and lead a campaign against the ever troublesome Parthians.[4] For a time there seemed to be the prospect of internal peace and goodwill brought about, maybe, by the influence of Octavia, anxious for harmony between her brother and husband. But it was not to last.

When in the spring of that year Antony left for the East he took Octavia with him, but then suddenly, when only half way, he sent her back to Rome. The reason given was that she had become pregnant, but this is not convincing. In view of what occurred later there were other reasons. It seems that Antony was already bent on a break with Octavian and a return to Cleopatra, for soon afterwards he sent a messenger to her asking her to meet him in Antioch, the capital of Syria, where they would plan for the future. It was agreed that in the following year Antony would mount a massive invasion of Parthia which would be incorporated into the empire and which would open the way to lands further east and on to India. They would then turn their combined forces on Rome and dispose of Octavian (and Octavia), and Cleopatra's dream of becoming queen of the largest empire the world had ever known would be fulfilled.

The plans evolved in Antioch, however, ended disastrously.

---

[4] Sixteen years before, in 53 BC, they had inflicted one of the heaviest defeats ever on a Roman army at the Battle of Carrhae which had never been adequately avenged.

Antony's invasion of Parthia proved a total failure. His army became divided and the Parthians, avoiding pitched battles and relying on guerrilla tactics, inflicted heavy casualties. With the coming of winter he had to make an ignominious retreat during which many died from cold and hunger. It resembled in some ways Napoleon's retreat from Moscow except that Antony, unlike Napoleon, did not desert his men but stayed with them to the bitter end, enduring their privations and doing what he could to keep up their spirits. By the end of the year he reached the coast of Syria where Cleopatra came to his aid with reinforcements and supplies.

The Parthian debacle was a turning point in Antony's career. Until then Cleopatra had been dependent on him and the power of Rome for support; now he was dependent on her and the wealth of Egypt. It was unfortunate for him that at the same time as he was suffering the bitterness of defeat, Octavian was celebrating a notable victory. His very able commander, Marcus Agrippa, had inflicted a decisive defeat on the fleet of Pompeius Sextus, thus removing the threat to Rome's grain supply and regaining suzerainty over Sicily. At the same time he warded off a threat from Lepidus, the third member of the Triumvirate, to expand his domain. Because he was basically weak and ineffective he was allowed to survive, and disappeared from the pages of history in which he had never shone brightly.

Cleopatra's growing ascendancy over Antony soon became marked. She persuaded him to abandon another invasion of Parthia and return with her to the delights of Alexandria. She was particularly anxious to keep him close to her as Octavia, his legal wife, had arrived in Athens, hoping to lure him back to her. She had been sent by her brother whose motives, as so often, were indistinct. It might be that he was seeking an entente with Antony, to share power with him equally, but he may have had a more devious idea – expecting that Antony would treat Octavia offensively, which would cause anger in Rome and damage his reputation. Cleopatra was in a strong position to maintain her hold over him as she was backed by the resources of Egypt and the fascination of Alexandria as well as her own bewitching personality. But she was taking no chances and saw to it that Antony was kept away from Octavia who was then ordered brusquely back to Rome (perhaps as Octavian had hoped).

Cleopatra also maintained pressure on Antony not to mount

another invasion of Parthia, which he could hardly do in any case without forces supplied by her. Instead he had to be content with a raid into Armenia, an easy prey which he had no difficulty in overcoming. But having done so he made a cardinal error. He proclaimed for himself a formal Triumph to be held eastern-style in Alexandria which, he should have known, would cause great offence in Rome. Triumphs were voted for by the Senate and were a uniquely Roman affair, accompanied by great popular festivities. To hold one on his own initiative in a foreign city, invoking foreign gods, was considered a major affront; and it was all grist to Octavian's mill, creating an image of a besotted Antony, gone native and caught in the wiles of an insidious oriental queen.

Worse was to follow. In a spectacular ceremony known as The Donations of Alexandria, Cleopatra was proclaimed Queen of Kings and Antony assumed the grandiose title of Autocrator ('Ruler Absolute'). At the same time Caesar's son by Cleopatra, Caesarion, then aged eleven, was declared his true heir rather than Octavian and proclaimed King of Kings, and Cleopatra's sons by Antony were assigned large domains, many of which were still unconquered and in any case were not Antony's to give. In effect this amounted to a declaration of war. Octavian was being denied his birthright and branded a usurper, and to nominate Caesarion as Caesar's legal heir could not be justified. At the time of his birth Caesar was still married to Calpurnia and bigamy was disavowed by both Roman and Egyptian law. In the following year, at Cleopatra's insistence, Antony declared Octavia divorced. No reconciliation was then possible. By 34 BC preparations for battle were under way. War was officially declared by Octavian in 32 BC, but he was at pains to make it clear that it was on Cleopatra rather than on Antony. He did not want it to be regarded as a civil war but as one against a dangerous foreign enemy.

In assessing the strength of the two sides it would seem that at first the advantage lay with Antony. He had behind him all the resources of Egypt, which included the Mediterranean's most powerful navy, as well as the support of a number of allies or 'client states' in Asia Minor. Also, despite his erratic behaviour, he still had support in Rome. Generous, warm-hearted and exuberant he was a more attractive character than the cold, underhand Octavian (whose sex life, although less public than Antony's, was no less licentious). And although lately Octavian had been gaining ground in Rome he had also made a number of enemies, especially among ardent republicans who suspected (rightly as it proved) that he was out for kingly powers. And so it was that after the declaration of war many high-ranking citizens (including two consuls and some 300 senators) left Rome to join forces with Antony. But he too had disadvantages, notably the unreliability of some of his allies and his dependence on Cleopatra; also the Roman legionaries in his army were not of the highest quality, including as they did local conscripts whose loyalty and skill were variable. If he had struck at once, however, he must have prevailed, but he let time pass during which he became weaker while Octavian was gathering strength, always fostering the idea that Antony was bent on a separate eastern empire with Alexandria outshining Rome, as its capital.

The Battle of Actium, which decided the fate of the Roman Empire, was complex and long-drawn-out. In the autumn of 32 BC Antony and Cleopatra arrived in Greece with large land and sea forces preparatory to a descent on Italy, but the decision was taken that this should not be carried out that year. It might well have been successful, but it was thought that an invasion by a largely foreign army would stir up strong patriotic opposition; better to defeat Octavian's army on neutral ground and then come to an agreement. The fleet and the army, therefore, went into winter quarters and the place for this was not well chosen. The Ambracian Gulf through the Actium Peninsula was a safe anchorage, but gloomy and unhealthy and with limited access to the Ionian Sea. During the long months Antony's forces were compelled to stay there morale sank low; many died from disease, there were numerous desertions and much discord.

Anthony's Roman supporters strongly resented the presence of Cleopatra whom they looked on as an oriental queen of evil repute whose influence on Antony and the conduct of the war was disastrous. They urged him to send her back to Egypt, but this he would not do; after six years he had come to love her and to depend on her, and it was she who had provided most of his fleet. In any case Cleopatra would not have gone; how much she was in love with Antony may be doubtful, but he was essential to the dream she was harbouring of the two of them enthroned in Rome to be succeeded by Caesarion and an Egyptian–Roman dynasty. And so she had to keep him by her lest he might think of making a deal with Octavian.

During the winter months Octavian and his brilliant lieutenant, Marcus Agrippa, were not inactive; they succeeded in almost completely blockading the forces of Antony. With the coming of summer Antony hoped to be able to fight a set-piece land battle, but Octavian, realising the strength of his position and that time was on his side, would not be drawn.

For several months there was a deadlock, but by the beginning of September Antony and Cleopatra could wait no longer. The former was in favour of a break-out by land forces, but the latter insisted on a naval engagement in which she envisaged her ships being victorious and the way to Rome and the fulfilment of her dreams being open. That Antony was not optimistic about the outcome of such an encounter is shown by his insistence on encumbering his ships with sails, masts and rigging so that he could if necessary make a longer voyage to the safety of Egypt. It seems to have been established beforehand that in the event of the battle going against them Cleopatra would sail off with her ships (along with the considerable treasure she had with her) back to Egypt where she would raise forces to confront Octavian again. This arrangement could not have failed to come to the notice of the ships' crews and the effect on their morale was devastating. When battle was joined the worst happened.

It is not clear how it came about as accounts of the battle are obscure and contradictory, but it is certain that Cleopatra led the way with 60 of her ships, and Antony followed soon after. It seems likely that his plan of campaign had been only to evacuate Greece and build up fresh forces in Egypt. But it went drastically wrong. Most of his ships were unable to follow him and were captured or sunk by the better-manned and disciplined ships of Agrippa. And the land army was left to its fate. The general in charge attempted to fight his way out, but morale in the ranks was so low that all succumbed to the terms of surrender offered by Octavian. The victory of Octavian and Agrippa was complete.

On the way back to Egypt Antony transferred to Cleopatra's flagship, but he kept apart from her. He was steeped in gloom: not only had he suffered a heavy defeat but also an ignominious disgrace; he had deserted his fighting men at the height of the battle and trailed off after his lover. This was something he could never live down.

On arrival in Egypt he continued to isolate himself, brooding

14

on his fate. Was this what had come to the descendant of Hercules, God of War, and the roistering reincarnation of Dionysus? He tried to steel himself to fall on his sword like other defeated Romans, but this at first he could not bring himself to do. He kept hoping that he would live to fight another day, but bad news came pouring in: the surrender of his army in Greece without a blow being struck and the desertion of all his one-time allies, anxious to come to terms with the victorious Octavian. It was only a matter of time before he arrived in Egypt to deliver the *coup de grâce*, but this was delayed as he first had to return to Italy to deal with local troubles there.

During this time, although Antony remained atrophied, Cleopatra was spurred into action. She may have known in her heart that her day of reckoning had come, but she was determined that her son, Caesarion, should be preserved to claim his inheritance in due course. And so she conceived an audacious plan by which he would escape to the East, perhaps to India, out of harm's way. This involved dragging ships overland from the Mediterranean to the Red Sea, a mammoth operation which was achieved successfully, only for the ships then to be destroyed by hostile Arabs.

Cleopatra then bent all her efforts to coming to terms with Octavian. For the survival of her children she was prepared to make any concessions – abdication, forsaking Mark Antony, lavish payments – but they were to be of no avail. At the same time she prepared for her own death. She was said to have experimented with various poisons, including the bites of asps, on condemned prisoners to see which were quickest and least painful. She also had a mausoleum built in which she stored the treasures of the Ptolemies along with combustible material so that they could all go up in flames rather than fall into the hands of Octavian.

In July of 30 BC Octavian had returned to the East and was advancing on Egypt. Then at last Antony stirred himself from his torpor and led a cavalry attack on the vanguard of Octavian's army, a successful one, and he hastened to Alexandria to break the news to Cleopatra. That night he had a splendid banquet in which he was once again Dionysus in full fling. But it could not last. The next day he had to watch the Egyptian fleet surrender to Octavian's, and soon after his cavalry did the same. The wish to be on the winning side, and Antony's tarnished reputation, impelled them to desert.

15

All hope was now extinguished. Only suicide remained. Antony gave his sword to his slave and told him to run him through, but rather than this the slave ran it through himself, so it was left to Antony to do the deed which he did, but not fatally, so he lay there horribly wounded, but still alive.

Meanwhile Cleopatra with two attendants had taken refuge in the mausoleum. On hearing of Antony's condition she sent for him and, as the mausoleum was barred and bolted against looters and the forerunners of Octavian's army, he had to be hoisted in through an upper window. Cleopatra then gave full vent to her grief, sobbing uncontrollably. Relations between them may have been strained lately, but their love had not died, and he was in her arms when he later died.

Cleopatra then awaited the arrival of emissaries from Octavian. She hoped to be able to hold them at bay outside while she negotiated from within about her children and her treasures – her strongest bargaining counter. But they managed to find a way in and prevented her from suicide, holding her in check until the arrival of Octavian for a historic confrontation. Cleopatra was then 39, in disarray, her beauty faded and her body bruised and scarred. Nevertheless Octavian thought it prudent to keep his eyes on the floor. He did not trust himself to look on her. It soon became clear that he was unrelenting. He would make no concessions or promises. He had no need to: her children were or soon would be in his power, her treasure was his, and she was captured alive to be shipped off to Rome to be the focal point in his Triumph. But in the midst of her collapse she did have one victory, in that she was able to avoid this humiliation.

It cannot be certain exactly how Cleopatra died. There are many accounts of it. Octavian left her in close custody but not close enough. Not all her guards were immune to her charms. One act of clemency from Octavian was to allow her to take charge of Antony's burial and to make visits to his tomb. It seems that on her return to the mausoleum after one of these she was able to find the freedom to deck herself out in her royal robes and then to take her own life with dignity and style as befitting a queen. According to legend a peasant farmer had been allowed in with a basket of figs in which was concealed a poisonous asp. This was never found, but on her arm there were two marks which could have been bites. Her two attendants also managed to kill themselves.

And so Octavian was robbed of his prey, but he saw to it that Cleopatra's reputation was thoroughly besmirched for future generations. She was to go down in history as a dangerous voluptuary from whose wiles no man was safe. This is the image posterity has wanted to believe, and has made the most of. No other qualities are allowed her. Shakespeare put into the mouth of Mark Antony the words:

> The evil that men do lives after them;
> The good is oft interred with their bones.[1]

So it was with Cleopatra.

---

[1] *Julius Caesar*, Act III, scene 2.

2

MARY QUEEN OF SCOTS (1542–1587)

Tragedy has been the lot of most queens, but to few has it come in such measure as to Mary Queen of Scots, Queen Regnant of Scotland, Queen Consort of France and in the eyes of some the rightful Queen of England. Of her three husbands one, an imbecile, died young; the second was murdered; and the third driven into exile to rot in a foreign gaol. And she herself, sometimes adored but more often excoriated, became a widow at 17, a deposed queen at 25 and a prisoner for 19 years, her life ending on a scaffold in a decayed English fortress.

Mary Stuart or Mary Queen of Scots, as she is more generally known, was born on 8 December 1542, and a month later she became Queen of Scotland on the death of her father, James V. He too had come to the throne as a baby when his father, James IV, was killed at the Battle of Flodden. Further back in history there was another parallel, when in 1290 on the sudden death of Alexander III, his successor was a young girl of seven, Margaret Maid of Norway. It had been intended that she should marry the son of King Edward I of England, the future Edward II, and if this union of the crowns had taken place much bloodshed and warfare would have been avoided, but Margaret died during a tempestuous crossing from Norway to Scotland. In 1542 there was also a plan for the union of the crowns between Mary and the heir to the English throne (the future Edward VI), but this miscarried and again bloody and unnecessary warfare was to follow.

At first the prospects for such a marriage had been bright. The Earl of Arran, Mary's cousin and the heir-presumptive, was appointed Regent (or Gouverneur) and at that time he was in favour of the alliance. He came to an agreement with Henry VIII in the Treaty of Greenwich whereby Mary would remain in Scotland in the care of her mother until she was ten, when she would marry Prince

Edward and come to live in England. The matter seemed to have been settled peaceably and reasonably, but it was soon to be disrupted.

Henry VIII, then in his last years, had become a headstrong and ill-tempered tyrant and interfered arbitrarily in Scottish affairs. This was greatly resented and stirred up the opposition of those who had always been opposed to the union of the two crowns, fearing that it would mean the subjugation of Scotland by its more powerful neighbour. And then too there were religious complications: Scotland at that time was in the throes of the Reformation; Protestantism was spreading rapidly but there were still many who clung to Roman Catholicism and wanted no connection with the Protestant Church as set up by Henry VIII in England. Preferable was Scotland's historic alliance with France in opposition to England ('the Auld Alliance' as it was called). They would have liked the infant Mary to become betrothed to a French prince, but that for a time had been impractical as Catherine de Medici, wife of the Dauphin, seemed to be sterile; after ten years of marriage there had been no issue, but then in 1544 a son was born and following him others came in profusion.[1]

The position was thus transformed and the French faction in Scotland became stronger. Especially influential was David Beaton, Cardinal-Archbishop of St Andrews and Papal Legate, a man of enormous wealth, unrestrained self-indulgence and flagrant promiscuity. Soon after the death of James V he produced what was alleged to be a will of the late King bequeathing the government of the country to a group of nobles headed by himself, but this had all the hallmarks of a forgery and was strongly disputed. However, as head of Scotland's Roman Catholics he was a force to be reckoned with, and the Earl of Arran, weak and irresolute, and fearful of a resurgence of French influence, felt he had to come to terms with him and switched from the English to the French faction: the Treaty of Greenwich was revoked and the infant Mary pledged to the newly born son of the Dauphin rather than to Prince Edward.

Predictably such a volte-face enraged Henry VIII. Then in the throes of an agonising disease and with his temper ungovernable, he ordered vicious reprisals against the Scots for their breach of

---

[1] See the chapter on Catherine de Medici.

19

faith. An English army under the command of the Earl of Hertford[2] was ordered to invade Scotland and wreak havoc wherever it went, and this it did barbarously – wrecking villages, ruining crops, demolishing monasteries, even setting fire to the city of Edinburgh. But this 'rough wooing', as it came to be called, did not have the desired effect. The Scots were not to be intimidated and help from France was soon to be forthcoming.

Meanwhile the eight-month-old queen, the fount of all this turmoil, was taken for safety to the fortress of Stirling, believed to be the most impregnable in Scotland. There she was in the care of her mother, the French Princess Mary of Guise, a strong-minded and capable woman, tall and graceful, and determined at all costs to preserve the throne of her daughter.[3] Before her marriage to James V she had been wedded to the French duc de Longueville, but had been left a widow at 22. She then had approaches from Henry VIII after the death of his third wife, Jane Seymour, but these, perhaps prudently, she had resisted. Her marriage to James V was not altogether happy: she had borne him two sons both of whom had died, and she had had to come to terms with James's libidinous lifestyle.[4] The birth of a daughter was a grievous disappointment to him and may have hastened his death, but Mary's succession to the throne was unopposed.

The Queen Mother was, of course, a strong supporter of French interests in Scotland, in particular the betrothal of Mary to Prince Francis.[5] She was also a fervent Roman Catholic and brought up her strictly in that faith. Protestantism, however, continued to spread in Scotland and there were strong reasons for this. The Catholic Church had become excessively wealthy and many of its pastors were idle and immoral. Public wrath, stimulated by the ringing oratory of John Knox among others, was mounting; and nemesis was to overcome David Beaton the Cardinal-Archbishop. He had ordered a horrifying death for a gentle and saintly Protestant preacher, George Wishart, and had then sat by comfortably, gloating while he was hanged and eviscerated. But this was too much for

---

[2] Later in the reign of Edward VI he became Lord Protector Somerset.

[3] She had been crowned in 1543 when barely a year old.

[4] He had fathered six sons and two daughters out of wedlock.

[5] He had become the Dauphin on the death of his grandfather, Francis I, and the accession to the throne of his father, Henry II.

a group of Protestant lairds who gained entrance into the bishop's castle of St Andrews and murdered him brutally.

In the following year (1547) King Francis I died and his successor, Henry II, showed himself more willing to send military help to the Scottish Catholics. At nearly the same time King Henry VIII died, and there was hope that this would mean an end to English harassment of Scotland and acceptance that Mary would marry the Dauphin rather than Edward VI, as he had now become. But these hopes were dashed when Lord Protector Somerset invaded Scotland, destroying and looting and inflicting on a Scottish army a crushing defeat at the Battle of Pinkie Cleugh. The safety of the infant queen then became a matter of major concern as she was shifted from one stronghold to another, the situation becoming more critical when she was struck down by a fever, thought for a time to be mortal. It had become evident that she could only be safe in France, and in August 1548 French ships arrived in Scotland to take her there. Her mother did not accompany her, remaining behind to take care of her interests in Scotland.

The arrival of the six-year-old Queen Regnant of Scotland and the likely Queen Consort of France aroused great interest. There were many who sought after her. One of the first was her formidable grandmother, Antoinette de Bourbon,[6] who was well pleased with her: 'She is very pretty indeed and as intelligent a child as you could ever see.' On others too she made a favourable impression, notably King Henry II who said that she was the prettiest and most graceful princess he had ever seen. But pretty and charming though she might be, her education needed taking in hand; her ways were Scottish and to French eyes somewhat uncouth and, surprisingly with a French mother, she spoke no French. So the best tutors were found for her, and she was to prove an apt, even precocious pupil. She learned French (and other languages) readily, her Scottish rough edges were eliminated and she was soon taking part in theatrical performances and poetry recitals, and conversing on art and music like an adult. She also gained a reputation for her dancing and her dress sense. Altogether she became the cynosure of all eyes.

The set-up at the court of Henry II was unusual.[7] The King

---

[6] Matriarch of the Guise royal branch. Mother of ten children, she lived to the age of 87.

[7] See the chapter on Catherine de Medici.

himself tended to be morose and cheerless, with few pleasures in life. At an early age he had been coerced into marriage with Catherine de Medici, daughter of a rich Italian banker and a relation of Pope Clement VII; but she had no other attributes: she was not beautiful and for ten years had failed in what was mainly required of her, the begetting of children. Because of this her position at court was insecure, and though by the time of Mary's arrival several children had been born, it remained so for the time being. Much the most influential figure at court was the King's long-term mistress, Diane de Poitiers (later Duchess of Valentinois). Some 19 years older than Henry, she had held him in thrall since childhood and continued to do so until his early death. She liked to put her oar in wherever she could, ordering not only Henry's life but also that of Catherine and her children which, surprisingly, Catherine accepted so that there was little hostility between them. She also took it upon herself, although hardly in a position to do so, to insist that outwardly the court of Henry II was respectable and untainted. She lost no time in taking Mary under her wing, supervising her education, refining her ways and plying her with worldly advice.

The most important matter to be confronted by Mary was her relationship with her future husband, the Dauphin. Perhaps because of the great pains involved in his conception, he was seriously handicapped both physically and mentally; malformed and immature, he was found to be almost ineducable, his only interest being hunting. However, Mary determined that she had to love him and succeeded in doing so, her attitude to him being always maternal – kindly and understanding and not expecting too much. And he reciprocated, becoming totally devoted to her.

In 1558, when Mary was in her sixteenth year, a delegation from Scotland arrived in France to negotiate the terms of her marriage contract. Of course Diane de Poitiers insisted on presiding over proceedings, but no difficulties were to arise. It was agreed that after their marriage the Dauphin would be titular King of Scotland, and on the death of his father he would be King Regent of both Scotland and France; furthermore their citizens would have joint nationality. If Mary died without an heir, the throne of Scotland would go to the next of kin by blood (at the time this would be the feckless Earl of Arran now Duke of Châtelherault). If there was a male heir he would be king of both countries, if a female then owing to the Salic Law, only Queen of Scotland.

These terms seemed to be lenient to Scotland, but there was also a secret covenant by which Mary contracted that if she died without children the throne of Scotland would go to the King of France in perpetuity, which would mean that Scotland would in effect become a dominion of France. Of course Mary had no right to do this; it amounted to a betrayal of her country, and she has been strongly criticised for doing so. In her defence it has been said that she was only fifteen and a half at the time and under strong pressure from her Guise uncles, the Duke of Guise and the Cardinal of Lorraine, and did not realise the full implications of what she was doing; but if she was the intelligent child she was said to be, this is not altogether convincing. Certainly it seemed to be the case that Mary had become 'frenchified'; France was her greatest love and Scotland a sideline.

The wedding of Francis and Mary in Notre Dame occurred soon after the signing of the contract on 24 April 1558. It was the first time for 200 years that a Dauphin had been married in Paris and no expense was spared for a magnificent occasion. The citizens went wild with excitement, desperate to catch a glimpse of the new Dauphine who, of course, stole the show, towering over her little husband as he limped along beside her. Wine flowed in fountains, largesse was scattered into the crowd, and it was with difficulty that order was maintained.

Within a year of the wedding Henry II died, accidentally killed in a joust celebrating the betrothal of his daughter Elizabeth to Philip II of Spain. And so at the age of 16 Mary became Queen of France. As such her power was considerable, as her poor inadequate husband, now Francis II, was helpless and relied on her for guidance. She in turn relied on her two power-hungry uncles, who took over the government of the country. But not for long, as after a reign of only 17 months Francis died, and Mary four days before her eighteenth birthday became a widow. This prostrated her with grief as she had become sincerely devoted to Francis despite his weaknesses, and was always to maintain that he was the great love of her life. Mary would then have liked to remain in France, but it was impressed on her by her Guise uncles that she had to go to Scotland, where her presence was needed urgently.

During the 13 years since she had been away there had been great changes in the country. The spread of Protestantism had been irresistible. The malpractices of the Roman church – the luxury, idleness and concupiscence of its leaders, their enormous wealth and their assumption of powers to which they had no right – had caused great discontent. Mary de Guise, who had been Regent since 1554, had attempted to stem the flow, but unavailingly. By the time of her death in 1560 a group of Protestant noblemen, calling themselves the Lords of Congregation, had taken over the government of the country (illegally) and set about suppressing Catholicism; and religious controversy had intensified with the arrival back in the country in 1559 of John Knox.

This extraordinary man had begun life as a notary and become a Protestant pastor in middle age when, because of his violent language[8] and rash behaviour, he had been sent into exile and had spent time as a galley slave. Later he had come to England but had had to make a hurried exit on the accession of Mary Tudor because of a bombastic anti-feminist diatribe he had written, 'First Blast of the Trumpet Against the Monstrous Regiment of Women', in which he had held forth on the inadequacy of women to govern, describing them as 'weak, frail, impatient, feeble and foolish creatures'. In 1559 he felt able to return to Scotland where, because of his spellbinding oratory and mesmeric personality, he became leader of the Protestants and as such one of the most powerful men in the country.

This then was the man Mary had to confront on her return to Scotland in 1561. It seemed they were bound to be sworn enemies. He lost no opportunity to lambaste her. When she left Scotland as a child he had written: 'she has been sold to the devil and despatched to France to the end that in her youth she should drink of that liquor that should remain with her all her lifetime for a plague to this realm and for her final destruction'. And on her return that she brought 'sorrow, darkness, dolour and all impiety'. By then his anti-Catholicism had become fanatical and he was seeing himself as an instrument of God to root it out.

At first Mary was hopeful that she might be able to come to terms with him. She was no Catholic fanatic like Mary Tudor and would have been appalled at the idea of Protestants being burned at the stake. Soon after her return she summoned Knox to a meeting,

---

[8] Of the appointment of Mary de Guise as Regent he had written that: 'to place a crown on the Queen Mother was as seemly a sight as to put a saddle on an unruly cow'.

an interesting confrontation of which, unfortunately, no unbiased account exists, and it cannot be known who had the upper hand; but subsequently Knox wrote of Mary that she was a 'dangerous adversary – such craft as I have not found in such age'. And he acknowledged too that, though he himself was impervious to it, she had 'power by which men were bewitched'.

It became clear, however, that agreement between them was impossible. Compromise and conciliation were not in Knox's nature, and fury broke out when Mary celebrated Mass, Knox thundering that 'one celebration of Mass was more terrible than the invasion of an army of ten thousand'. At times his language became ever more vitriolic; it is likely that he was behind an order from the Edinburgh Council that 'monks, friars, priests, nuns, adulterers, fornicators and such filthy persons should be driven from the city', an order countermanded by Mary. He even went so far as to say that it was the duty of subjects to disobey a Catholic monarch because he (or she) was dangerously wrong; which was clearly treasonable and might have brought him to a horrific death, if Mary had been so minded.

Except for outbursts of abuse from Protestant extremists Mary was well received in Scotland at first. People could not but admire her grace and beauty, and she behaved at first with tact and discretion. To exchange France for Scotland required these qualities. Compared with the former, the latter was a backwater. Life at court was sombre and economical; there was little art and music, and rugged Scottish lairds were far removed from the elegant aristocracy of France. But Mary did not despair; she had French money at her disposal and she soon transformed Holyrood into something more elegant and sophisticated, importing quality furniture, carpets and wall hangings, and inviting poets and musicians to raise the tone.

At first conditions of life were favourable. Mary appointed a Privy Council, headed by her half-brother James Stewart, later Earl of Moray (illegitimate son of James V), which saw to the government of the country. Usually she was present at their meetings, but it seems that on these occasions she was more interested in her needlework than in affairs of state. And she was able to spend time in her favourite occupations of hunting and dancing (described by John Knox as 'an invention of the devil'). At the same time her personal needs were attended to capably and devotedly by a retinue including the Four Maries – Beaton, Seton, Livingston and Fleming.[9]

Life was certainly not, however, all pleasure. There were crucial problems to be confronted of which the most pressing was establishing a pact with Queen Elizabeth of England, who regarded her with hostility. There were many at that time to whom Mary was the lawful English Queen: the marriage of Henry VIII to Anne Boleyn, Elizabeth's mother, had been declared invalid by the Pope, which made Elizabeth illegitimate. In that case Mary, being next by lawful descent from Henry VII, should be Queen. However, in his will Henry VIII had nominated Elizabeth in the line of succession and had excluded Mary, and Elizabeth had been crowned Queen and had the support of the majority of English people.

The position of both queens was precarious and both needed to come to an agreement, but this could not be reached. Mary was willing to abandon her claim to replace Elizabeth, but insisted on being nominated her successor should she die childless, thus revoking the will of Henry VIII. But Elizabeth, while always prevaricating, was unwilling to do this. And so there was tension and rivalry between them. In this conflict the advantage lay with Elizabeth – nine years older, shrewd, cold and self-controlled, in contrast to Mary – warm-hearted, generous and emotionally unstable.

The other great problem confronting Mary was that of marriage, which was of concern to all the royal courts of Europe, as it could affect significantly the European balance of power. As both Queen Dowager of France and Queen Regnant of Scotland, and youthful and affluent besides, Mary was a prime matrimonial target; but in current conditions there were barriers against any marriage she might make. Opposition and strife would inevitably be stirred up. She had been interested in Don Carlos, son and heir of Philip II of Spain, which would have made her the richest and most powerful monarch in Europe; but such a match was violently opposed by both England and France, and it proved impracticable as Don Carlos was even more disabled than Francis II – undersized, hunchbacked and epileptic; and he eventually had to be confined because of

---

[9] Usually associated with the haunting lament of one of them on the eve of her execution: 'Yestreen the Queen had four Maries / The night she'll ha'e but three; / There was Mary Beaton and Mary Seton / And Mary Carmichael and me.' But this is not historical. There was no Mary Carmichael, and not one of them, as in the ballad, ended up on the gallows.

homicidal tendencies.[10] A betrothal was also considered with her brother-in-law Charles IX, the infant King of France (nine years younger than Mary), but this would have upset Spain and England and was barred by his mother, Catherine de Medici, who was emerging as a formidable power in the land. Marriage to a Scottish nobleman was also a possibility, but this would have provoked ferocious interclan strife.

The matter was of greatest concern to Queen Elizabeth, who would be most affected by any marriage of Mary. Her determination was to prevent any union between Mary and a foreign prince, and to queer her pitch she herself had been dallying with the youthful princes of France. Some 20 years older than them, it is hard to believe that she was serious. It is likely that she had no intention of marrying anyone and only went through the motions for political purposes.

Her preference for a husband to Mary was an English Protestant whom she could dominate and whose issue might unite the two crowns. But her choice here was eccentric: her discarded lover Robert Dudley, later Earl of Leicester.[11] Such an idea was surely insulting, but because she thought it might bring her the reversion of the English crown, Mary did not reject it out of hand. It is possible that agreement between the two queens might have been reached if they had ever had a meeting, and arrangements for this were made: a date and a place (York) were fixed, and details as to ritual and expense (always a main concern with Elizabeth) thrashed out.[12] But at the last moment the meeting had to be put off owing to England becoming involved in a war with France concerning the persecution of the Huguenots.

Mary, then, was constrained on every side and overburdened with advice, and by 1565, when she was 23 and longing for a husband whom she could love and trust, she broke free and made a choice on her own initiative, one which was to prove disastrous.

Henry Stuart Lord Darnley was Mary's step-first cousin, grandson of her grandmother, Margaret Tudor, by her second marriage to the Earl of Angus. He was four years younger than she and had spent most of his life in England until coming to Scotland in 1565

---

[10] Said to have been brought on by an accident to his head while chasing a chambermaid.

[11] An unpopular figure and in bad odour following the death of his wife, Amy Robsart, in mysterious circumstances.

[12] For some reason Elizabeth's entourage was to have included an elephant.

at the age of 19. There he made an immediate impression on the Queen. He was tall, good-looking and gifted – an accomplished musician, a skilful sportsman and an elegant dancer. But beneath the surface there were serious flaws: he was syphilitic and his outward charm concealed a selfish, headstrong character; he had been pampered and spoilt as a child and had grown up to believe that whatever he wanted was his by right. But Mary became infatuated by him and was blind to his faults. He was 'the best proportioned long man she ever saw' and the first dancing partner she had known who was taller than herself. She was warned of his shortcomings but was not to be put off and within five months they were married, secretly and without papal sanction, necessary in the case of close relationships.[13] A public ceremony followed a few weeks later and Darnley, who had already been loaded with titles and honours, was proclaimed King Henry of Scotland.

The marriage, as was expected, met with strong disapproval. Darnley had already made himself disliked and, as he was a Catholic (albeit a flexible one), there was strong opposition from Protestant lairds, a group of whom under the leadership of Mary's half-brother, the Earl of Moray, rose in rebellion.[14]

Inevitably John Knox condemned it, inveighing against Darnley's dissolute way of life and referring darkly to his 'having in his company gentlemen willing to satisfy his will and affections'.[15] Of greatest moment was the disapproval of Queen Elizabeth, who at one time seemed to have been promoting the match, but she angrily dismissed the marriage as 'unmeet, unprofitable and perilous to sincere amity between two queens'. It is likely that her main objection to it was that she had not been consulted.

Mary's love for Darnley did not last long, hardly more than a year, and was to be replaced by bitter hatred. His behaviour during that time was intolerable – dissolute, self-seeking, querulous. As with all spoilt children the more he was given the more he wanted, in particular the crown matrimonial, that is, having equal powers with the Queen and these to be continued after her death. The withholding of this became a standing grievance for which he blamed Mary.

---

[13] Also illegally, as it was without the consent of the Scottish council.

[14] This came to be known as 'the Chaseabout' owing to no battles being fought, only endless manoeuvring.

[15] An allusion to his suspected homosexuality. He had been described at the time as 'more like a woman than a man, beardless and lady-faced'.

Relations between Mary and Darnley came to the boil with the arrival in Scotland of David Rizzio, an Italian in the service of the Savoy embassy. He had first caught Mary's eye by his ability as a musician, of which she was always in need for her recitals; but their relationship developed and in 1564 she made him one of her secretaries. In appearance he was totally different to Darnley – swarthy, hunched and not at all beautiful – but he had a lively wit and a flow of worldly conversation which made a welcome change from the gruff parochial talk of the Scotsmen by whom Mary was usually surrounded. Certainly she found him attractive, and showed it. It is unlikely that they were lovers, but there was a degree of intimacy that was imprudent, and enough to stir up public resentment and frantic jealousy in Darnley.

By 1566 there were many who wanted to see Rizzio removed from the scene, and in that year a number of Scottish noblemen, including Darnley, put their name to a bond with this objective in view. Knowledge of this bond was widespread and Mary was warned of it but did not take heed of it. Rizzio could be eliminated, either by imprisonment or by assassination. On the insistence of Darnley the latter was decided on and, moreover, not secretly but in the glare of publicity in the presence of the Queen, to punish her for the wrongs to which he thought she had subjected him.

The events of 9 March 1566 are not clear-cut. There have been varying accounts of them, some from eyewitnesses, some from those who learned of them subsequently. On that night the Queen was having a small supper party in Holyrood House, which included Rizzio, when a group of conspirators broke in. It was headed by the Earl of Ruthven, a murky and disreputable character who, among other evils, was believed to practise necromancy. He was to claim later that it was not his intention to murder Rizzio on the spot, but this is scarcely credible. Certainly this was what happened: he was dragged out and stabbed as many as 50 times.

In the ensuing chaos Mary, who was six months pregnant, was roughly manhandled and threatened with death. She managed to survive by pretending to come to terms with the conspirators and going through the motions of pardoning them. But she was not to be set free; she was to be kept in confinement for the time being and was placed in the custody of her husband. However, Darnley then defected on his fellow conspirators and contrived for Mary to escape from Holyrood. This was followed by a nightmarish journey of 25 miles through the night on horseback, with dangers threatening all the way. Darnley's behaviour could not have been worse: he rode on a separate horse while Mary rode pillion behind someone else. When they fell behind Darnley kept beating their horse to go faster, and when Mary protested about the danger to their unborn child he answered brutally: 'In God's name come on! If this baby dies we can have more.' He then galloped on ahead, leaving Mary and her rider to fend for themselves. Miraculously, after what she had endured in the last three days, Mary arrived safely and in good shape at Dumbarton Castle where supporters awaited her, and nine days later she was to ride into Edinburgh at the head of an army some 8,000 strong.

Soon afterwards Mary was struck down by a serious illness, for a time feared to be mortal. It was combined with a deep depression which must have been brought on by the physical and mental stress she had been enduring and by the contumacious behaviour of her husband which was at times treasonable. There were rumours, albeit unconfirmed, that he was hatching wild plots to oust Mary and take over the government of the country in the name of his newborn son, James,[16] with himself as Regent, and to this end had been soliciting the aid of the Pope and Philip II of Spain on the grounds that Mary was not a true Catholic and had been allowing too much toleration of Protestantism. Mary made little attempt to conceal the fact that she longed to be free of her husband. She had hoped that this might be achieved by divorce, but this depended on the consent of the Pope which might not be forthcoming; also it would cast doubts on the legitimacy of her baby son.

There were others besides herself at that time who wanted to see Darnley dead. His accomplices in the murder of Rizzio sought revenge for his desertion of them and were fearful of what he might reveal about their part in the plot. In November of 1566 a number of prominent Scottish noblemen (Morton, Lethington and Argyll among others) were secretly plotting the death of Darnley. If divorce was not possible then it would have to be by what was euphemistically called 'other means'; in plain language, assassination.[17] In this the lead was taken by one who was to have

---

[16] The future James VI of Scotland and James I of England was born on 19 June 1566.

[17] They put their names to what became known as the Craigmillar Bond by which Darnley would be killed and whoever did the deed would be defended by the other signatories.

a fateful role in Mary's life. James Hepburn, Earl of Bothwell, then some 30 years old, had had a wild and adventurous career. He was described by a contemporary as 'glorious,[18] rash and hazardous'. Of great bodily strength, vicious and dissolute, he had always lived dangerously and had seen the insides of several prisons including the Tower of London. His favoured way of settling any dispute had been by the drawn dagger rather than by compromise. His spell was a powerful one and, increasingly, Mary succumbed to it.

Few murders in history have caused such a sensation and been so deeply investigated as that of Darnley, and events are still surrounded by an aura of mystery. There is much conflicting evidence and many questions have not been fully answered. Here it is not intended to delve into all these complexities. The main outline of what happened is reasonably clear.

At the end of 1566 Darnley (not yet 21) was suffering acutely from tertiary syphilis; his hair and teeth were falling out, he was covered in pustules and was stinking vilely. In this condition Mary could not but feel some pity for him and arranged that he should have treatment (mainly mercury and sulphur baths) in a house in the outskirts of Edinburgh known as Kirk O'Field. Here he was at the mercy of his enemies, who decided on immediate action to implement the 'other means' they had in mind. As might be expected, Bothwell was the ringleader and took the decision that the assassination should be effected by the blowing up of Kirk O'Field. This was a strange choice, as Bothwell's usual method was cold steel; and it had difficulties, notably the inconspicuous transport of a large quantity of gunpowder into Kirk O'Field, packing it tightly in the room below that of Darnley and then setting it alight. However, this was achieved and at 2 a.m. on 10 February 1567 there was an almighty explosion and Kirk O'Field was reduced to rubble. But this was proved to be unnecessary, as it seems that Darnley and the servant who slept in his room became aware that something was afoot and made off into the garden where, it later transpired, they were set upon and strangled.

News of the murder caused shock and bewilderment throughout Scotland and, indeed, throughout Europe. The question in everyone's mind was: who was responsible? Few had doubts that Bothwell

---

[18] In the sense of vainglorious rather than heroic.

was at the centre of it, but what of the Queen? Was she involved, and to what extent? The presumption at the time was that she was privy to the plot and had given her consent to it; but this has not stood up to the test of time and today it is generally accepted that she had no prior knowledge of it. She had always had a horror of any form of violence and, much as she might have been exasperated by her husband, she would not have agreed to him being blown up. Certainly her movements and behaviour on the night of the explosion gave no indication that she was expecting an event of that sort; and afterwards her shock and horror seemed to have been genuine.

Unfortunately her later behaviour did nothing to allay suspicions. It was expected that she would set up an immediate enquiry into the murder, but this she seemed disinclined to do, perhaps dissuaded by some of her ministers whose consciences were not clear, having given their name to the Craigmillar Bond, pledging the death of Darnley. It was on the initiative of Darnley's father, the Earl of Lennox, that Bothwell was put on trial for the murder before the Privy Council where he was acquitted for lack of evidence, although there was a general suspicion that this was a false verdict.

Afterwards Bothwell became increasingly high-handed. Within a week he convened a meeting of political and religious leaders (including eight bishops, nine earls and seven barons) who were induced to sign a bond in which they affirmed Bothwell's innocence and expressed the hope that Mary being 'now destitute of a husband', might consider Bothwell in that role.[19]

A week later on 24 April Bothwell became outrightly despotic, waylaying Mary en route from Stirling to Edinburgh and carrying her off to his castle of Dunbar. It was to appear later that this 'abduction' had not perhaps been forcible and that Mary had gone voluntarily. Dazed and lonely, she was desperate for a strong guiding hand and it seemed to her that this was what Bothwell could provide. He was bent on becoming king and at Dunbar, having ravished her, he coerced her into agreeing to marriage. There was an obstacle to this in the form of his wife, Lady Jane Gordon, but she readily agreed to a divorce which was granted straight away by a Protestant court. Two weeks later Bothwell was created Duke

---

[19] This became known as Ainslie's Bond after the name of the tavern where it was believed to have been signed.

of Orkney and he and Mary were married in a Protestant ceremony; the celebrations were low-key in contrast to the festive occasion of Mary's marriage to Darnley. This, Mary's third marriage, was to last for no more than four weeks. For her these were weeks of pain and remorse as Bothwell was a harsh and repressive husband, making her give up innocent amusements like hunting, music and cards and raging furiously if she so much as looked in the direction of another man, while he himself retained relations with other women including his ex-wife.

But Bothwell had overstepped the mark. Opposition to him soon began to mount even from those who had been his associates in the murder of Darnley and had later supported him in the Ainslie Bond. He was accused by the Privy Council of murder and illegal marriage.

In June 1567 rebel lords began to muster their forces and Bothwell mustered his. Their armies confronted each other at Carberry Hill near Musselburgh. Each side occupied a strong position and was unwilling to take the offensive. The rebels paraded in front of them a banner depicting Darnley dead below a tree and a child, representing his son James, kneeling beside him with the motto, 'Judge and revenge my cause, O Lord!' But this did not provoke the royalist forces into an attack, and so the two armies waited, inactive through a scorching summer's day. At times attempts were made for a truce, but these were unavailing because Mary would not forsake Bothwell and let him be taken prisoner by the rebels. It was even proposed that the matter should be settled by single combat between Bothwell and one of the rebel lords. Both were willing but Mary intervened to prohibit it. In the end Mary and Bothwell were compelled to come to terms; their army, maddened by thirst, was melting away and there were no signs of expected reinforcements. Bothwell was to be allowed to make off in search of fresh forces while Mary surrendered to the rebel lords on condition that there would be a parliamentary enquiry into the murder of Darnley.

Before leaving, Bothwell gave Mary a list of the lords who had signed the Craigmillar Bond and these included the two leaders of the rebel army, the earls of Morton and Argyll to whom Mary addressed the pertinent but in the circumstances tactless remark: 'I am told that all this [the rebellion] is done in order to get justice against the King's murderers. I am also told that you are the chief of them.'

Mary had expected from the rebel lords treatment befitting a queen, but this was not accorded her. Not only did she suffer discomfort and hardship, but also virulent abuse from the rank and file of the rebel army. She was greeted by shouts of 'Burn the whore! Burn the murderess of her husband!' Since her marriage to Bothwell she had become a hate figure. She was then conducted to Edinburgh where she was lodged not in Holyrood but in a private house without any attendants and few clothes, and once again crowds gathered to shriek abuse at her. She had once been their beloved, beautiful queen but now, bedraggled, undressed, frantic (and four months pregnant) she presented a very different picture. She had hoped to be taken from Edinburgh to her son in Stirling, but she was to find that there was a different destination for her. The rebel lords wanted her out of the way, incommunicado and in tight security, and the place chosen was an island on Loch Leven.

Mary was to remain a prisoner there for ten months. It is possible that she might have come to terms with the rebel lords if she had been willing to divorce Bothwell, but this she would not do, partly because her love for him was not dead and partly because of her pregnancy; she did not want the legitimacy of her offspring to be put in doubt.

Bothwell was soon to be quit of Scotland. He had been outlawed and stripped of his titles, accused of murdering Darnley, abducting the Queen and marrying her by force. He had been unable to raise fresh forces and had been driven into the north of the country and had then taken refuge in Norway where by an unlucky chance he had fallen into the hands of an old enemy (kinsman of an ex-mistress) who had clapped him in gaol and then handed him over to King Frederick who kept him a prisoner in gruesome conditions until his death eleven years later, by which time he was 'distracted of wits and senses'.

Soon after the confrontation at Carberry Hill the rebel lords (principally Morton, Maitland and Balfour) had taken out a warrant for Mary's detention, stating that: 'she appeared to fortify and maintain the said Earl of Bothwell and his accomplices in their said wicked crimes'. They also hunted down and put to death brutally all Bothwell's minions who had had any connection with the Kirk O'Field explosion. This they did ruthlessly in order to distract public attention from their own far greater guilt.

Among those hauled in was Bothwell's tailor, George Dalgliesh, whose arrest was to have historic consequences. Under torture he confessed to the possession of a silver casket belonging to Bothwell, containing letters and 'divers evidences and parchments' which proved to be deeply incriminating of Mary, showing that her 'abduction' had been a put-up job and that she was involved in the murder of Darnley. In time these documents were to give rise to endless debate and disagreement but, strangely, at first they were not made public – all the more strange because at the time the rebel lords were actively engaged in blackening Mary's name. As will be seen later this was not to be the only thing that was strange about the so-called 'casket letters'.

On the island fortress of Loch Leven Mary was in the custody of Sir William Douglas (half-brother of the Earl of Moray). Also present was his mother, Lady Margaret Douglas, a formidable old battleaxe who had a strong dislike of Mary and saw to it that her imprisonment was strict and rigorous. In the first weeks of her imprisonment Mary became seriously unwell and on 20 July she was devastated by a miscarriage (of stillborn twins). A few days after, when she was at her weakest, she was visited by a leading rebel (Lord Lindsay) who bullied her brutally into signing an Instrument of Abdication by which she resigned the crown to her son James and agreed to the regency of her half-brother, James Stuart Earl of Moray (illegitimate son of James V). A week later James, at the age of 13 months, was crowned King as James VI amid general rejoicing.

At that time Mary had few friends. The rebel lords were united against her, Moray was stern and unsympathetic, and John Knox took the opportunity to inveigh against 'the Scarlet Woman' and 'the Whore of Babylon'. But this was to change. It was not long before Moray had made enemies and some Scottish lairds had resumed their habitual feuding in which some of them upheld the cause of Mary. Mary herself staged a marked recovery both bodily and mentally, and it soon became evident that her physical allure was as potent as ever, and that there were those in Loch Leven castle who were not immune to it. Sir William's younger brother, George Douglas, became infatuated by her and wanted to marry her, but this became known to Sir William who ordered him off the island. This was not the end of the affair, as from the mainland he was to have a leading role in Mary's escape.

By 1568 Mary, encouraged by news of growing support, became determined to break free. Her first attempt came to nothing; she had disguised herself as a washerwoman and bribed a boatman to row her across the loch, but although her face was well hidden her hands were not and these, sleek and slender, were not those of a washerwoman, so the boatman refused to proceed, although he did not report the incident. Five weeks later, however, on 2 May a second attempt, engineered primarily by another young admirer, Willie Douglas, was to succeed, and Mary reached the mainland where she was greeted enthusiastically. Popular opinion had evidently veered considerably in the last months, and within a week a powerful group of nobles, churchmen and other notables had given their name to a bond pledging their support, and Mary had renounced her abdication on the grounds that she had signed it under duress and it had been ratified by an illegal parliament.

The Regent, Moray, was aghast when he heard of this, and took prompt action to rally his forces. His army and that of Mary were to give battle in the village of Langside (now a suburb of Glasgow). Although Mary's forces outnumbered those of Moray by about two to one, owing to the ineptitude of her commanders she suffered a reverse and was forced into flight southward. After a horrendous journey of more than 90 miles, suffering every kind of hardship, she reached Dumfries where it was necessary for her to make a crucial decision. There were three options open to her: she could continue the struggle in Scotland where support for her was growing; or she could take refuge in France where as Queen Dowager she should be received honourably; or she could take a ship to England and plead for military aid from her cousin and rival Elizabeth. This was an uncertain and dangerous course, and her advisers urged her not to take it, but she insisted – with fatal consequences.

Mary landed at the Cumberland port of Workington on 16 May 1567. She immediately sent word of her arrival to Lord Lowther, the Deputy-Governor of Carlisle, who was much taken aback and at a loss to know what treatment should be afforded her – that for a queen or for a refugee from justice. He sent to London for guidance and in the meanwhile Mary, with an entourage of some 40, was lodged in Carlisle Castle.

When the news reached Queen Elizabeth she too was shocked and uncertain of what action to take. It was indeed a thorny question. Her attitude for some time had been that Mary had been deposed

36

illegally and was still Queen of Scotland, but there could be no question of her being reinstated by force of English arms. Besides, she was a Roman Catholic and a claimant to the English throne and as long as she was at liberty in England she posed a threat, as Roman Catholics might rally round her. At the same time Elizabeth was unwilling to send her back to Scotland to the tender mercies of the rebel lords who might put her on trial and condemn her to death, which would be a fearsome blow to the principle of monarchy and set a dangerous precedent. Elizabeth decided, therefore, that she would dissemble and play for time.

She gave orders that Mary was not to be allowed to come to London but was to be detained in Carlisle where the treatment of her and her entourage was to be honourable, but that 'not one of them should be allowed to escape' and all incoming and outgoing letters should be 'apprehended' as her great fear was that Mary would seek aid from France or Spain. Such treatment amounted in fact to imprisonment, but modified so that it should not seem to be so. But to keep her in any form of custody needed a reason, and Elizabeth laid it down that she would not meet Mary face to face and talk of her release until she had been cleared of the crimes of which she was accused. This would mean putting her on trial, but such would be beneath the dignity of a queen, so it was ordained that there should be a commission of enquiry into the activities of the Earl of Moray, the Regent, and other Scottish lords who were bidden to attend and put their case. This was unwarranted interference in the affairs of a sovereign state and gave rise to the suspicion that Elizabeth, like Edward I and Henry VIII before her, was aiming at a takeover of Scottish royal powers. Moray, however, decided to agree to this arrangement as Mary at large in England was as much a danger to him as to Elizabeth, and the last thing he wanted at that time was an English invasion of Scotland.

Agreement from Mary was harder to obtain. She had been bitterly disappointed that she had not been taken directly to Elizabeth to plead her case. Instead she had been kept isolated in the north and moved for greater security from Carlisle to the remote castle of Bolton in Yorkshire where she was out of touch with events, and conditions there were rigorous.[20] To deal with her Elizabeth sent

---

[20] Among other hardships was a shortage of appropriate clothes and Mary appealed to Elizabeth to send her some from her ample wardrobe, but in this Elizabeth proved niggardly and sent her only a few of her less presentable cast-offs.

up one of her most trusted and able ministers, Sir Francis Knollys, to assure her that 'no creature living was more anxious than herself to help', but at the same time she imposed strict conditions – that Mary give up for ever her claim to the throne of England, that she would seek no aid from abroad and that she would forswear the Mass. Knollys soon established a close rapport with Mary, perhaps even falling a little in love with her, writing back to Elizabeth of her 'eloquent tongue, discreet head and stout courage'. Under his influence Mary agreed to what Elizabeth asked of her. 'I am in her hands', she said ruefully, 'and she can dispose of me as she will.'

The commission of enquiry was convened at York in October 1568. Sitting in judgement were three English noblemen headed by the Duke of Norfolk, who seemed to be unclear as to the purposes of the enquiry and what was expected of him. The result was that proceedings became confused. It was not thought proper for Mary to attend, but Moray and other rebel lords were there in force, set on doing all they could to blacken Mary's name so that she remained imprisoned in England. To this end Moray brought to light the Casket Letters which had remained dormant for the last 18 months, no one paying much attention to them. Now Moray saw to it that copies of these with translations were put before the judges. As had been seen, these were deeply incriminating of Mary, and the effect of them at first on the Duke of Norfolk was shattering. He became convinced of her guilt and sent urgently to London to find out what action he should take. However, he soon subsided, being persuaded that the letters were forgeries and that Mary was completely innocent – so much so that he entertained ideas of marrying her. But by then Queen Elizabeth realised that the enquiry had become chaotic and ordered that it should be transferred to Westminster where it would be under her eye.

When it was set up again a further ten judges were added (including Elizabeth's ex-lover the Earl of Leicester and her guiding genius William Cecil). Once again proceedings became disordered, quite unlike any other court of law. Moray and his Scottish commissioners came armed with copies of the Casket Letters as well as 'A Book of her Articles' which listed further crimes of Mary, including conspiring with Bothwell to do away with her infant son James to make way for her children by Bothwell to succeed her on the throne. Mary herself was kept at a distance in

Bolton Castle and was offered the alternatives of answering the charges against her in writing or by word of mouth to noblemen sent to her for this purpose; but both of these she refused, nor would she confront her accusers face to face which would be beneath her dignity. 'I am not equal to my rebels,' she declared, 'neither will I commit myself to be weighed in equal balance with them.' She was only prepared to testify before Queen Elizabeth, who would not hear her. She did, however, bring counter-charges against Moray and others of complicity in crimes including the murder of Rizzio.

The outcome of this great legal charade was a stalemate. Everything was left inconclusive. The charges against Mary were not proven, nor were those against Moray and the rebel lords. Actually this state of affairs suited Elizabeth. Although Mary was not found guilty there was enough evidence for keeping her in some form of captivity as 'a lawful prisoner'. In this respect Elizabeth's devious tactics had paid off. She was also content that no guilt should be brought against the rebel lords, although their records were far from clear. Not only were they afforded a safe passage back to Scotland but they were enriched by a subsidy of £500 – unusually liberal for Elizabeth.

Although it might seem that Elizabeth had been successful, it must be doubtful whether the results were the best possible for her. These entailed Mary being kept a prisoner in England for 19 years, during which time she was a constant thorn in the flesh and finally forced Elizabeth to take action which drove her to distraction. If in 1569 Mary had been allowed to go free she would doubtless have gone to France where she would have been received graciously but, because of the murder of Darnley and her marriage to Bothwell, with no great honour. She would probably have died in comparative obscurity, instead of which her execution in England after long years in captivity turned her into a holy martyr.

It might have been expected that at the end of the Westminster enquiry the Casket Letters would have attracted little further attention, but this was far from the case. Fifteen years later the original documents were to disappear, somewhat mysteriously, so that only copies and translations remained, but controversy over these was to rage for centuries to come with no generally accepted final verdict. There will always be an element of doubt concerning the innocence or guilt of Mary.

In 1569 the immediate problem was where and in what circumstances Mary was to be detained. As a reigning monarch (still regarded as such by some) her treatment had to be special, and it was decided that she should be put in the charge of the Earl of Shrewsbury, England's wealthiest nobleman, to be lodged in one of the seven estates he owned in the Midlands. This involved the Earl in considerable trouble and expense (as the allowance made to him by the government was sparse), but during the 15 years he was Mary's governor he was to prove kindly and accommodating as well as finicky and insistent. His wife, the notorious Bess of Hardwick (four times married and immensely rich) was to be less sympathetic and she saw to it that Mary's life was not without rigour.

It was unfortunate that the first of Shrewsbury's houses to which Mary was taken was that at Tutbury in Staffordshire, a derelict medieval castle – depressing, far from weatherproof and with foul sanitation so that a fetid smell always pervaded it. Here Mary soon became unwell and was moved first to Wingfield Manor in Derbyshire and then to Chatsworth where her treatment was lenient. She lived in semi-state with an entourage of some 40 and was allowed reasonable freedom to take fresh air as well as occasional visits to the curative waters of Buxton. She was closely supervised at all times, but not closely enough to prevent secret letters coming in and going out, and some of these were incriminating; for England at that time was rife with plots and insurrections, and most of these were focused on Mary, even though she was not always aware of them. Within a year of her imprisonment there was a rebellion in the northern counties where Roman Catholicism was strongly prevalent. Mary had no part in it and it soon petered out, but others were to follow.

Two years later in 1571 a wildly impractical scheme came to light, orchestrated by a cosmopolitan financier, one Robert Ridolfi, involving an invasion of England by Spanish forces from the Netherlands, the assassination of Queen Elizabeth and the enthronement of Mary wedded to the Duke of Norfolk; such a union had been on the cards for some time and, rather strangely, had been looked on with some favour by Mary. But the plot was soon exposed and although Ridolfi managed to escape abroad, Norfolk, who had blundered into it somewhat cluelessly, was hunted down and executed. If full justice had been done Mary too should have been put to death as it was evident that she was aware of what was going on, although not closely involved and having no part in the proposed assassination of the Queen. In the event no proceedings were taken against her, as Elizabeth dreaded – as she was always to do – condemning her cousin to death.

In the following years there were to be yet more conspiracies as religious attitudes hardened and intolerance became more bitter. This was initiated in 1570 when Pope Pius V excommunicated Elizabeth, formally deposing her as Queen, and it being intimated later that assassination of her would be no mortal sin. Already by then the forces of the Counter-Reformation were gathering strength. In 1568 an Englishman, William Allen, set up a seminary in Rome to train young missionaries in the campaign of reconverting England to Catholicism. As well as religious indoctrination they were taught to expect torture and death and to have no fear of them, rather to glory in them if they brought about the end of heresy. Allen always insisted that their sole purpose was to preach the gospel and save souls and that they had no political intentions, but as they came with the blessings of the Pope and the King of Spain they were deeply suspect. William Cecil was convinced that their real purpose was to overthrow the government and the Church of England and replace Elizabeth by Mary on the throne. Accordingly they were banned and, if apprehended, put to death barbarously.

Fear of Catholic designs in England increased with the accession to the Papacy in 1572 of Gregory XIII, who took a more aggressive view of the campaign in England, openly encouraging the assassination of Elizabeth and giving his blessing in 1579 to an abortive invasion of Ireland.

This intensification of religious strife inevitably affected the position of Mary. At one time she had seemed to be interested in converting to Protestantism, but by 1574 this had been put aside and she declared herself a firm, unwavering Catholic; she had no qualms about introducing Catholic priests into her household illegally, disguised as domestic servants or doctors. For some time she had been carrying on an indiscreet secret correspondence in code with the Pope and the kings of Spain and France, and this had become known to the vigilant English secret service organised by the Secretary of State, Sir Thomas Walsingham. Following the discovery of another plot in 1783 organised by Sir Francis Throckmorton and the assassination of the Protestant Dutch king, William the

Silent, in 1584 the government became seriously alarmed about the safety of Queen Elizabeth, and it was decided that Mary had to be put under more rigorous supervision. To his great relief the Earl of Shrewsbury was replaced as her governor first by Sir Ralph Sadler and then by Sir Amyas Paulet, a man of a very different hue – a stern unbending Puritan with an uncompromising sense of duty and a strong disapproval of Mary and all she stood for.

And so Mary was transferred from Chatsworth back to the hardships and squalor of Tutbury where a harsh and inflexible routine was imposed on her. By then Cecil and Walsingham had come to the conclusion that if Elizabeth and the Protestant church were to be preserved, Mary had to be eliminated, and this they set about effecting ruthlessly. In the first place they pushed through Parliament an Act of Association by which it became treasonable not only to participate in a plot but also to be the beneficiary of a plot, even if one had no knowledge of it. This, they thought, would ensnare Mary; but to make sure, Walsingham engaged in a devious and unscrupulous stratagem. In 1586 he became aware of a plot being put together by a callow, reckless youth, Anthony Babington, and instead of moving in at once and crushing it, he decided to infiltrate it with double agents and agents provocateurs so that Mary became deeply compromised.

She was provoked into writing an incriminating letter which left no doubt as to her participation in the plot. This recklessness on her part is surprising and may have been prompted by the harsh treatment she was receiving. As her movements became further restricted, her communications with the outside world were cut off and her retinue diminished, she came to long for death and martyrdom. 'I am only left with my royal blood and Catholic religion', she declared.

By August of 1586 Walsingham was ready to strike. Babington and his fellow conspirators were arrested and put to death, and in September Mary was moved to the grim fortress-prison of Fotheringay Castle, where on 15 October commissioners from London arrived to put her on trial. It might have been that Mary would have had no part in this. It was clearly illegal. There was no justification for the sovereign of one country to put on trial for treason the sovereign of another. Like her grandson, Charles I, in the next century, she might have shunned it altogether. But this she did not do. She wanted to state her case bravely and dramatically.

During the trial she was put to every disadvantage: she was allowed no counsel to speak for her, nor witnesses called for her defence, and she had no access to the documents of the prosecution while her papers and notes were taken from her. Nevertheless, though her body might have been weakened by long adversity, her mind was clear, and she remained calm and self-possessed throughout. Boldly she proclaimed to the court:

> I am myself a queen, the daughter of a king, a stranger, and the true kinswoman of the Queen of England. As an absolute queen, I cannot submit to orders, nor can I submit to the laws of the land without injury to myself, the King my son and all other sovereign princes. For myself I do not recognise the laws of England nor do I know or understand them as I have often asserted.

She also made plain that she had only ever conspired to effect her escape from captivity – never to assassinate her cousin and take her place on the throne.

It was a foregone conclusion that she would be found guilty (of 'compassing and imagining since June 1 diverse matters tending to the death and destruction of the Queen of England'). But there was to be a delay of three months before Elizabeth could bring herself to sign her death warrant. During this time she was at great pains to find ways of avoiding this. If Mary were to admit her guilt and beg forgiveness she might be spared by an act of clemency; but this Mary resolutely refused to do. Elizabeth even let it be known that she would welcome her secret assassination and indicated to Paulet that he might see to this, but Paulet, severe and brutal though he might be, was no murderer and would have nothing to do with the idea.

Apart from the repugnance Elizabeth felt at the thought of putting to death a cousin and a fellow sovereign, she could not but be concerned also by the strong feelings that Mary's execution would arouse in the courts of Europe. The last thing she wanted at that time was war with the major powers, and the person who might have stirred this up was Mary's son James, King of Scotland. But James had no filial feelings. He had been brought up to regard his mother as a murderess and adulteress and her religion as devilish. Above all he did not want to compromise in any way his succession to the throne of England. For this he would make any sacrifice; he was even prepared to consider the fantastic notion of marriage to Elizabeth, 30 years older than he though she might be. And so he took no positive action, merely remarking callously that his mother 'must drink the ale she had brewed'.

Meanwhile further hardships and humiliations were being inflicted on Mary. She was told bluntly that as 'an attainted, convicted and condemned woman', she could expect no royal privileges. But this no longer concerned her unduly: her thoughts were no longer on her royal status but on her martyrdom, which she was longing for. Elizabeth was at last prevailed on to sign her death warrant on 1 February 1587 (although she was later to pretend she had never meant to), and a week later a deputation arrived at Fotheringay to break to Mary that she was to be executed the following morning – news which she received with total calmness. 'I thank you for such welcome news,' she said. 'You will do me great good in withdrawing me from the world out of which I am very glad to go.'

During her last night Mary made no attempt to sleep, but spent the time drawing up a will and bestowing her few remaining possessions on her attendants. Few concessions were made to her by her captors: she was not allowed a Catholic priest for her last confessional; it was only with difficulty that she obtained permission for some of her servants to be with her at the end; and her request that she should be buried in France was refused.

Although she had such little time for preparations, she was able to see to it that her execution was a memorable occasion for those who witnessed it. Throughout she remained serene and dignified with no trace of fear, bidding those round her to rejoice for her rather than to weep as her troubles were now done. She came in a black dress but this was taken off to reveal a bodice of scarlet. Then after granting wholehearted pardon to the executioner and brushing aside the attempted ministrations of Protestant divines, she proceeded to the scaffold and laid her head on the block. A special axeman had been hired for the occasion but he failed to sever her head with one blow. Another was needed, and her remains were then treated with scant respect. Her head was held up to the cries of 'So perish all the Queen's enemies', and the golden hair was found to be a wig and came off, revealing underneath closely cropped grey hair. Her body was then stripped of all clothing to be embalmed and then placed in a heavy lead coffin which remained unburied in Fotheringay Castle until 1612 when, on the orders of James I, it was interred in Westminster Abbey.

And so at the age of 45 Mary's tragic life came to an end. Few monarchs have had to contend with such a 'sea of troubles'.[21] Certainly there had been indiscretions and follies, but retribution had been extortionate. Her last great wish, however, was to be granted: that of a martyr's death which would be for ever memorable. She was not to be forgotten. In many media – poetry, drama, film and television – she was to be vividly and variously commemorated. Not many lives have given rise to such strong emotion.

---

[21] Shakespeare, *Hamlet*, Act III, scene I.

3

CATHERINE DE MEDICI, QUEEN OF FRANCE
(1519–1589)

Catherine de Medici was the wife of one French king, Henry II, and the mother of three others: Francis II, Charles IX and Henry III. She was also mother-in-law of the King of Spain. It is one of the anomalies of French history that she, the offspring of a wealthy Italian banking family with no royal blood in her veins, should have been the effective ruler of France for nearly 30 years, for most of which time the country was in tumult from wars of religion. It was perhaps beyond the capacity of anyone, certainly of Catherine, to bring these to an end. For her failure to do so, however, and for the horrific events which occurred during that time, notably the massacre of Saint Bartholomew's Day, she has borne the main blame. Her reputation, unjustly, has been that of a ruthless and devious despot, interested only in boosting her own power and that of her family. Her well-meaning but unavailing attempts to bring peace have been given less publicity.

Catherine was born in Florence on 13 April 1519. Her father, Lorenzo de Medici, Duke of Urbino, was head of the ruling house of the city, which had made a great fortune out of banking; her mother, Madeleine de la Tour d'Auvergne, came from a wealthy aristocratic French family. The Pope at the time, Leo X, was her great-uncle, and he was followed (not immediately) by another member of the Medici family, Clement VII.

Catherine's childhood was tumultuous. Her mother died two weeks after giving birth to her and her father a week later so that, in the words of a contemporary poet, she was 'left lying in her cradle between two coffins'. Pope Leo saw to it that she was brought to Rome where he created her Duchess of Urbino and placed her in the care of her aunt, Clarice Strozzi, who became a surrogate mother to her. Pope Leo died when Catherine was two and was succeeded by Hadrian VI, a severe character (he had once been Grand Inquisitor of Spain) and no friend of the Medicis. He sent Catherine back to Florence where she was downgraded; but Hadrian died two years later (in 1523) and was followed (after active vote-rigging) by Clement VII who restored Catherine to the dignity and honour due to a member of her family. Pope Clement was fully aware that Catherine, one of the few remaining legitimate members of the Medici family and possessed of great wealth (mainly from her mother) would be a valuable pawn in the plans he was evolving for extending papal power in Italy. These mainly revolved around an illegitimate son he had fathered years ago when he was a cardinal. At the time Giulio de Medici had been passed off as the bastard son of Duke Lorenzo II (more seemly from a layman than from a prince of the church), which made him Catherine's half-brother.

But Pope Clement's schemes were to be sharply set back when his principal ally, King Francis I of France, was decisively defeated in 1525 by his arch-enemy, the Holy Roman Emperor Charles V[1] at the Battle of Pavia. Following this the armies of the Emperor, mainly savage German mercenaries, poured into Italy and in 1527 descended on Rome which lay helpless before them so that Pope Clement was forced to flee from the Vatican, leaving the city to be ravaged by a horde of hungry unpaid soldiers who robbed and raped at will. Nothing had been seen like it since Rome was overrun by the Goths more than 1,000 years before.

In the chaos which then pervaded Italy Catherine (aged eight) was trapped in Florence where, according to the varying fortunes of the war, her treatment was sometimes kindly but more often harsh and brutal, especially when Florence came under siege and she was in great danger from angry, starving mobs who blamed all their troubles on the Medicis. This traumatic experience made a lasting impression on the young Catherine.

In 1530 Pope Clement was able to return to Rome and saw to it that Catherine was brought back there in comparative safety. By then she was considered to be of marriageable age (eleven) and because of her wealth and the fame of her family she had many suitors. As was usual the choice was not left to her, but was assumed by Pope Clement who decided on Henry Duke of Orleans, the second son of the French King, Francis I.

---

[1] Once Charles II of Spain and father of Philip II (husband of Mary Tudor, Queen of England and nephew of Henry VIII's first wife, Catherine of Aragon).

For Catherine marriage into the French royal family was a great honour; she had no royal blood in her veins and it was almost unknown for French princes to marry commoners. But Pope Clement knew that Francis I, despite his defeat at Pavia, still harboured designs for expanding French suzerainty in Italy, and he was in a position to offer him not only large sums of money but also sovereignty of several Italian cities including Pisa, Parma and Modena. Such bait Francis found irresistible. And so in 1533, when they were both 14, Catherine and Henry were married in a magnificent ceremony in Marseilles presided over by the Pope.

The man Catherine married had had no less a troubled childhood than she. At the age of five his mother had died and then came a long and gruelling experience. After the Battle of Pavia Francis I had been taken prisoner and was being held until he agreed to the rigorous terms being imposed on him by the emperor Charles V. As these included the cession of the province of Burgundy he held out against them stubbornly, but then became seriously ill and could bear imprisonment no longer, and pretended to agree. But Charles V did not trust him and insisted on holding his two eldest sons, Francis the Dauphin aged eight and Henry aged seven, as hostages until the terms of the treaty had been implemented. This proved prudent as it soon became evident that Francis was stalling and doing all he could to avoid his obligations; and as he did so the treatment of the two young princes in a Spanish prison became more severe, even brutal, and their term of imprisonment, originally expected to be no longer than a few months, extended to four and a half years. This was to have a lasting effect on Henry. Predictably it resulted in a strong aversion to Spain as well as resentment against his father for letting him remain incarcerated for so long. He also became taciturn and withdrawn, hardly ever laughing or smiling and having few pleasures in life.

Catherine was not well received at the French court. Her lack of royal blood and the commercial origins of her family told against her. She was dubbed 'the Italian woman' and 'the tradesman's daughter'. Life might have been more tolerable for her if she had been a great beauty, but this she was not. A diplomat at the time wrote: 'her mouth is too big and her eyes too prominent and colourless for beauty'; although he did concede that she had 'a shapely figure, a beautiful skin and exquisitely shaped hands'. Her position became more precarious when a year after marriage Pope

Clement VII died, leaving most of her dowry unpaid, and was succeeded by Paul III who not only renounced the dowry but also the papal alliance with France so that Catherine was of no further use to the French king who declared that he had come to her '*toute nue*' (stark naked).

More serious was the uneasy relationship between Catherine and her husband. Henry treated her civilly and dutifully but there was no love between them. Since an early age Henry had been in thrall to a woman 19 years older than himself, Diane de Poitiers, a lady of great beauty and determination. For 23 years she maintained her hold over him, and certainly did not allow it to weaken when he married, continuing to consort with him, to manage his affairs and even to some extent those of Catherine, whom she treated with cool condescension. Surprisingly Catherine, at heart proud and strong-willed, made no great objection to this situation. Perhaps she realised the insecurity of her position and Henry's need for Diane. And marital fidelity was not the order of the day at the court of Francis I, a lusty 40-year-old who let no opportunity pass and set a tone of pervasive prurience.

Catherine's standing in France in her first years, then, was fragile and unsettled, and it became more so with the passing of time when she seemed to be incapable of bearing children. Of all her troubles this was the most despairing. She was fully aware that giving birth to an heir was expected of her above everything. In her anguish she resorted to all manner of weird remedies, consulting astrologists and quack alchemists who prescribed such horrors as draughts of mules' urine and vilely stinking poultices to be applied to her 'sources of life'. She even went so far as to have peepholes bored so that she could spy on Henry and Diane in bed to see if there was anything lacking in her love-making. But for ten years these measures had no success.

During this time there was much talk of Catherine's marriage to Henry being annulled to make way for a more fertile wife,[2] and this was intensified when in 1536 Henry's elder brother, Francis the Dauphin, died suddenly and he became heir to the throne. As Dauphine Catherine became more vulnerable and felt she had to take action, and decided on a bold course. She knew that the matter

---

[2] That it was Catherine who was deficient was shown in 1537 when Henry fathered a bastard son.

rested ultimately with her father-in-law, Francis I, with whom she was on good terms, and so she gambled all by humbling herself meekly before him and imploring him to do whatever he thought best for the kingdom of France, and said she would comply. In this she judged shrewdly as she knew that Francis, despite gross faults, was generous at heart and always susceptible to femininity in distress, and he did indeed respond kindly, laying it down that Catherine's marriage to Henry was indissoluble.

For whatever reason Catherine's apparent sterility came to an end suddenly in 1544 when she gave birth to a son, Francis, named after his grandfather. From then on children came in profusion – nine in 12 years, of which seven survived infancy. This was a turning point in Catherine's life: until then she had felt inadequate and unwanted and had kept in the background; now she began to emerge as a character in her own right. This was carried a stage further when three years later in 1541 on the death of Francis I her husband succeeded to the throne as Henry II and she became Queen of France. Still, however, she did not push forward into the realms of politics. Henry would not have welcomed this and in any case she was preoccupied with child bearing. And Diane de Poitiers was still very much to the fore. When Henry became king she became ever more demanding and Henry, unable to resist her, heaped her with honours and riches. The title of Duchess of Valentinois was bestowed on her and she was imposed on Catherine as lady-in-waiting where she took it upon herself to take charge of the upbringing of her children. On state occasions she was always in evidence, sometimes being accorded precedence over Catherine who showed great self-restraint in tolerating such humiliating situations.

Like his father, Henry II always had ambitions of extending French rule in Italy and in furtherance of this in 1552 he declared war on Charles V, Emperor of Austria and King of Spain, over disputed territories there. But his armies were unsuccessful and by 1559 he had been compelled to cede nearly all French territory in Italy. While he was away Catherine was left as Regent but with only limited powers, and in 1557 she had to take urgent action when a Spanish army invaded northern France from the Netherlands and inflicted a heavy defeat on the French at St Quentin in Picardy, only 80 miles from Paris. This caused great alarm and many citizens (including Diane de Poitiers) fled from the city. But Catherine rose to the occasion, rallying such forces as were available and raising money to pay for them. In the event these were not put to the test as Philip II (King of Spain since the abdication of his father, Charles V, in 1555) did not press home his advantage; but Catherine had won great admiration for her qualities of leadership. This was a significant event in her life, marking the end of a retiring subservient role and the emergence of a formidable power in state affairs.

In 1559 it seemed as if France was set on a steadier and more pacific course; that year peace was made with Spain and to cement the friendship of the two countries a marriage was arranged between Catherine's 13-year-old daughter Elizabeth and Philip II of Spain (twice married before and 20 years older). But then out of the blue came tragedy. To celebrate his daughter's marriage Henry II proclaimed a splendid tournament and issued a challenge to all comers to compete with him in a joust. He was strongly warned against this both by court astrologers and by Catherine, who had had pre-visions of disaster, but he insisted on going ahead – at first with success, but in his final combat he had a mortal accident when wood splinters pierced his eyes and penetrated into his brain so that he died in agony a week later. For France this was a disaster as Henry was developing into a wise and well-respected king, and in his place came his eldest son, Francis II, a weak and sickly youth of 15 who was clearly going to need a lot of propping up. This Catherine was anxious to give him, but she did not have the field to herself.

In the previous year Francis had been married to Mary Stuart (known to history as Mary Queen of Scots). She had been Queen of Scotland since babyhood on the death of her father James V, and became Queen of France on the accession of Francis II; she was also claiming the throne of England as being the only legitimate great-granddaughter of Henry VII.[3] Through her mother, Mary of Guise, Mary was also a member of a powerful and strongly ambitious branch of French royalty, the House of Lorraine, which claimed descent from Charlemagne. This included the Guise family whose influence was greatly enhanced at the accession of Francis II as he was dominated by Mary and gave high office to two of her Guise uncles – Francis

---

[3] Roman Catholics did not accept that Henry VIII had been lawfully married to Queen Elizabeth's mother, Anne Boleyn.

Duke of Guise who commanded the army, and Charles Cardinal of Lorraine who took charge of civil affairs. Although this arrangement did not suit Catherine she felt obliged to go along with it as she did not yet feel strong enough to take control of government herself. For the time being she was lying low.

Francis II was to reign for only 16 months. He had always been frail and prone to illnesses and it was not unexpected that he should have died young. His death in 1560, however, was a turning point in French history, for it marked the assumption of political powers by Catherine. Until then she had apparently been content with a subordinate and deferential role, but with the accession of her second son, Charles IX, at the age of ten, she was ready to assert herself and take control. And this she did decisively. She at once had herself declared Regent with the grandiose title of Gouvernante de France and a special seal was created for her bearing the legend 'Catherine by Grace of God, Queen of France, Mother of the King'. Her position was then made clear: the power of the Guise family was trimmed (although not altogether), the Duchess of Valentinois was ordered from court and made to give up the crown jewels and other gifts that had been bestowed on her; and Mary Stuart, Catherine's daughter-in-law and the other Queen Dowager, returned to her native Scotland. And so at the age of 41 Catherine, offshoot of an Italian banking family, became the effective ruler of France and was to remain so almost until her death nearly 30 years later. And these were to be some of the most troubled years in France's history, encompassing bitter religious strife and bloody civil war.

For some years the Protestant religion had been spreading throughout France. Its adherents, known as Huguenots, came from all ranks of society from princes of royal blood to the humblest peasant. At first they had been regarded by the country's rulers as a scourge to be eliminated by force. But it was soon to be found, here as elsewhere, that religious beliefs could not be suppressed by persecution; to the contrary it inflamed them. This was recognised by Catherine who sought to end the strife by a policy of moderation and tolerance, hoping that this would bring about compromise. But in this she was mistaken. Religious fanaticism was too deeply ingrained. Her policy of granting limited rights to Huguenots pleased no one. Huguenots were resentful that they had not been granted more, while Catholics were furious that they should have been given any at all; and both sides vented their fury on Catherine.

In 1562 the First Religious War broke out and was to be marked by horrific atrocities on both sides: Catholics massacred rebel Huguenots who for their part murdered priests and monks, desecrated churches and destroyed sacred relics; all of which intensified passions and made the chances of a peaceful settlement between them more remote. Particularly provocative was the assassination of the Duke of Guise, commander of the royal forces, by a demented Protestant who asserted that he had been put up to it by a leader of the Huguenots, Admiral Gaspart de Coligny (nephew of the Duke of Montmorency, Constable of France and a strong Catholic). This caused a blood feud between the two families which later was to have fearful consequences.

During the war, which came to a temporary halt in 1574, Catherine, while always remaining a Catholic, did not give up in her efforts to find a peaceful accord; and some agreements were made, although always soon broken. She also did all she could to make her second son, Charles IX, into a plausible monarch. This was not easily done: like his elder brother Francis, and indeed like all his four brothers, he was weak and ill-favoured, shy and retiring, and subject to ungovernable rages. There was little of majesty about him and few powers of leadership; balls and court occasions he detested, his only pleasure being hunting wild animals in which he showed an unhealthy delight in the kill and the evisceration of corpses.

Catherine was clear that as King he would need strong and prolonged support from her, and one way in which she sought to enhance his stature was by maintaining a large and glittering court, perhaps as many as 10,000 strong, containing in addition to the usual throng of courtiers and servants a group of about 50 beautiful young maidens known as 'the Flying Squadron' who, dressed as goddesses, would provide 'chaste and innocent amusement' for the gentlemen. Lavish entertainment was laid on – balls, banquets, masques – the enjoyment of which, Catherine hoped, might bring together Catholic and Protestant and take their minds off religious differences. But this was not to be.

In the same vein Catherine organised for Charles a tremendous royal tour of the whole of his dominions. The idea of this was that Charles (aged 14) would become acquainted with all sorts and conditions of his subjects and they in their turn would be overawed by the magnificence and mystique of monarchy. Perhaps too some of the scars of civil war might be erased. It was all organised on a vast scale with a retinue of several thousand including government officials, foreign ambassadors, prelates and all sorts of entertainers as well as a large armed escort. It was expected that more time would be spent in displays and festivities than in travelling, so also included were such items as triumphal arches, gold plate, silk hangings and gilded furniture, even a royal barge. The tour was a great achievement, covering some 3,000 miles and lasting 28 months. During that time the great host battled through snow storms, floods and scorching heat, and was often in danger from robbers and religious fanatics. In the course of it Charles and Catherine did indeed encounter a variety of people – grandees, scholars, mendicants and the chronically sick. How much of lasting value the tour achieved cannot be known, but it did not bring peace, as civil war broke out again soon after their return.

The Second War of Religion was initiated by a rebellion against Spanish rule in the Netherlands. French Huguenots wanted to send help to the Dutch rebels, but this Catherine would not do, although she was uneasy about a large Spanish army in a neighbouring country which might later be used against France. Philip, most intractable of Catholics, had been strongly opposed to Catherine's concessions to the Huguenots, regarding them as mortal sin, and he might have been tempted to send an army into France to crush all Protestants; and to guard against this Catherine had hired a force of Swiss mercenaries. In the event they were not needed against Spain, but Catherine did not disband them, which led the Huguenots to believe that they might be used against them, and so warfare broke out.

The war followed much the same course as previously. At first the Huguenots had successes particularly in the south of the country, but later most of their gains had to be given up. Both sides relied heavily on mercenaries and help from abroad – Catholics from Spain and Protestants from England and Germany. In pitched battles the Catholics usually had the upper hand although not decisively, and when a temporary peace was agreed it was not because of a great victory but because both sides were exhausted and financially broke. As before, the war was fought brutally and ruthlessly: old customs of knightly chivalry went by the board and most battles were followed by the slaughter of prisoners. And in this Catherine was as guilty as anyone: gone was her moderation and pursuit of compromise. She saw that such policies had failed and brought her nothing but odium and distrust. For a time she became vindictive and avenging. 'Let them bc killed or sent to the galleys', she said of prisoners after one battle. In particular she sought the elimination of Huguenot leaders, and for this she was prepared to use any methods, however nefarious – poison, hired assassins even the black arts. These had always fascinated her; she paid great heed to astrologers, and during her great tour had made a point of meeting the famous Nostradamus.[4] And so she resorted to necromancy to get rid of her enemies. Stories were abroad of poisoned apples and noxious gloves that brought death to their wearers, as well as full-scale bronze effigies on which spells would be cast. And some Huguenot leaders did die mysteriously. It was not for nothing that she became known at that time as 'the Black Queen'.

In spite of Catholic victories in battle it had become clear by 1570 that the civil war had again reached a stalemate, and in that year another peace treaty (St Germain) was agreed which gave Huguenots greater rights than they had had before, and so caused outrage to hard-line Catholics. But there was for a time a period of comparative peace during which Catherine sought prestigious marriages for her children.

Some of these were strangely misconceived, especially those involving Queen Elizabeth of England who, she thought, might be a suitable wife for her son Charles IX, although he was 19 and Elizabeth 37. But the Virgin Queen held aloof, although she did not reject the suit out of hand as she needed France as an ally against Spain, so she prevaricated until Charles lost patience and married instead the enchanting Elizabeth of Austria, daughter of the Habsburg emperor. Not to be put off, however, Catherine then proposed her third son, Henry Duke of Anjou (future Henry III) as a marriage partner for the English queen: but, effeminate and eccentric, he soon faded from the scene. Still Catherine persevered, and most bizarre of all, put forward her youngest son, Francis Duke of Alençon; tiny, humpbacked, pockmarked from smallpox and 23 years younger, he was hardly a partner for 'Gloriana',[5] but Elizabeth did not turn him down immediately; it suited her politics to keep him (and Catherine) in suspense.

---

[4] French physician and astrologer and author of a book of prophecies.

[5] He had been christened Hercules, but when this name became palpably absurd he was renamed Francis, his eldest brother having by then died. For more on him see the chapter on Queen Elizabeth I of England.

Just as improbable as the marriages Catherine failed to arrange was the one she did bring off between her daughter Marguerite (known as Margot) and the 17-year-old Henry, King of Navarre, nominal leader of the Huguenots. There were strong considerations against such a union: apart from religious differences they were second cousins and so within the limits of consanguinity, thus needing a dispensation from the Pope which he was unwilling to grant. There was too strong personal antipathy. Henry, a strong, vibrant character, was later as Henry IV to be one of France's greatest kings, but Margot found him uncouth and illiterate (and malodorous); and he, although a great lover of women, had no love for her. But Catherine was convinced that the marriage might heal the country's religious rifts and pressed forward with it. There was strong opposition from hard-line Catholics and Huguenots, notably from Henry's mother, Jeanne d'Albret, Dowager Queen of Navarre and an implacable Protestant who regarded with horror any union with Catholics and any contact with, as she thought, the loose and pernicious morals of the court of the King of France. She gave way eventually but only after great pressure had been brought to bear on her. Another person whose agreement was necessary for the proposed marriage was the highly esteemed Huguenot leader Admiral Gaspard de Coligny, who strongly disliked the idea of it, but was won over to it as being the most likely means of preventing another civil war. He was to be a key figure in the catastrophic events of the following years.

The wedding, which took place on 18 August 1572, was hardly a hallowed occasion as it was evident that the bride and bridegroom had no love for each other, and during the ceremony Henry, being a heretic, was not allowed inside Notre Dame and had to wait on a platform outside while a proxy acted for him at the altar.

Soon afterwards a confused and dangerous situation arose. King Charles IX, then aged 22, had for some time been moving away from the dominance of his mother and falling under the spell of Admiral Coligny, whom he had come to regard as a wise and benevolent father figure, and was even showing some sympathy with his Protestant beliefs. This liaison infuriated Catherine who felt that her control of her son was slipping away, and decided that Coligny had to be eliminated – a fateful decision which was to precipitate one of the most appalling events in French history.

For the assassination of Coligny Catherine conspired with her younger son, Henry Duke of Anjou, and members of the Guise family who had never forgiven Coligny for his alleged responsibility for the murder of Francis Duke of Guise in 1563. It was settled that an assassin would be hired to kill him on 22 August in Paris, four days after the wedding. There could not have been a worse time and place, for Paris at that time was tense and overcrowded. People had poured in for the spectacle of the royal wedding and these included many Huguenots who were regarded with suspicion and hatred by the predominantly Catholic native Parisians. The city, sweltering in the hottest summer in memory, was a tinderbox ready to ignite, and nothing was more likely to make this happen than the killing of the leader of the Huguenots. And Catherine must surely have realised this. Yet she and her fellow conspirators let the plot go ahead.

In the first instance the assassination was botched. Coligny was wounded but not mortally and seemed likely to recover, his reputation enhanced by near martyrdom. It was then that Catherine and her co-conspirators, including by then the weak and feckless Charles IX, took the decision not only to finish off Coligny but also to put to death all the Huguenot leaders in Paris at that time. To justify their action rumours were spread abroad of a sinister Huguenot plot to take over the government. The result of this was uproar and a bloodbath on an unprecedented scale. Parisian mobs went wild and on 24 August 1572 (St Bartholomew's Day) massacred all the Huguenots – men, women and children – that they could find. It was reckoned that between 3,000 and 4,000 people lost their lives. And this was not the end of the matter. Anti-Huguenot riots spread to other parts of the country, and the final toll was perhaps as many as 30,000. For many years these ghastly events were to blacken the history of France. More than ever it became a divided country. Huguenots who until then had professed loyalty to the crown did so no longer, and their anger and hatred were focused on Catherine. It was generally believed that she bore the main responsibility for what had happened. It cannot be believed that she deliberately intended the slaughter of thousands, but by the killing of the Huguenot leaders it was she who set it in motion.

Abroad, news of the massacre had a mixed reception. Philip II of Spain announced: 'For me it is the best and most joyous news

I could receive at present'; while the Pope let it be known that for him it was, 'A hundred times more pleasing than 50 victories like Lepanto',[6] although he revised his opinion somewhat when he realised that the massacre had not been organised officially but was mainly due to uprisings of unruly mobs. In Protestant countries, however, there was horror and shock, notably in England where Queen Elizabeth made no secret of her outrage.

The massacre of Saint Bartholomew's Day might have meant the end of Catherine's ascendancy. Hatred and contempt were poured on her. To some she had always been 'the Florentine shopkeeper'. Now she became 'La Serpente' and 'the supreme embodiment of human craft and wickedness'. The worst possible interpretation was put on all her actions – that she had deliberately engineered the massacre and that she had enfeebled her sons to preserve her own power. Her earlier attempts to come to terms with the Huguenots were overlooked, as were her moderation and acts of clemency. But in spite of being execrated and distrusted, Catherine did not withdraw from the scene. Her determination to preserve the Valois dynasty in the rule of her sons was undaunted. In the wake of the massacre Charles IX had become a physical and nervous wreck and in need of all the support he could get, and this she gave him.

At the same time she set herself the task of finding a throne for her third son, Henry Duke of Anjou, and after some hard canvassing secured for him in 1573 election to the kingdom of Poland. He did not stay there long, however, as on the death of his elder brother in 1574 he became King of France as Henry III. Henry was Catherine's favourite son and she had great hopes of him as a powerful and enlightened ruler, but these were in vain. For, charming and brilliant though he might be, he was essentially a lightweight dilettante and had his quirks: he loved to adorn himself in exotic attire (often feminine) covered with jewellery and reeking of perfume; he also surrounded himself with wild young men known as *mignons* on whom he bestowed great favours, so that he became known as the Prince of Sodom. He also had some weird religious practices – writing love letters in his own blood and praying in a chapel lined with skulls. Such freakishness was not uncommon among crowned heads and might not have been fatal, but he was also frivolous and innately indolent: affairs of state were neglected

---

[6]Lepanto was a notable victory at sea by a Christian fleet over the Turks.

and he shied away from difficult decisions. Catherine was always ready to help and to buoy him up, but he was apt to be wilful and to go his own way and was unappreciative of her efforts on his behalf. Although often treated disdainfully, she remained always devoted to him. 'He is my life', she once declared, 'and without him I wish neither to live nor to be.'

In the years following the massacre, Catherine's main troubles came from her youngest son, Francis Duke of Alençon. A spoiled younger son, like King John of England, he was consumed by an ambition for a throne of his own and ready for any act of treachery to get one. He had been engaged in two unsuccessful plots against his elder brother, Charles IX, and was lucky to have escaped the death penalty. He had been imprisoned until the accession of Henry III when he took part in a madcap venture to free the Protestant Dutch from the tyranny of the King of Spain, but this had ended in fiasco.

He died young at the age of 29 which meant that the heir to Henry III was his cousin (and brother-in-law) Henry King of Navarre of the House of Bourbon and a leader of the Huguenots. As has been seen, he had been forced into an unhappy marriage at an early age with Catherine's daughter Margot, but they had soon become separated. In 1578 Catherine compelled Margot to be reunited with Henry, and she tried to persuade him to revert to the Catholic faith to which he had once belonged. If he had done so his position as heir-presumptive to the throne could not have been challenged, but on this matter he proved intractable – not, as might be expected, for theological reasons, as he was the most pragmatic of religionists, but because he needed Huguenot support.

This failure on the part of Catherine marked the beginning of the end of her dominance. In 1587 civil war flared up again and Henry III, still dabbling in esoteric religious practices and subject to worthless favourites, was incapable of dealing with the situation and looked for support from his mother, but Catherine's powers were seen to be waning. In her negotiations with the Duke of Guise, leader of the Catholics, he hardly seemed to take her seriously. 'She was like Satan,' he said, 'promising the world to Christ. All very well but not his to give.'

The year 1588 was to be one of destiny. It was heralded in by strange and sinister portents in the sky as well as natural phenomena on earth (famine, floods and the densest fog ever to envelop Paris).

Astrologers everywhere predicted doom: 'Yet will the whole world suffer upheavals', said one; 'Empires will dwindle and from everywhere will be great lamentations. If the end of the world come not,' said another, 'there would happen at least a universal change.' The overwhelming event was of course the defeat of the Spanish Armada, but French history too was to be set on a different course.

King Philip of Spain, fearful that Henry III of France was a doubtful ally who might even give aid to England, took action to stir up the French civil war with the result that forces of the Duke of Guise were able to infiltrate into Paris. In the ensuing chaos Henry III fled the city, leaving it to his mother to come to terms. Although by then 69, obese and hardly mobile, Catherine, clambering over barricades and brushing aside hostile troops, entered into negotiations with Guise. With the forces of the latter dominant in Paris and gaining ground outside, the French King had to accept the humiliating terms of the Edict of Union – no toleration of Protestants, Henry of Navarre excluded from the throne and the Duke of Guise to be commander of the King's army. It seemed the triumph of the Catholics was complete. But then suddenly came a reversal of fortune. Henry III, wishing to assert his authority and freedom from dependence on both Guise and Catherine, dismissed the ministers that had been imposed on him and appointed others more favourable to himself. He also instigated the assassination of not only the Duke of Guise but also of his brother, the Cardinal of Guise. 'I am king now', he proclaimed triumphantly to his mother, but to Catherine it was no triumph but disaster. She foresaw all too clearly the vengeance that would follow, leading to the downfall of the House of Valois. Two weeks later she was dead.

Her passing caused no great stir, so much had she become a figure of the past, and a deeply tragic one. She seemed to have failed in everything she set out to achieve: her three sons had been weak and ineffective kings and the Valois dynasty seemed doomed. All but two of her ten children had predeceased her and the dream she had had of Medici descendants in all the courts of Europe had vanished. One thing she was spared – the assassination eight months after her death of Henry III by a fanatical friar. The religious settlement she had sought was as far away as ever and her reputation was indelibly tarnished: she was to be blamed for all the disasters that had occurred since her arrival in France and little credit was given for her good intentions. She did have gifts – courage, cunning, political skills and strength of character – but she lacked statesmanship and depth of understanding. Great ignominy was to be heaped upon her, more than she deserved.

Perhaps the last word should go to her son-in-law, Henry of Navarre, a great King of France who had little reason to love her: 'I ask, what could a woman have done, left as she was by the death of her husband with five little children, and with two families in France who were reaching for the crown – ours [i.e. the Bourbons] and the Guises? Was she not forced to play strange roles in order to deceive first one and then the other, and in order to protect, as she did, her sons, who successively reigned through the wise conduct of that shrewd woman? I am surprised that she never did worse.'

4

CHRISTINA QUEEN OF SWEDEN (1626–1689)

Christina, the hermaphrodite Queen of Sweden, succeeded to the throne when she was six. At the age of 18 she assumed royal powers which she held until her abdication ten years later. For the remaining 34 years of her life, in spite of being no more than an ex-queen of a minor state with no great wealth nor beauty and with a bodily deformity, she was always a prominent figure and a force to be reckoned with on the European scene.

The birth of Christina in 1626 caused deep disappointment. Her parents had been married for six years with no surviving children, and a son and heir was eagerly awaited and had been foretold by soothsayers and other necromancers. Instead of which came a puny little girl, her body covered with hair and one shoulder higher than the other. Her mother, Marie Eleanore of Prussia, beautiful but neurotic, was appalled by what she had brought forth and would have nothing to do with her. But her father, Gustavus Adolphus, magnanimous as always, concealed his disappointment and, taking the pathetic creature in his arms, thanked God for her and prayed for her preservation.

Gustavus Adolphus was one of the great European monarchs. Coming to the throne at the age of 18, he succeeded in the next 20 years in transforming Sweden, a poor, bleak, infertile country, into a leading European state with mastery of the Baltic and the principal upholder of the Protestant faith. A military commander of genius, he was greatly beloved by his troops because of always being in the forefront of the battle and insisting on sharing all their dangers and hardships. He had other talents too – he was a scholar and musician and conversant in eight languages.

He was killed in battle when Christina was six years old, and the government of the country was then vested in a Council of Regency which did not include Christina's mother. Gustavus was devoted to Marie Eleanore but was aware of her limitations and idiosyncrasies, and did not want her to be in charge of Christina's upbringing. She could not, however, be excluded altogether, as on becoming a widow she overcame the repulsion she had once felt towards her daughter and became affectionate and possessive, which Christina did not welcome, disliking the black draped rooms in which her mother confined herself and dreading her morbid tastes for dwarves, hunchbacks and other human oddities.

When Christina was a baby Gustavus had prayed that 'she might be as a son to him', a prayer which was perhaps to be granted more differently than he intended. In furtherance of this he had drawn up a programme of education, masculine in character with emphasis on academic rather than feminine accomplishments, which suited Christina ideally as she proved to be a receptive, even precocious student with a lively questioning mind and an 'insatiable desire to know everything', as well as a capacity for long and arduous hours of study. At the same time she developed into a sturdy tomboy with unfeminine traits – careless of her appearance, uninterested in clothes and negligent of personal cleanliness and hygiene. 'Tidiness is only for the idle', she once proclaimed.

Christina came of age on 8 December 1644, and this was marked by a splendid ceremony in which she made a point of taking the oaths as King of Sweden. For a time afterwards she was prepared to be guided by Axel Oxenstierna, who for 21 years had been the right-hand man of her father and who during her minority had coached her in matters of statecraft. Later, however, they were not always to agree, particularly as regards the terms on which to bring to an end the Thirty Years War. Christina was anxious for peace as she had ambitions to establish a brilliant court which would attract scholars, artists and musicians from all over Europe. And in this she was to succeed brilliantly, her court becoming widely famed for its erudition and conviviality, as well as for its permissiveness – for Christina was no prude and the moral tone was loose. Her own sexual orientation was unclear. It might seem to be lesbian but there was only one case in her life of a homoerotic affair – with a beautiful and gracious lady-in-waiting, Ebba Sparre; it did not last long and Christina made no attempt to prevent her marrying. Generally she preferred the company of men and was to have a close relationship with many, although she always made it clear that this stopped short of marriage.

But, of course, marriage was expected of her in order to produce an heir to the throne. She had had a childhood romance with her cousin, Charles Gustavus of Palatine and there was talk of them being wedded, but later on she let it be known that this would not happen, and he had to be content with being nominated as her successor. She felt a stronger love for the Count de la Gardie, son of the High Marshal. On him she poured great honours and riches so that people had hopes for marriage, but once again she shied away and he was to wed the sister of Charles Gustavus.

The avoidance of marriage was to be a besetting problem for Christina. 'I would rather die than be married', she once declared. She had a particular horror of pregnancy. 'I could never allow anyone to treat me as a peasant does his field ... I am as likely to give birth to a Nero as to an Alexander.' She considered that she had done all that was necessary in designating her cousin as her successor.

Christina's coronation was not celebrated until 1650, six years after she came of age. This was a magnificent occasion with no expense spared, despite the near bankruptcy of the country. But by then her health was in a parlous state. Overwork, hyperactivity and an unhealthy diet of spiced greasy foods had taken their toll, and she was beset by illnesses – fevers, fainting fits, pleurisy among others. Orthodox Swedish medicine – mainly blood-letting, enemas and weird folk cures – had no effect. But in 1651 a new force came into her life which was to transform her.

Pierre Michelon Bourdelot was of humble birth, the son of a barber-cum-surgeon. He had made a study of medicine and had original ideas on the subject, particularly the importance of psychology. A man of limitless ambition, he had moved in high circles and had had popes and kings among his patients. He saw at once that at the root of Christina's ill-health was her way of life, which was too strained and overburdened: oppressive affairs of state and long-drawn-out intellectual discourses were weighing heavily on her, and what she needed was light relief. Being a man of charm and plausibility he soon found favour with her and she allowed him to take charge of her life. Under his auspices she became lighthearted, even frivolous: instead of attending scholarly seminars she delighted in Italian love songs to the accompaniment of guitars; at the same time she distanced herself from tedious government business and royal ceremonies, and while still enjoying the company of learned men was ready to make mock of them, insisting cruelly on elderly decrepit academics joining in hearty games and dances and making an exhibition of themselves.

Most notorious of her new ways was her behaviour in church. Although well versed in the scriptures, she was not naturally pious, and made no attempt to conceal her irritation with ritual she found tedious, playing with lapdogs during services and flapping impatiently with her fan when sermons went on too long. Predictably such behaviour caused scandal among grave Lutheran divines, as also did her intimacy with Bourdelot. He had always been unpopular, particularly in the medical profession where he was regarded as a charlatan and a braggart, and ill-feeling against him was becoming widespread. It must be doubtful that he and Christina were ever lovers, as his days proved to be numbered when the Queen's attention digressed to other men.

One who was to have profound influence on Christina was the French Ambassador Pierre Chanut who, as well as being an accomplished diplomat, was also a distinguished scholar. It was perhaps he who first sowed in Christina's mind the thought that she was out of her element in Sweden, a country not to everyone's liking with its long, dark, wintry nights, pervasive forests and rigorous climate. How much more attractive were the lands of the South with their sun-drenched landscapes and fruitful exotic gardens! And how more congenial the people! Instead of austere, God-fearing Scandinavians were to be found charming, articulate and indulgent Latins. Besides, she was finding herself being drawn more and more towards the mystique of the Church of Rome with its splendid ceremonies, a church in which it seemed to her that there was greater freedom than in the stern precepts of Luther.

By 1651 Christina was longing to be rid of the formalities and obligations of monarchy. She longed for a life in which she could give free rein to her unconventional personality. Only a year after her coronation she was talking openly of abdication. To the newly arrived English Ambassador, who had come to negotiate a commercial treaty, she poured out: 'I have it in my thoughts and resolution to quit the crown of Sweden, and to retire myself unto a private life, as much more suitable to my contentment and the great cares and troubles attending upon the government of my kingdom.' When she announced her intention to the Senate there was consternation and a delegation came to implore her not to proceed with the idea; and for the time being she held back.

65

But the intention did not die and by 1654 she was resolved both to abdicate and to convert to Rome. About the former she was open but about the latter she had to be secretive, for the Roman Catholic Church was banned in Sweden and if it became known that the daughter of Gustavus Adolphus, the great upholder of Protestantism, had succumbed to popery there would be outrage. Nevertheless, secret negotiations took place, at first with the Jesuit confessor of the Portuguese Ambassador who reported Christina's state of mind to the General of his order, who lost no time in despatching two eminent Jesuit scholars to Sweden to add their voices. Someone else who had great influence on her was another diplomat, Don Antonio Pimentelli, Envoy Extraordinary of the King of Spain. Like Chanut he was a man of commanding presence, and after the departure of Bourdelot became Christina's main favourite. It was he who organised her journey through Europe after her abdication, accompanying her to Rome where for years he was her mainstay until superseded by a younger man.

Before making public her change of religion it was essential for Christina to come to terms about abdication. In the first place she had to ensure that she would be succeeded by Charles Gustavus, who could be relied on to be generous; and this she achieved by an Act of Succession. More vital, though, was a financial settlement, for if she was to maintain a princely state, which she was determined to do, she would be dependent on a grant from the Swedish Senate, and there might be unwillingness there to subsidise an ex-queen living abroad who had converted to Catholicism. So for the time being she had to let it be assumed that she would remain a Protestant and be living in Sweden.

Christina formally abdicated on 6 June 1654. In the Senate it was a moving ceremony in which, in spite of her idiosyncrasies, great affection for her was shown and perhaps hope that she would have a last-minute change of mind. The official who should have divested her of her crown and royal insignia refused to do so, so she had to do it herself. After an emotional speech, during which many were in tears, she was escorted out by Charles Gustavus, the new King to whom she swore allegiance; but she did not attend his coronation later in the day. She felt it necessary to slip quietly away and leave the country as soon as possible before it was realised that she would not be staying in Sweden to spend the money granted to her there.

After her secret flight from Sweden, Christina and her entourage made for Denmark where she was soon recognised and news of her arrival spread at once. There was great curiosity about the queen who had renounced her throne. 'Who is this lady', it was asked, 'who light-heartedly resigns what most of us fight and long for in vain?'

At first Christina seemed to have no clear purpose as to where she was going to go. For nearly a year she lingered in the Low Countries while Europe buzzed with rumours about her, in particular about her conversion to Roman Catholicism. In Brussels six months after her abdication she made a secret profession of her new faith, and she hoped that it might remain secret, as news of it would cause tumult in Sweden and endanger her financial settlement; but this was to prove impossible.

It was not until September 1655 that Christina set out south for Rome; with her went an entourage of some 200 including confessors, political advisers, soldiers of fortune and entertainers; but only four Swedes and five women. It was to be expected that she would travel unconventionally – sometimes by coach, sometimes astride a horse with a gun slung over her shoulder; sometimes in feminine attire and sometimes dressed as a man. Wherever she went she attracted widespread attention and could rely on a warm, sometimes ecstatic, welcome. One intriguing encounter on the way was with King Charles II of England, then in exile during the rule of Cromwell. He was said to have wanted to marry her, but nothing came of this – a pity, as a combination of Old Rowley[1] and the Amazon Queen would have been interesting.

By the time Christina reached the Alps rumours of her conversion were so rife that she felt it was time to come into the open about it. And so in Innsbruck on 3 November 1655 in a splendid public ceremony she solemnly renounced the Lutheran faith of her fathers and professed her allegiance to the Church of Rome; this was followed by a sermon from a Jesuit preacher on the text: 'Hearken, oh daughter, and incline thine ear; forget also thine own people and thy father's house.' As in all pious ceremonies Christina was unable to be too serious and was ready to joke and to shock. When the same evening she attended a light comedy performed by Italian players, and some people expressed surprise, she replied that it was most appropriate 'after the farce I played in this morning'.

---

[1] Charles was so called after a well-known thoroughbred stallion of that name.

As Christina progressed into Italy her welcome became ever more enthusiastic. Everywhere she was greeted by fanfares, triumphal arches, banquets and general rejoicing; in deference to her reputation as an intellectual, scholarly seminars were also laid on, presided over by local sages. It had been planned that her first entry into Rome should be incognito with a magnificent formal celebration days later, but Christina could never be under cover for long and huge crowds awaited her. The official welcome was indeed spectacular. No expense was spared. Cannons boomed, rockets soared and wine flowed freely. A silver coach designed by Cavaliere Bernini had been provided for her entry into the Vatican but, typically, she decided to ride astride a beautiful white horse that had been presented to her. The steps of St Peter's were lined with cardinals as she strode up in riding habit dressed more for the hunting field than for an audience with the Pope. But as a prize convert to the Faith all eccentricities of dress and behaviour were forgiven and, having kissed the pontifical toe, she was received graciously by Pope Alexander VII who bestowed notable favours on her, including the honour of dining with him, normally forbidden to women; although it was necessary for her to be at a separate table on a lower level.

After a stay of several days at the Vatican Christina moved to a palace which had been prepared for her, the Palazzo Farnese, designed by Michael Angelo for Pope Paul III and containing many art treasures. Once installed she soon became the centre of Roman social life with leading figures in art and politics vying for invitations. But all was not well. In the course of her travels she had become strongly attached to two brothers, Francesco and Ludovico Santinelli, charming and entertaining but villainous and out for what they could get; and Christina allowed them to get a great deal: anything of value in the Palazzo was in danger of being misappropriated, and Christina was so defrauded that her finances became critically depleted.

At the same time her relations with the Pope went sour. He had had visions of her as a prominent and outspoken crusader for Catholicism in the forefront of religious ceremonies and setting an example of piety and charity. But she had not come up to expectations: her religious practices had been low-key and she had not been notable for good works. Moreover the Pope had heard from his spies that money was short and she might become a financial liability, and rumours were abroad of impious behaviour at the

Farnese where there was evidence that Christina was keeping a disorderly house. But the situation was to improve later with the arrival on the scene of a man of outstanding ability and good nature: calm, erudite and articulate. Cardinal Decio Azzolino had become a cardinal at the age of 31 and was soon to become Secretary of State. He was believed to be the one man whom Christina deeply loved.

With her restless disposition Christina was not likely to be content for long with life in Rome: she was missing the trappings of royalty and the honours that had once been paid to her, to say nothing of a (usually) reliable income. After only four months her thoughts were turning to new ventures. In particular the kingdom of Naples attracted her attention. At the time it was under the dominion of Spain, but there was much discontent. In the last years there had been frequent changes of regime (five kings of different nations in two years) and there were those who were ready for yet another. Naples was a turbulent country but beautiful and prosperous and with a warm gentle climate. The prospect of becoming its Queen greatly appealed to Christina and she determined to see if this could be achieved. For it to happen she would need the help of France, then at war with Spain, and so she set about entering into secret negotiations. To cover her tracks she announced her intention of passing through France on her way to Sweden; but for this she did not have sufficient finance. The Pope was approached for help and, perhaps not sorry to see her go, made her a gift of money and provided a fleet of galleys to take her and her suite to Marseilles.

When seeking permission to travel through France, Christina had requested to Cardinal Mazarin, the dominant figure in the country during Louis XIV's minority, that she should come incognito with no ceremony. But this was not likely to happen. She was welcomed into the country by the duc de Guise, the Grand Chamberlain, who escorted her to Paris, and on the way crowds everywhere greeted her enthusiastically. Her reputation had preceded her and people were expecting the unconventional. As always she was ready to stir things up and to shock, which she did by her louche behaviour and blasphemous language. A lady accompanying her to the theatre recalled how 'in her praise of places that pleased her she would swear by God, throw herself back in her chair, tossing her legs about and assuming postures hardly decent'. But, 'rough, brutish and libertine' though her ways might be, such was her charm and vibrant personality that it was found 'not difficult to pardon all irregularities'.

In Paris she made a triumphal entry into the city astride a grey horse in her usual motley array of garments (breeches, petticoats, boots, cavalier hat), and crowds flocked to catch sight of the famed Amazon Queen. One person eager for an early glimpse was the young King Louis XIV, then aged 18, who visited her with his brother in disguise, but whom Christina soon recognised and declared him 'born to wear a crown'.

The following day she arrived at the court of Anne of Austria, the Queen Regent who, like others, was taken aback by her unkempt appearance and rough and ready ways but, like others too, was charmed by her and delighted in her company. For a week Christina was entertained lavishly – balls, banquets, ballets and plays – but behind the scenes she was carrying on high-powered negotiations with Mazarin about an invasion of Naples. On the face of it there seemed to be no reason why Mazarin should espouse her cause as an ex-queen, almost penniless and with no hereditary claim, but it happened that she fitted in with his long-term plan which was to secure the throne of Naples for Louis XIV's younger brother, Philippe of Anjou. But for this he was not yet ready and in the meantime Christina – middle aged, almost certainly barren, favourably disposed and ready to nominate Philippe her successor – was a convenient stop-gap. And so he gave a secret undertaking to provide an invasion force. This achieved, Christina lost no time in returning to Italy, all pretence of travelling on to Sweden abandoned.

In Italy, partly because of a plague in Rome and partly because of increasing money troubles, she settled in Pesaro in the north where she continued to lay plans for an invasion of Naples, bombarding Mazarin with one plan after another; but Mazarin with other matters on his mind was vacillating, and after six months in June 1657 Christina decided that she had to return to France. There her welcome was in contrast to that of the previous year – no triumphal progress nor invitations to court, only an allocation of a small apartment in the chateau of Fontainebleau where for the time being she was kept at a distance.

Mazarin had not lost interest in the invasion of Naples, but it was put off and ultimately abandoned as a result of an ugly incident which occurred at the end of 1657. By then Christina was suspicious that details of the Naples operation were being leaked by a member of her staff, and was intercepting incoming letters. From these it became clear that the culprit was Giovanni Monaldesco, her Grand Equerry, a man she had trusted completely and who had been designated as Commander-in-Chief. On being confronted with incriminating letters Monaldesco could not but confess his guilt, and Christina decreed that he must die immediately. This was high-handed in the extreme: she was a guest of the King of France, staying in one of his palaces, and an on-the-spot execution would be at the worst murder and at the best a gross violation of hospitality. Members of her suite, including her confessor, pleaded with her for remission, but she was intractable: he must be executed there and then. The task of executioner was assigned to Ludovico Santinelli who made a botched job of it, as Monaldesco was wearing a breastplate and to finish him off it was necessary to cut his throat. All the while Christina was in a chamber next door, imperturbable and resolute.

When news of the killing broke there was outrage. Mazarin was appalled and, realising what harm it could do, urged Christina to put it down to a private vendetta. This she stalwartly refused to do, affirming that it was an act of justice by a queen on a traitor. But it was not as simple as that: she was an ex-queen and at the time she was in a foreign country under foreign jurisdiction. The rulers of France made no secret of their displeasure: Christina was left to languish in Fontainebleau, shunned and uninvited to court functions. The Naples project was put in abeyance and finally abandoned.

When Christina returned to Rome in the spring of 1658 her fortunes were at their lowest ebb: the Naples project was fading out, money from Sweden was diminishing (and much of it falling into wrong hands), and following the murder of Monaldesco her reputation was seriously tarnished, particularly in the eyes of Pope Alexander VII who in a fit of anger at that time described her as 'a woman born a barbarian, barbarously brought up and living with barbarous thoughts'. Moreover the Palazzo Farnese was no longer available to her so that she had to live temporarily and awkwardly in a palace belonging to Cardinal Mazarin.

From this sorry predicament she was to be rescued by Cardinal Azzolino, who showed great magnanimity in taking her under his wing. He had risen rapidly in the hierarchy of the Church and was setting his eyes on the pontificacy itself, and it would do his reputation no good to be closely associated with the disgraced Christina. But he was to devote himself to her cause wholeheartedly and she was to trust him and fall completely under his spell.

One of the first things he did was to dissociate her from Naples, and he saw that the best way of doing this was to replace this venture with one of a similar nature; so he encouraged an idea of hers to form 'a league of Christian princes' to make war on the Turks who were ever more encroaching into Europe. In the event nothing was to come of this owing to lack of response from the Christian princes, but it occupied her energies for a time and did something to mend her fences with the Pope.

Azzolino also found her an ideal residence. The Palazzo Riario was smaller than the Farnese and in the outskirts of the city, but it was attractive and more manageable, with an exceptionally beautiful garden in which she took great delight. Here she was to create a permanent home in her own style and brought to it the furniture, art treasures and library she had been able to take out of Sweden and which had since been in store in Antwerp. But first it became necessary for her to go on her travels again.

For some time money from Sweden had become irregular. This was partly because the country's finances were in a parlous state owing to constant wars and partly because of mismanagement and corruption in the administration of Christina's estates. For some time she had been contemplating a visit to put things in order, and when in 1660 her cousin King Charles Gustavus died it became urgently necessary. So long as he was alive he would always do all he could to help her, to whom he owed his throne and with whom he had once been in love. But he was succeeded by a Council of Regency acting on behalf of his son, a delicate child of five. From the new rulers Christina could expect little goodwill, especially as its chief member was one Magnus de la Gardie whom she had once loved but whom she had jilted and later sent into exile. And so, reluctant as she was to be parted from Azzolino and having pawned her jewellery and borrowed all the money she could, she set out with a small suite for Sweden in July 1660.

The news of her intended visit caused shockwaves in Stockholm. It was well known there how much trouble she might stir up, as Christina, daughter of the country's most famous king, was still popular despite her eccentricities and change of religion. It soon became evident that these fears were well founded. As soon as she landed Christina made no effort to be conciliatory. Far from veiling her religious beliefs she flaunted them (more than she had ever done in Rome), and showed little restraint or tact in her dealings with government ministers. She even declared brazenly that in the event of the death of the young King she would be his successor, but this caused such a storm that she was compelled to retract and confirm her abdication. The Council of Regency did all they could to make her visit as short as possible and this they did not by a major showdown but by a number of pinpricks, restricting her religious practices and insisting on the banishment of her blameless chaplain. And these ploys were to prove effective so that after five months she was writing to her Governor-General: 'For God's sake make haste to settle my affairs, so that I can leave as soon as possible this country where I am so cruelly persecuted ... I would rather die miserably elsewhere than live in Sweden subjected to daily insults.'

As in 1654 Christina left Sweden in haste, and it was not possible for her to proceed at once to Rome. Her finances were still in disarray and she had to stay for over a year in Hamburg where she put them under the control of a Jewish banker, Diego Texeira, who managed in spite of many difficulties to keep her more or less solvent. During this time she corresponded frequently and emotionally with Azzolino who was watching over her interests in Rome. From these letters (some of them in code) it is evident that she was deeply in love with him and that he regarded her with affection and care. Nevertheless, at that time he was not anxious for her to return to Rome, for the death of Pope Alexander VII was expected soon and in the conclave that would follow he would have an active part: at 38 he was too young to be considered for the Papacy itself (*papabile*) but he had a keen interest in who was elected, and he might find Christina's presence close to him an embarrassment.

Christina arrived in Rome in June 1662. Pope Alexander VII was not to die until 1667, but by then her relations with him had been restored, and she was greeted by a bevy of cardinals who conducted her straight to the Vatican where, hot and dusty from the road and in her customary melange of garments (boots, breeches and transparent skirt) she was received graciously by His Holiness.

While she had been away Azzolino had been putting in hand the refurbishing of the Palazzo Riario, but it was not yet ready for occupation so it was necessary for Christina to get by for several months in a smaller house in the garden. But then began one of the happiest periods of her life, when she unpacked her treasures from Antwerp and set about creating her new home. In this Azzolino had a major role, taking on the management of her household where his greatest achievement was in ridding her of the dishonest rogues who had found their way into her service. Her eyes were at last opened to the thievery of the Santinelli brothers and others, and they were given short shrift. At last she had a sound, dependable entourage, and at the same time she herself underwent a character change, becoming more mellow and considerate. For a time, life was idyllic.

She was not to be content for long, however, with a tranquil, low-profile existence. She was soon thirsting for action. She still had visions of leading a crusade against the Turks, also of forming an alliance to protect Catholic minorities in Protestant countries. More ambitious still was her idea of becoming Queen of Poland.

The throne of Poland was elective, and since 1648 it had been occupied by John Casimir, an ex-cardinal, whose reign had been plagued by wars and insurrections, and in 1668 he had been persuaded, not unwillingly, to abdicate. For the ensuing election there were four candidates of different nationalities, and Christina lost no time in joining them. She thought she was in with a chance as she was a member of the Wass dynasty whose members had been for generations sovereigns of Sweden and Poland; she was also a strong Catholic and a figure of renown and had the backing of Pope Clement IX – but this was not as compelling as it might have been as he had already given his blessing to two of the other candidates. Strong and unqualified support came from Azzolino, then Secretary of State at the Vatican and so carrying some weight. In letters to the Papal Nuncio in Poland, intended to be passed on to the principal voters, he described Christina with some hyperbole as 'a heroine remarkable for her piety, her wisdom and her virile courage'. And being aware that there would be strong prejudice against a woman: 'All the world now looks upon the Queen not only as a man but as superior to all men ... born to command an army and to endure the privations of war.' Another weakness in Christina's bid was that she was unmarried and unlikely to bear children and on this point Azzolino was blatantly deceitful, stating that she would soon be married with every possibility of fecundity

(41 though she might then be). Christina was less definite, saying only that she would marry no one to whom the Polish Diet objected.

At the time of the election Christina was in Hamburg and for a time in Sweden, drawn there once again by financial troubles; and it seemed that in the later stages her enthusiasm for the project was cooling. It may be that she was having second thoughts about ruling a turbulent foreign country whose language she did not speak and with whose ways she was unaccustomed; and it may too have been a consideration that she would be at a distance from Azzolino. As it happened the matter did not arise: it became known that her sex and celibacy were an insuperable barrier and her name did not go forward for election.

Christina returned to Rome in 1668 where she received a warm welcome. The newly elected Pope, Clement IX, was an old friend and paid her the signal honour of a public banquet in the Vatican, and then paid her a visit in the Palazzo Riario. He also made her a handsome allowance so that her finances for once were on a more or less even keel. Azzolino too had been honoured as Secretary of State, and as such was one of the most powerful men in Rome. So, for the time being, all boded well for Christina.

The sky, however, was not entirely cloudless. The Pope's health was unsound and it was feared that he would not live long. The responsibilities of his office weighed heavily on him and, in particular, he was haunted by the spectre of the invasion of Europe by the Mohammedan Turks. This danger had been increasing lately, and at the end of October 1669 came news of the fall of Candia, the capital of Crete and the main bastion against the invaders. To Clement this was a mortal blow: he went into a decline and died six weeks later. Although he had been pope for only two years he was to leave behind him a lasting reputation for kindliness and integrity.

His death was a serious setback for Christina and Azzolino. There would be an election for the new Pope who might be less sympathetic and might appoint a different Secretary of State. At the age of 46 Azzolino was still too young to be considered for the Pontificacy, but if he was to retain his position he would have to see to it that the new Pope was favourably disposed, and this was realised keenly by Christina who entered into the fray with alacrity.

The election of a pope at that time was a devious business. In theory the cardinals assembled in conclave and sought guidance from the Holy Spirit, but in practice they were motivated by more worldly considerations. They came from different countries of whose interests they were aware, and they knew what was expected of them by their heads of state. Nevertheless, they went through the ritual of being shut into small, bare, inhospitable cells where they pondered and decided on how to cast their votes. At first it seemed likely that Azzolino's favoured candidate would win easily. Cardinal Vidoni was well fitted by age and experience and had widespread backing, but such was the manoeuvring in conclave that if this became known it would stir up opposition in other factions. Azzolino was well aware that he must keep secret the candidate he was backing but, mistakenly as it proved, he and Christina went further and put it about that they were opposed to Vidoni. This was being too clever by half, for other factions, who were equally well versed in conclave stratagems, smelled a rat and stirred up support for someone else.

The consequence was that there was a deadlock, and for four long bitter months the cardinals were incarcerated in their cells in direst discomfort while they vainly sought God's will. And at the end of that time they could only agree on a compromise candidate, a frail elderly man of nearly 80, who had only been created cardinal a few months before, who had no wish for the position of pope and had to be coerced into it. As was to be expected, however, everyone – including Azzolino and Christina – made haste to make obeisance to him and to let it be known that they had always supported him, and were responsible for his election. During the long months of impasse Christina had been frantically active, not always advisedly, somehow getting long letters to Azzolino behind closed doors, full of advice and news of the current state of opinions in Rome. Of course, the result was a great disappointment to them: in spite of their manipulations they had failed to get the appointment of their candidate.

Christina, however, soon recovered from this blow. It was not in her nature to live a quiet, withdrawn life and she was soon again the brilliant hostess, entertaining the grandest in the land, and a pivotal figure in literature and the arts. She gave particular encouragement to music and the theatre and was to be seen on many occasions in her box at the opera, usually amid a cluster of cardinals. Her activities became somewhat constricted with the death in 1676 of the elderly, good-natured Pope Clement X and the accession of Innocent XI, a sterner and more forbidding character who disapproved of theatres and took a strong line about the cut of ladies' dresses and how much they covered up. He even ordered the painting-over of naked bosoms in public statuary. He and Christina had little in common, and she took delight in flouting him and transgressing his ordinances.

As she grew older Christina lost none of her sparkle. She was as vital as ever. 'I love the storm and fear the calm', she once pronounced, and it was a love that never left her. To the end she was always ready to embroil herself in political controversy, seeking a role in the peace treaty between Sweden and Denmark, pressing the urgency of a crusade against the Turks and incurring the wrath of Louis XIV of France by condemning his 'dragooning' of the Huguenots.[2] 'Soldiers are strange apostles,' she said. 'As our Lord did not make use of them, they cannot be the best.' And her range of interests was as wide as ever. She still loved to preside over serious scholastic discourses, and her delight in collecting works of art was undimmed. By the time of her death she was the owner of some 160 sculptures and a unique gallery of paintings. Other interests she had too, notably in archaeology and astronomy, and she still spent long, fruitless hours in chemical experiments, trying to find the philosopher's stone which would turn base metals into gold. But her greatest love was for music. 'Music', she wrote, 'is something more touching than the other arts. It seems that it is made specially for the soul, harmony bringing with it a kind of sympathy which charms.' Many musicians were to benefit from her patronage including the greatly renowned Scarlatti and Corelli who for a time held the post of Master of her music.

In old age under the wise, restraining influence of Azzolino, Christina became calmer and more prudent, although she still liked to make her presence felt and to dabble in affairs of state. But her health became more unstable and her appearance ever more bizarre. A Frenchman who saw her the year before she died left a vivid description:

Very small of stature, exceedingly fat and corpulent. Her complexion, voice and face are those of a man; but she has

---

[2] That is, billeting soldiers on Huguenot households to their great discomfort.

a big nose, large blue eyes, blonde eyebrows and a double chin, from which sprout a number of isolated tufts of beard ... Imagine as regards her costume, a very short black skirt revealing a pair of men's shoes. A very large bow of black ribbons instead of a cravat. A belt drawn tightly round the coat over the lower part of the stomach, most clearly revealing the rotundity of this.

Christina died on 19 April 1689 at the age of 63. She had asked for a simple burial service 'with no pomp and all other such vanity', but it was not thought that she meant it and her funeral was on a magnificent scale, her body lying in state for four days and then interred in an outsize tomb in the crypt of St Peter's. Her will provided for 20,000 Masses to be said for her soul and the consecration of two chapels.

Striking personality as Christina certainly was, it has to be questioned whether such splendour was suitable. Essentially she was a maverick – individualist and iconoclast. Her inheritance and dubious sexuality combined to create a unique character of which the dominant trait was ambition. She decided early on that Sweden was too small a stage for her genius; she sought greater scope and appreciation. Closest to her heart was military glory, in the steps of her heroic father. Hence the aggressive pose, the wearing of mainly masculine attire and her persistent fishing in troubled waters. But she was aiming too high. None of her great schemes came off: she failed to mount a crusade against the Turks and to become Queen of Naples or Poland; and if she had ideas at times of acting as arbiter between heads of state or becoming a power behind the Papacy, they were illusory.

Although unsuccessful in politics, there was much that Christina achieved in scholarship and the arts. She brought much fine music to Rome and aroused among Romans a greater interest in their classical past. Her popularity and pervasive influence were due to a magnetic personality and a steely determination to go her own way, responsible only to God.

5

QUEEN ELIZABETH I OF ENGLAND (1533–1603)

Elizabeth I was queen of England for 44 years, one of the most momentous periods in the country's history. During that time the nation was transformed from an insignificant backwater into a major European power, the might of Spain was set at nought and the Protestant religion was finally established. The period also saw England's greatest attainments in the arts, notably music and literature. In all these achievements the part played by Elizabeth was central.

Elizabeth was born in Greenwich Palace on 7 September 1533, and rarely has a birth given rise to such dismay, particularly from her parents, Henry VIII and his second wife Anne Boleyn, who were desperate for a son. The fates had endowed Henry with many great gifts – scholarship, physical strength, musicianship and prodigious vitality – but one had been withheld which he valued above all others: a son to succeed him. For the sake of this he had been ready to pay a terrible price. He had annulled his marriage to his first wife, the devoted and virtuous Catherine of Aragon, and in order to do so had replaced the ancient Roman Church with the Protestant Church of England, thus making way for Anne Boleyn whom he loved to distraction and who, he felt sure, would bear the son he so much wanted. To Anne too the birth of a son was urgently necessary. Her life depended on it. A love affair with Henry of seven years had ended in pregnancy and a secret marriage, but by then Henry's love for her had begun to wane and she knew the only way in which it could be revived was by bearing him a son. Otherwise she would be cast aside and he would look elsewhere. The birth of Elizabeth was not the end of the line for Anne. She was to survive for three years yet, but after miscarrying with a stillborn son a year later there was little hope left for her.

In the meanwhile the birth of Elizabeth was suitably if not

enthusiastically celebrated. Te Deums were sung, church bells rung, and at her baptism (not attended by her father), the Garter King at Arms prayed that, 'God of his infinite goodness would send prosperous life and long to the high and mighty Princess of England, Elizabeth'. She was also declared the only legitimate offspring of the King, thus in effect bastardising Mary, his daughter by Catherine of Aragon.

Elizabeth's position as heir-presumptive did not last long. When she was three her mother was put to death and she was declared illegitimate. Her father then married Jane Seymour, who gave birth to the future Edward VI but died immediately afterwards. There followed an agitated period when in 1540 Henry married Anne of Cleves and in the same year divorced her; he then married Catherine Howard whom he had beheaded 18 months later; and finally he married Catherine Parr whose great achievement was to outlive him.

By then he had degenerated into a brutal and unpredictable tyrant from whom no one was safe. Elizabeth had to be extremely careful in all she said and did, but it seems she never completely lost her father's love. She was provided for and, illegitimate though she might be, was named in his will as in line to the throne after Edward and Mary.

During these anxious times her life was greatly enriched by an excellent education. At the time of the Renaissance it was customary for well-to-do young ladies to be educated fully. The idea that all they needed in the way of education was some light reading, a little music and needlework belonged to a later age. When still a child Elizabeth was grounded in the classics, and under the aegis of a renowned and enlightened teacher, Roger Ascham, proved an exceptional scholar. When she became Queen she was the intellectual superior of most of those around her, able to speak six languages, ready to discourse with university dons on points of scholarship and to communicate with most foreign ambassadors in their native tongues or, at least, in impromptu Latin.

After the death of Henry VIII Elizabeth lived for a time with her stepmother, Catherine Parr, who was kindly disposed towards her and like her had intellectual leanings so that they had interests in common. This arrangement was not to last long as within no more than four months of Henry's death Catherine married again (for the fourth time). Her husband was Thomas Seymour, uncle of

Edward VI, Lord High Admiral, with robust charm, licentious ways and boundless ambition. He had at one time had thoughts of marriage to one of the princesses – Mary or Elizabeth – but any such idea had been firmly vetoed, and he then turned his attention to the Queen Dowager with whom he had had a love affair some years before, and she accepted him readily.

His arrival in her household, however, brought troubles. He cast his nets wide, and it was not long before the youthful Princess Elizabeth was caught in them. At first there had been only comparatively harmless horseplay – slap and tickle, no more – of which Catherine Parr was aware and to which she took no exception. But later when it appeared that a love affair was developing, she took a strong line and Elizabeth had to go. It might be thought that such a minor matter was of little significance, but it did not rest there, for soon afterwards Seymour was arraigned for high treason.

Soon after the death of Henry VIII, Edward Seymour, Thomas's elder brother, had made himself Duke of Somerset and Protector of the Realm – in effect dictator. This had given rise to great jealousy and resentment, particularly from Thomas who acted secretly and rashly to undermine his brother which became noticed and in 1549 he was imprisoned in the Tower while evidence was sought to incriminate him, and this included his goings-on with Elizabeth who was rigorously interrogated about them. Strong pressure was brought to bear on her – at times by dire threats, at others by gentle persuasion – to confess to evil and seditious intrigues; but she remained firm throughout that she and Seymour had done nothing wrong. Not that this did the latter any good as he was executed soon afterwards.

It might have been that Elizabeth would be distressed by this, as it was apparent that she had become fond of Seymour and had not found his advances altogether unwelcome. But she showed no sign of emotion. Later she wrote bluntly: 'There died a man with much wit but very little judgment.' It is likely, however, that the incident had a lasting effect on her. During her life she was always to treat matters of love and marriage guardedly, and this could have originated with the Seymour affair. She may also have gained from it strength and determination; the severe cross-examination she endured may have hardened her and prepared her for a more gruelling one that lay ahead.

Apart from the attentions of Thomas Seymour, Elizabeth's life was on an even keel during Edward VI's reign. She was broadly in agreement with the Protestant legislation that was enacted and was unmoved by the downfall of Lord Protector Somerset and his replacement by the Duke of Northumberland; and she prudently kept aloof from the plot of the latter to put Lady Jane Grey[1] on the throne on the death of Edward VI. When this collapsed and Mary rode in triumph into London, she was by her side.

In the new reign, however, Elizabeth was going to have to walk warily, as her relationship with her half-sister was precarious. They had certain things in common: they were both daughters of Henry VIII, and both had been bastardised and disinherited, and then to some extent reinstated when they were included in the line of succession to the throne. But there was much to divide them. Mary always believed that it was Elizabeth's mother, Anne Boleyn, who had brought about the downfall of her mother, Catherine of Aragon, and it was because of her that the Roman Church, to which she was passionately devoted, had been replaced by the Protestant Church of England. Under great pressure from her father she had been compelled to renounce the Pope and acknowledge the King as head of the Church in England, but these were not her true beliefs and on coming to the throne she was determined that the Church of Rome should be restored. As for Elizabeth, she had to be Protestant: the legitimacy of her birth depended on the Protestant faith; to Roman Catholics she was a bastard. The crucial question when Mary became Queen was: how would Elizabeth survive the restoration of the Papacy? Would she remain a Protestant or would she convert to Catholicism? And could she do this convincingly? Because at the same time she must not lose faith with the strong body of English Protestants who looked on her as their champion. It was a tightrope she had to walk.

At the beginning of her reign Mary was inclined to be moderate. She hoped to persuade rather than coerce people to rejoin the true faith, as she saw it. There were as yet no signs of the faggots of Smithfield. Mary, however, entirely underestimated the strength of the opposition there would be to the reintroduction of the Roman Church. There were zealous Protestants who were as devoted to

---

[1] Lady Jane Grey was the granddaughter of Henry VIII's youngest sister, Mary, and so Elizabeth's first cousin once removed. Unlike Mary and Elizabeth there were no doubts about her legitimacy.

their faith as Mary was to hers. There were, too, Protestant priests who had married and would be unwilling to renounce their spouses. But the most powerful opposition would come from the owners of lands that had once belonged to the Church. They would resist to the death the restitution of these.

Elizabeth found that she would have to decide soon whether or not to convert to Catholicism. At first she prevaricated and said she could not attend Mass until she had had instruction in Roman doctrines, but she soon became aware that she had to convert at once. Her life depended on it, as also did her succession to the throne. But it was not certain that even conversion would save her. There were those close to the Queen, especially the Spanish Ambassador, the Count of Feria, who thought her sly and untrustworthy and only playing for time.

The great change in Queen Mary's relationship with the people of England came with her marriage to King Philip of Spain. This was bitterly unpopular. Philip, as fanatical a Roman Catholic as Mary, reigned over one of the largest empires in history, covering not only Spain but also the Netherlands, parts of Germany and Italy and colonies in South America; and the dread was that England would be sucked into this conglomerate and be enslaved by foreigners and Papists. Soon after the betrothal was announced there was a serious rebellion, led by Sir Thomas Wyatt, which nearly toppled Mary. When it was put down, everyone who was suspected of having had any part in it was rounded up, including Elizabeth. She strongly denied having been involved but was sent to the Tower for two months where she was grilled relentlessly in order to obtain a confession of complicity. She remained steadfast that she had known nothing of it, and Sir Thomas Wyatt, even after the most gruesome torture, insisted that she was innocent.

When she was released from the Tower Elizabeth was sent to a royal lodge in Woodstock in Oxfordshire where she was kept under strict but not unduly rigorous confinement. Her journey there by river had been something of a royal procession with large crowds turning out to cheer her on her way. People were already looking to her as the future sovereign who would deliver them from Papacy and the domination of Spain. Such popularity, of course, made her situation more dangerous. At the same time Queen Mary was sinking ever lower in popular esteem as tragedy crowded in on her: deserted by a husband she adored; a pregnancy that came to nothing; and an awareness that at 40 she was becoming older, less attractive and in failing health. The Roman Catholic Church had been restored by Act of Parliament, but Protestantism was unbowed. In her dementia Mary felt it her duty to consign Protestants to the flames, not as a punishment but a salvation – but the heroism of these martyrs (some 300 in all including bishops and one archbishop as well as humble folk) strengthened rather than weakened the Protestant faith.

In her state of mind Mary might well have ordered the execution of her half-sister; but support for Elizabeth was to come from an unexpected quarter. Mary's husband, Philip, had impressed on her that Elizabeth had to be kept alive. His reasons were not humanitarian but diplomatic. Certainly for him there were objections to Elizabeth becoming Queen of England, but there were even greater ones to the next in line to the English throne, Mary Stuart. She was already Queen of Scotland, and about to become Queen of France; and if she were also to become Queen of England (as was her birthright), an alliance of the three countries would be a serious threat to Spain. In any case, Philip was already entertaining ideas of marriage to Elizabeth himself, should Mary die and he again became a widower. So he gave orders that Elizabeth should not be harmed, and for Queen Mary his word was law.

In her last years Mary's depression continued to deepen. Her husband made only rare visits and there was by then no prospect of a child being born to her. There was also the realisation that she would be succeeded by Elizabeth, who was likely to restore the Church of England. One final blow remained. As some had foreseen, England became drawn into a war on the side of Spain against France, and as a result lost her last remaining possession on the Continent, Calais. Mary was desolated by this and affirmed that when she died the word 'Calais' would be found engraved on her heart. She was, though, spared the knowledge that her name was to be reviled more than any other English sovereign with the epithet 'bloody'.

Elizabeth's accession was greeted with wild acclamation. Church bells were rung, bonfires lit and vast quantities of liquor consumed. People looked forward to a new, less repressive regime. At the age of 25, with no experience of state affairs, Elizabeth found herself at the centre of government. It was fortunate for England that she was blessed with exceptional qualities, for the situation that confronted her was desperate: the country was riddled with religious divisions; due to indecisive wars and bad harvests its finances were in chaos; and there was a threat of foreign invasion. In addition Elizabeth's right to the throne was widely disputed. To orthodox Roman Catholics the marriage of her mother Anne Boleyn to Henry VIII was illegal and she was, therefore, illegitimate, in which case the rightful sovereign was Mary Stuart. As she was a firm Roman Catholic this view was strongly opposed by English Protestants who asserted that Elizabeth had been nominated in the line of succession in the will of Henry VIII, and that in any case 'the crown once worn taketh away all defects whatsoever'.

The main danger at first came from a union of Scotland and France. When the French King Henry II died seven months after Elizabeth's accession, his successor, Francis II, husband of Mary Stuart, was proclaimed not only King of France but also of England, Scotland and Ireland. He himself was a puny weakling of 15 who soon died and on the accession of his younger brother, Henry III, power in France passed to his uncles, the Cardinal of Lorraine and the Duke of Guise, who were bent on strengthening Mary's position in Scotland where her mother, Mary of Guise, had been acting as Regent during her minority. From there with the aid of French troops they envisaged invading England and installing Mary as Queen.

England's only ally in Europe had once been King Philip of Spain, but this alliance had become weaker and in time was to turn into strong hostility with the restitution of the Protestant Church and the refusal of Elizabeth to accept him as her husband. For a time England's situation was perilous, but this was to ease with the seizure of power in Scotland by a group of Protestant noblemen known as The Congregation; and in France by the development of internal religious strife between Catholics and Huguenots. Elizabeth's position as Queen of England, however, was always to be insecure.

Elizabeth's good judgement was soon shown by her choice of ministers, notably William Cecil whom she appointed Secretary of State.[2] Judicious and discreet (and when necessary ruthless) he was to be at the Queen's right hand until he died 40 years later.

Cecil's immediate concern was that the Queen should marry

---

[2] He had managed to survive service under Henry VIII, Edward VI and Mary. 'I have gained more', he once wrote, 'by my temperance and forebearance than ever I did by my wit.'

immediately and appropriately. The safety of the realm and the Protestant religion could not be assured while the heir to the throne was Mary Stuart. The life of Elizabeth would always be in danger as long as she was heir-presumptive. But in this matter Elizabeth was to be disingenuous. She would not turn the idea down out of hand, but neither would she commit herself.

To those who came begging her to be married she might reply vaguely that God would provide in due course or, sententiously, that she was already 'bound to a husband which is the kingdom of England'. It cannot be known for certain why she shied away from marriage. It may be that she did not like the idea of a man about the house, making his presence felt, laying down the law and generally getting under her feet. It has been suggested that there may have been physiological factors which prevented her from giving birth or even consummating a marriage; but the evidence for this is inconclusive. There were, of course, political difficulties about any marriage. One to a foreign prince was likely to entangle her in European affairs – the marriage of her half-sister Mary to the King of Spain had given ample warning of this – while one to an English nobleman would give rise to jealousy and internal rifts.

While the Queen's marriage was being vehemently debated the matter was complicated by her falling ardently in love with a most inapposite suitor. Robert Dudley (later Earl of Leicester) was a younger son of John Dudley, Duke of Northumberland, who had been executed following the abortive attempt to put Lady Jane Grey on the throne instead of Mary, following the death of Edward VI.[3] He had many attractive and dashing qualities – in sport, dancing, jousting and most forms of entertainment – but he was for certain married. His wife, Amy Robsart, was a quiet, retiring figure who suffered from bad health, possibly cancer. The Queen made no secret of her attachment to him and loaded him with honours and riches including the lucrative post of Master of the Horse. This, of course, gave rise to feverish chatter that they would marry but for the existence of Amy Robsart. Then, when the affair was at its height, Amy died in somewhat mysterious circumstances, falling downstairs and breaking her neck while alone in her house

---

[3] His grandfather, Edmund Dudley, known for his extortionate methods of taxation in conjunction with Sir Richard Empson in the reign of Henry VII, had also been executed on a charge of treason.

in the country.[4] These facts were confirmed by a coroner's verdict, but inevitably tongues wagged and there was speculation, both at home and abroad, as to whether she had been murdered. It was then that Elizabeth might have made a fatal error. If she had married Dudley there would have been an uproar which she could hardly have survived, but unlike Mary Queen of Scots in a similar situation, her head ruled her heart, and although Dudley continued to be around, marriage to him was ruled out.

The main need of England at the time of Elizabeth's accession was freedom from religious strife, which had been raging furiously during the last three reigns. The Queen hoped to achieve this by reintroducing the Protestant Church of England but with modifications to conciliate Roman Catholics. So she took the title of Supreme Governor rather than Supreme Head of the Church, and offensive references to the Church of Rome were removed from the English Prayer Book.[5] It was also laid down that priests should wear vestments and were not free to marry. But heed had to be taken of the strong feelings of English Protestants, and so services were to be held in English, not Latin, while the Real Presence of Christ in the communion service was denied, as also was the miracle of transubstantiation of the communion bread and wine into the body and blood of Christ. At the same time candles and crucifixes were discouraged, as also were prayers to saints and the veneration of holy relics.

Elizabeth herself was well versed in the scriptures and attended church services regularly, but she had her prejudices. She had always been averse to long-drawn-out arguments about the minutiae of religious doctrine and she had a particular dislike of overlong sermons; and showed it, often nodding off and being always ready to interrupt when anything was said which she did not like. Her great love was for the singing of choirs, especially of contemporary music by such composers as Thomas Tallis and William Byrd. She was always to persist in her attempts to steer a middle course between Protestant and Papist, disliking all extremism and being in favour of as much toleration as possible. Her attitude generally was that people should conform outwardly to the main tenets of

---

[4] Unusually, all her servants had been sent off to a local affair on a Sunday.

[5] For example prayers were no longer offered for deliverance from 'the Bishop of Rome and his detestable enormities'.

Christianity but could think what they liked in private; there should be no delving into their innermost thoughts, or as was said, 'to make windows into men's souls'.

With doubts being cast on her rights to the throne Elizabeth set herself to strengthen her position by winning the love and support of the English people, and for this she had unique gifts. What is known today as 'star quality' (or charisma) she had in abundance. Wherever she went she was always the centre of attention and somehow made people feel she cared for them and loved them. She knew by instinct what they felt and wanted, and identified with them. And this love was genuine. She spoke from the heart when she declared: 'There is nothing so dear, no worldly thing as the hearty love and goodwill of my subjects.' She was constantly reiterating also the people's love for her. 'It was', she said, 'of such a kind as has never been known or heard of in the memory of man... It is such a love as neither persuasion nor threats nor curses can destroy.'

A feature of Queen Elizabeth's reign was the 'progresses' she made each summer. These were large-scale stately tours, sometimes visiting royal palaces (such as Greenwich, Nonsuch or Hampton Court), sometimes staying with eminent noblemen. With her on these journeys went her whole court, a full retinue of servants (grooms, butlers, cooks, hairdressers, laundresses among others) as well as loads of furniture, tableware, carpets and bed linen – anything that might be needed. Altogether there might be as many as 400 wagons, more than 2,000 packhorses and an accompanying staff of more than 1,000. This vast concourse could travel between 10 and 12 miles a day and could not venture far afield – 90 miles from London at the most. On arrival at its destination it caused almighty problems for the host. Much was expected of him. Not only did he have to provide accommodation, food and drink, but also lavish entertainment. The cost and inconvenience of these visitations were prodigious, but to the wealthy and ambitious with an eye on advancement at court it was considered worthwhile.

Not many festivities were as splendid as those laid on at Kenilworth in 1575 by the Earl of Leicester, a supreme master of revels. As well as enormous banquets of more than 100 courses there were performances of plays, country dances, water pageants and a firework display of such magnificence that 'the heavens thundered, the waters surged and the castle shook'. And in the midst of divine music and the arts came the grisly 'sport' of bear baiting which, it has to be said, the Queen greatly enjoyed.

Visits were also paid to some of the larger cities like Bristol, Norwich and Oxford, where the authorities went to great pains to brighten the place up – adorning buildings, laying gravel on roads and removing from sight all uglinesses such as gallows, stocks and piles of ordure. The Queen was often welcomed by lengthy orations, some, to the dismay of the less erudite members of her suite, in Latin. But she listened intently and was ready with a speech in reply, also in Latin. On these occasions she was at her best, taking every opportunity to show her love and sympathy for people. She mingled in the crowd and by a blend of graciousness and informality soon had everyone lost in wonder and awe. And she did not spare herself. She washed the feet of mendicants on Maundy Thursday and laid hands on those suffering from a scrofulous disease known as King's Evil. Her chaplain wrote of this: 'How often have I seen her with her exquisite hands, whiter than the whitest snow, boldly and without disgust pressing their sores and ulcers.' It was made known that on these visits the Queen expected a handsome gift, which often took the form of a silver bowl filled with gold pieces. These she might go through the motions of disdaining, on one occasion exclaiming: 'Princes have no need of money. We come for the hearts and allegiance of our subjects.' She nevertheless kept the gift.

The love and admiration which Queen Elizabeth commanded was not, it would seem, due to great beauty. There are doubts about this. Of course the flatterers at court praised it to the skies, but they would. A foreign diplomat of that time, who was comparatively disinterested, wrote that she was 'comely rather than handsome ... with a good skin, although swarthy, and with fine eyes', while another writer agreed that she had fine eyes, but that she had pale skin and fair hair. In determining her true looks little can be gained from portraits that have come down. These were not concerned with realism, portraying a lifeless face with little sign of humanity, immersed in sumptuous clothes laden with jewellery. They have been likened to an Indian idol or a wooden doll. It is necessary to distinguish between myth and reality.

The myth, built up by Elizabeth herself and writers and painters of the time, was of a chaste goddess – 'Fair Oriana', 'the Sun Queen', infinitely wise, just and beautiful. The reality, however, was different. Elizabeth was no demure goddess. She was, in fact, earthy, robust and somewhat coarse. Of feminine charms she was not lacking, but she drank heartily, danced vigorously and swore roundly. Her temper, as might be expected of a daughter of Henry VIII, was incandescent and she could be violent, striking out at her ministers and ladies-in-waiting, throwing shoes at them and even spitting at them. Although possessed of enormous energy she was not physically strong and suffered acutely from toothaches and headaches. Considering the strain under which she lived – with the threat of foreign invasion never far off and herself in constant personal danger – it is not surprising that at times her nerve cracked and she gave way to hysteria, 'lambasting all around both with blows and words'.

The Queen's working day was a full one. She had little need of sleep and rose early. There then ensued an elaborate toilette. There were no bathrooms in the royal palaces and little washing was done, but extensive use was made of rose waters and rare perfumes, also of primitive cosmetics. The Queen attached great importance to her skin being white, and to achieve this used a concoction of white of egg, powdered eggshell, alum, borax, white poppy seed and water 'that run from under the wheel of a mill', all beaten into a white froth. Her teeth might be treated with toothpick and cloth, and her hair was occasionally washed in a liquid called lye, a mixture of woodash and water. Later in life wigs became necessary; that there was a large number of these is shown by an account for 'six heads of hair, 12 yards of hair curl, 100 devices made of hair'. The most important moment was the choosing of a dress; these were always magnificent, often encrusted with seed pearls and diamonds and, as was the custom for unmarried ladies, cut low. Finally the Queen would feel ready to appear and set about the business of the day.

At first sight the Elizabethan court seemed magnificent indeed – the great Queen herself leading the dance and setting the tone, the brilliant courtiers in attendance, the masques and tournaments, the music of Byrd and Gibbons, the plays of Shakespeare. But, as with all courts, beneath the surface lay a different picture: the Queen outwardly the fair goddess but behind the mask a hard-headed virago; the courtiers flaunting their wit and wisdom but with their eyes fixed firmly on the main chance and scrambling for honours and riches; the furniture and trappings beautiful and costly but painfully uncomfortable; and the charade, which all had to play, of being madly in love with the Queen, plying her with flattery and going through the motions of a flirtation. Sir Walter Raleigh, one of the court's leading lights, could write of it:

> Go tell the court it glows
> And shines like rotten wood.

It has been seen how at the beginning of her reign Elizabeth attempted to bring unity to the Church of England and bring about an abatement of religious intolerance. But these efforts were not to succeed, and in the course of her reign religious strife was to become ever more intensive. This began in earnest when in the late 1560s the Vatican launched the Counter-Reformation to stamp out Protestantism, with England being specially targeted. In 1570 Elizabeth was formally excommunicated by Pope Pius V and it was later decreed that her assassination would not be considered a mortal sin. At the same time colleges were set up on the Continent to train priests in the work of reconverting the country. It was laid down that they were to confine their activities to preaching the gospel and were not to dabble in politics, but in view of the militant attitude of the Vatican they came to be suspected of being subversive agents bent on overthrowing the government, murdering the Queen and replacing her with Mary Queen of Scots. This suspicion became stronger with the arrival in the country of a new order of priests, the Jesuits, whose declared intention was to eradicate heresy by whatever means. They were regarded as a serious threat to national security, in particular to the life of the Queen, and were hunted down and, if caught, put to death brutally.

Religious intolerance was also to be stirred up by the arrival in the country in 1568 of Mary Queen of Scots, fleeing from her rebellious Scottish subjects. It has been seen in the chapter of this book devoted to her that her presence in England gave rise to a number of plots and rebellions, culminating in her execution, which caused widespread outrage.

Signing Mary's death warrant was for Elizabeth the most traumatic experience of her life. She had a low opinion of Mary and wanted her dead, but condemning a fellow sovereign to death in cold blood was something from which she shrank and which she did all she could to avoid. But the pressure was too great: the Privy Council, both Houses of Parliament and all leading Protestants were insistent that there was no safety for the government, the Church and Elizabeth herself so long as Mary was alive; and she herself knew this but still held back, trying to find a way out. She would have accepted secret assassination, but this could not be done; Mary's keeper, though stern and unrelenting, was no murderer. And so eventually she did sign the death warrant, but then tried to make out that she had not meant it to be carried out. It was the fault of the Secretary of State, William Davison, who had coerced her into signing and then not waited for confirmation.[6] But this attempt to put the blame on another was not generally believed.

In the latter part of Elizabeth's reign it was not only from Roman Catholics that the Church of England was endangered. A new form of Protestantism was gathering strength based on the teaching of the French theologian John Calvin. His followers, known as Presbyterians or Puritans, advocated a new form of church government ruled by elders (or Presbyters) rather than bishops and monarchs. Vocal, active and fiercely intolerant, they were becoming a powerful pressure group both in Parliament and in the country at large. Their religious practices were austere in the extreme. They led simple, hard lives devoid of pleasure. Such amusements as dancing, sports, the theatre and bear baiting[7] they regarded as sinful; and any form of church decoration – pictures, sculptures, stained glass – they abhorred as idolatrous and believed it was their Christian duty to destroy or deface them. For the Puritans Elizabeth had little sympathy: laws were passed curbing their activities, censorship was imposed on their writings and brutal punishments inflicted for minor breaches of the law. And the Queen also made a point of encouraging all sports and festivities, taking part in them openly herself; and giving strong support to the rapidly developing theatre. The Puritans, however, were not to be crushed. Their power and influence continued to grow and in time was to overwhelm (temporarily) both Church and state.

As has been seen, since becoming queen, Elizabeth had been under constant pressure to marry. Many and various prospective husbands had been under consideration including the King of Spain,

---

[6] Davison was sent to the Tower and threatened with death. From this he was saved, but he was dismissed from office.

[7] Not because of the pain caused to the bears but the pleasure experienced by the spectators.

the King of Sweden, the Archduke of Austria and the Earl of Leicester. But for one reason or another their suits had come to nothing so that by the time Elizabeth had been on the throne for 20 years and had reached the age of 45 it seemed likely that she would remain single for life. She herself was said to have declared: 'If I followed the inclination of my nature it is this: beggar woman and single far rather than queen and married.' But then after years of prevaricating and dodging the issue she suddenly showed signs of being seriously interested, which caused not only surprise but also consternation as her choice of partner was, to say the least, bizarre.

Francis Duke of Alençon was the youngest son of the French King Henry II and Catherine de Medici. He was 23 years younger than Elizabeth, undersized and misshapen; he was also a weak and untrustworthy character.[8] It was unimaginable that she should think of marrying a man such as he, but it seems to have been on the cards. Evidently she delighted in his wit and charm and petted him and called him her 'little frog' – hardly complimentary but betokening warm affection. She was also overheard telling the French Ambassador: 'You may tell His Majesty that the Prince will be my husband.' This appalled her ministers, who could not think what she was doing. At the time England was in need of an alliance with France to shore her up in her worsening relations with Spain, but not at the expense of such a marriage. However there need not have been any worry. It was to become apparent that Elizabeth was up to her old game of playing for time. She was a consummate actress and deceived everyone; and when it came to hammering out a marriage settlement between herself and Catherine de Medici there was little likelihood of agreement. It was a case of Greek meeting Greek.

By the 1580s, war with Spain was certain. By then Philip II had come to realise that he was not going to become Elizabeth's husband and England would not be reconverted to Catholicism without war. A hard-line Catholic, he put himself at the head of the Counter-Reformation with two main objectives: the crushing of the revolt of Protestants in the Spanish Netherlands and the conquest of England. For some time there was a state of undeclared war in which Elizabeth sent help to the Dutch rebels while Philip

---

[8] See the chapter on Catherine de Medici (p. 55).

stirred up trouble and sent troops to Ireland. There were also the activities of English privateers, Francis Drake and John Hawkins among others, who preyed on the Spanish ships transporting silver and other treasures to Spain from the mines of Mexico and Peru. This was blatant piracy but it had the tacit support of the Queen who took a generous share of the takings, while maintaining to the indignant Spanish Ambassador that she knew nothing about the matter.

But this undercover war could not last indefinitely, and by 1585 Philip was making preparations for a large-scale invasion of England. His plans were set back when in 1587 Francis Drake set fire to a number of Spanish ships in Cadiz harbour. But by 1588 the Great Armada, as it was called, was ready – consisting of 130 ships with 30,000 men on board of whom 2,000 were soldiers. The plan was to sail up the English Channel to the Spanish Netherlands where a further 16,000 soldiers under the Duke of Parma would be taken on board, and then to make a landing on the southeast coast of England. It seemed that such a mighty array would be irresistible. It is not necessary here to go into details as to how the Armada, battered by storms and English gunfire, ended up fleeing for refuge round the north of Scotland, eventually arriving back in Spain but losing more than half its number on the way.

It should be noted, however, that this event was a turning point in the history of England and of Europe. It marked the end of Spain as a great power and the emergence of England as one. The Counter-Reformation had foundered and Protestantism had been saved. It should also be recorded that at this time of extreme danger Queen Elizabeth was to be seen at her greatest. Somehow, in spite of an empty Exchequer, she mustered an army of 20,000 men under the command of the Earl of Leicester. She came among them at Tilbury and addressed them with words which show vividly the strength of the bond between her and her subjects:

> Let tyrants fear. I have always so behaved myself that, under God, I have placed my chiefest strength and safeguard in the loyal hearts and goodwill of my subjects; and therefore I am come amongst you, as you see, resolved in the midst and heat of the battle, to live or die amongst you all, to lay down for my God, and for my kingdom, and for my people, my honour and my blood, even in the dust. I know I have the body of a

weak and feeble woman, but I have the heart and stomach of a king, and of a king of England too, and think foul scorn that Parma of Spain or any prince of Europe should dare to invade the borders of my realm; to which, rather than any dishonour shall grow by me, I myself will take up arms, I myself will be your general, judge and rewarder of every one of your virtues in the field.

After the dispersal of the Armada the war with Spain (although never officially declared) dragged on until the end of Elizabeth's reign 15 years later. During this time there were no historic events. Philip II made no serious attempts to mount another invasion of England while Elizabeth was always restricted in what she could do by financial straits. She did, however, continue to send help to the Protestant rebels in the Netherlands and to the Huguenots in France, and there was still some activity from English privateers preying on Spanish treasure ships, but these had become less successful and after the death of Sir Francis Drake in 1596 were on a small scale. The only memorable naval engagement was at Flores in the Azores when a single English ship, *The Revenge* under Sir Richard Grenville, held at bay 15 ships of Spain for 15 hours.

At home religious disputation continued unabated, while the cultural life of the country flourished as never before, notably in music and the theatre. At court the scene was changing as the old guard faded away and new figures made their appearance. Leicester, by then obese and debauched, died in 1588, Walsingham in 1590 and William Cecil (by then Lord Burleigh) in 1598. In their place came Robert Cecil, undersized and hunchbacked but no less astute than his father; Sir Christopher Hatton, a smooth operator and skilful dancer; Sir Walter Raleigh, virile and adventurous with some literary ability; and, most conspicuous of all, Leicester's stepson Robert Devereux, 2nd Earl of Essex.

Essex had many gifts – charm, good looks, intelligence and courage – but he was also seriously flawed: he was arrogant, ill-tempered, reckless and extravagant. At an early age he caught the eye of the Queen who, 33 years older though she might be, could not but be fascinated by him. She bestowed honours and riches on him and took him into her Council of Ministers at the age of 26. She did not, however, give him a free rein as she was not blind to his faults and was bent on correcting them. 'I shall break him of his will,' she once declared, 'and pull down his great heart.'

It was evident to the Queen and to all who came in contact with him that Essex's ambitions were boundless. He sought to outstrip all other ministers and favourites, but at first his great desire was for glory on the battlefield. He was forever urging the Queen into military engagements with him in command, but here she was not easily persuaded. She was averse to war and the great cost it entailed, and she also disliked the thought of Essex being in danger. Against her better judgement, however, she did agree to his being put in command of a force sent to help the Huguenots in France; and almost at once her worst fears were realised. At a safe distance Essex went his own way, disobeying orders, embarking on wild ventures, spending money freely – and achieving little. He was ordered home and there was a flaming row but, as usual, by lavish applications of charm and flattery, all was forgiven.

In other operations in which he took part the story was much the same. He always fought with great courage but was a law unto himself; he was on occasions victorious, notably in an attack on the Spanish port of Cadiz in which he shared the command with the prestigious Lord Howard of Effingham who had been in command of the English fleet against the Armada. Cadiz was captured and held for a time, a number of Spanish ships were sunk, and several Spanish grandees were captured and held to ransom. But the Queen was not impressed. Great glory may have been won, but the treasure taken was in her eyes inadequate – not enough to cover the cost of the expedition, and that was the main consideration. The same was to happen in other similar engagements, so that she finally ordered them to cease. In England Essex had become a popular hero, but he was restless and discontented and concentrated his efforts in gaining the upper hand in the Queen's Council and strengthening his position by obtaining appointments to high offices for his friends and supporters.

Although hostilities against Spain were suspended, there was another theatre of war which could not be avoided. In the late 1590s there was a serious rebellion in Ireland, the fourth in Elizabeth's reign. The powerful and charismatic nobleman Hugh O'Neill, 2nd Earl of Tyrone, had raised the standard of revolt in Ulster and with help from Spain was threatening to overthrow English dominion in the country. This could not be tolerated and

Elizabeth, much as she disliked war and the cost of it, had to concede that the revolt had to be put down.

Essex was not long in coming forward to take command of this operation. He may well have hesitated as it was a formidable task, and he might have heeded the words of a foreign diplomat that Ireland might be called an Englishman's grave, but he decided that he had to go. His reputation at court lately had been slipping, as the Queen had been appointing Robert Cecil to the more important government offices. He knew that if he were successful in Ireland he would be widely acclaimed and his position would be unassailable, but if he failed he would be finished. It was a desperate gamble but he had to take it. He first had to overcome opposition from the Queen, who knew from experience that once out of sight he would act on his own initiative, recklessly and expensively, but partly owing to popular clamour, she had to agree. Essex was then provided with the largest English army ever to be sent to Ireland as well as being invested with special powers.

The Queen might well have had fears. On arrival in Ireland Essex became hesitant about his ability to overcome Tyrone and instead of confronting him in the north marched against lesser rebels in the south. He then entered into secret negotiations with Tyrone and to complete his treachery decided to return to England with an armed escort. His idea seems to have been then to confront the Queen and impose on her conditions including the dismissal of her ministers.

Elizabeth was stunned and aghast when Essex broke in on her when she was at her toilette in Nonsuch Palace. She decided that for the time being she had to temporise, as she knew that Essex commanded wide popular support. She also knew that he was rash and impetuous and, given enough rope, was likely to hang himself. So she negotiated, but she did deprive him of his public offices and then of his sources of income, and it was this that prompted him into desperate action. He conceived a wild plan for taking over the court, the Tower and the city, but this depended on a rising in his favour which was not forthcoming and he was forced to give himself up. He was then put on trial, condemned to death and executed. Although she had once loved him, the Queen showed no hesitation in signing his death warrant. The safety of the realm demanded it.

Two years of life were to lie ahead of Elizabeth after the death of Essex, and until the end she was as vital and active as ever. She brushed aside all notions that she was too old to do anything – hunting regularly, riding up to 15 miles a day and then perhaps leading the dance in a spritely galliard. She might also indulge her crude taste for bear baiting or bull fighting, and then in a sudden switch of mood attend a play of Shakespeare or listen to the celestial music of the Elizabethan composers.

For most of the time her health was reasonably robust, as it had always been. In the course of her life she had had only one serious illness, an attack of smallpox in the 1560s. She had also been much troubled by an ulcer on her leg which left her with a slight limp. Otherwise she steered clear of doctors and medicines and wherever possible tried to conceal any ailments, treating them with her own personal remedies, the main exception being toothache which, caused by eating too many sweetmeats, afflicted her sorely. Her mental powers never dimmed, nor her powers of command. As long as she lived, she ruled. She depended greatly on Robert Cecil – prudent, tactful and adept at managing her – although he had to be reminded on occasions that he should be constrained in the language he used to princes. She was still prone to great anger, when she would stamp her feet or spit with rage, and she kept a sword by her side which every now and then she would thrust through the wall hangings where she thought a possible assassin might be lurking.

In 1601, two years before she died, Elizabeth had a notable political triumph. In that year the Commons met in an ugly mood. Taxation recently had been high, to pay for the war in Ireland, and some of the methods employed for raising money had been nefarious, particularly the granting to individuals of monopolies – that is, the exclusive right to deal in certain commodities such as tobacco, salt and wine. These privileges had often been grossly abused, resulting in exorbitant prices being charged, and the Commons was bent on having them abolished. During her reign Elizabeth's relations with the Commons had been civil, cool and positive; sometimes flattering, sometimes rebuking. She recognised their right to authorise taxation, but made it clear that 'they must not presume to meddle with matters above their capacity, not appertaining to them'. In particular they must not touch on religious matters. Their speech was to be 'liberal but not licentious'. She summoned them as rarely as possible – 13 times in 45 years – and was always ready to disperse them when they had performed their vital task of voting taxes. But she was always aware that she must keep on the right side of them; after all they represented the people on whose love, she had often declared, her throne was based; and when in 1601 they assembled in fractious mood she acknowledged that they had a point.

Monopolies were a genuine grievance; as one member put it 'more derogatory to herself and more odious to her subjects'. Concessions had to be made and they would be made graciously and generously. In her speech from the throne, which came to be known as 'the Golden Speech', she conceded that there had been 'errors, troubles, vexations and oppressions', and these would be attended to. She then went on to make a highly emotional declaration of her love for her subjects: 'There is no jewel, be it never so rich a price which I set before this jewel, I mean your love ... and though God hath raised me high, yet this I count the glory of my crown that I have reigned with your love.' These words came from the heart and the Commons were overwhelmed; tears poured from their eyes as they bowed in submission.

By the beginning of 1603 it was evident that the Queen was sinking fast. Her memory was fading as was her eyesight and her comprehension of what was going on around her. It seemed that she had lost the will to live. A foreign diplomat who saw her at that time wrote that she was 'full of chagrin and weary of life'. Communication with her was difficult, often impossible; and on one subject she was particularly reticent – that of her successor. When it was put to her that it should be her cousin, King James VI of Scotland, she seemed to assent but would never make an open declaration. She continued to refuse all physics and nearly all food; for ten days she refused to go to bed, sitting on the floor in day clothes, propped up by cushions. The end came on 24 March when she was six months short of her seventieth birthday.

Her reign had been unique; her achievements monumental. No woman in English history, possibly in world history, has had such power and exercised it so shrewdly. Being human she did have faults and foibles. She could be indecisive and bad-tempered, vindictive and cruel,[9] and she had no qualms about the ends justifying the means; she was a past master in double dealing, and

---

[9] She had no compunction about the use of torture if thought to be effective.

in the art of dissimulation was second to none. Her tastes were not all aesthetic – some were crude and bestial, as for example her delight in being in at the kill in a hunt, ready to plunge a sword into a trapped stag. But these flaws were overridden by her phenomenal gifts: prodigious intellect, incisive wit, adroit political skills and a profound insight into human nature. At the time of her death there were discontents who looked forward to better times under a king (there had not been a king in England for 47 years), but the rule of the Stuarts soon caused them to change their minds and look back on the reign of Elizabeth as a golden age. For 200 years her coronation day was celebrated as a holiday.

6

CATHERINE I, TSARINA OF RUSSIA (1684–1727)

To have risen from scullion in the baggage train of the Russian army to wife of Russia's most powerful tsar, and then to become Tsarina as Catherine I in her own right, was the achievement of Martha Skavronska, daughter of a Lithuanian peasant who eked out a lowly living mainly as a grave digger.

At the age of three she was left an orphan and was adopted by an aunt who looked after her until the age of 12 when she was put into domestic service in the household of a Lutheran pastor in the small town of Marienberg. Of education she had none; she never learned to read or write. At the age of 19 (or thereabouts) she married a young soldier, a trumpeter in the Dragoons, which was considered an advantageous match for one of her humble station, but this was immediately upset when Lithuania was overrun by Russia and many of the inhabitants were carried off into slavery, in Martha's case to menial work with the Russian army where her treatment was of the roughest.

It was not long, however, before she began to attract attention, first of the local Russian commander, then of the Commander-in-Chief in Lithuania, and then of one of even greater eminence on whose shoulders she was to be carried to undreamed of heights. Alexander Menshikov, like Martha, came from lowly origins; it was reported that at one time he peddled pies in the streets of Moscow. But he was of unbounded self-confidence and ambition and somehow had worked his way into the favour of the great Tsar Peter I, studying closely his likes and dislikes, finding ways of humouring him and pandering to his every whim. In doing so he thought he could make use of the beguiling charms of Martha.

Several years before, Peter had put aside his wife and sent her into a nunnery. For some time afterwards he had relied on the attentions of a *maitresse-en-titre*, Anna Mons, but he had become tired of her and when he discovered that he was not her only lover, had dismissed her. Since then he had had a succession of transitory affairs, but Menshikov sensed that he was now looking for something more permanent, and it occurred to him that Martha might fill the bill.

In 1703 the Tsar announced his intention of paying a visit to Menshikov, who went to immense trouble to see that it was a splendid occasion – and among the attractions was Martha waiting at table, on whom the eyes of the Tsar were constantly turning. This was not lost on Menshikov who later detailed Martha to show the Tsar to his bedroom. A few weeks later the Tsar paid another visit, but this time Martha was not in attendance as a waitress. As expected her absence was remarked on, and when she was presented it was not in servant's attire but in something much more alluring. Menshikov had played his cards skilfully and it came as no surprise when a few days later an army officer arrived with orders to escort Martha to Moscow.

In 1704 Martha (renamed Catherine) bore her first child by Peter. It had taken her hardly more than a year to rise from scullion to mistress of the Tsar. It was her great achievement that she adapted to this transmutation readily and was to be the lasting love of the titan known to history as Peter the Great. A man of enormous strength and size (6 feet 8 inches tall) and prodigious energy, he was a phenomenon among rulers. When Catherine arrived on the scene he had been tsar for eleven years and during that time had taken upon himself the task of developing the vast, barbarous land mass of Russia into a modern, civilised state.

In this he had spared himself no pains. Eschewing pomp and majesty, he had thrown himself into every task however humble – carpenter, shipwright, metal worker – and delighted in them. He claimed to be the master of 14 trades. At the same time he had been the driving force behind everyone, impelling the laggards, overriding the prejudiced and searching out the corrupt. As might be expected such a workload took a heavy toll on his constitution, mighty as it was. He became physically exhausted and so stressed that he flew into violent uncontrollable rages when he would lash out in all directions and no one dared approach him; no one, that is, except Catherine. She alone was able to soothe him, taking his head on her lap and treating him like a child, which he loved, and he would always refer to her as 'little mother'.

Exalted as was Catherine's new status, she was nevertheless aware how precarious it was. It depended entirely on Peter. Without him she was nothing, just another concubine to be paid off; perhaps generously, perhaps not. So during Peter's long absences on government business or in wars against foreign powers she suffered agonies of anxiety. Should a stray bullet come his way, he would be succeeded by Alexei, his son by his legal wife (she in a nunnery) from whom Catherine could expect little sympathy. She implored Peter to let her accompany him, but this at first he would not allow, insisting that she stay behind to look after the increasing number of children to whom she was giving birth (eleven in all, of whom only two daughters were to survive into adulthood).

The brief times they had together then were precious, and of these perhaps the ones they cherished most were those spent in the new city Peter was creating in the far north of the country. He had always hated Moscow – a teeming metropolis with its golden domes and thousand churches side by side with squalid alleyways and fetid tenements. It epitomised the medieval, mystical Russia which he wanted relegated, and he wanted the country brought into a new age. It was also a lawless city and he could never forget the traumatic experience he had as a boy when he witnessed the slaughter of friends and relations by rebellious soldiers. Whenever he and Catherine were there they avoided the centre of the city and stayed in a safe haven in the suburbs.

So Peter had decided to build a new capital city. It might seem strange that he chose the desolate marshlands where the river Neva flows into the Baltic as its site. It certainly had great drawbacks – not only the bleak climate and terrain but it was also disputed territory, having once belonged to Sweden which still lodged a claim to it. But for Peter there was one overriding advantage: it would be a seaport, and one of his obsessions was for a large, modern navy. At that time Russia, vast though it might be, was almost entirely landlocked: most of the Baltic coast in the north belonged to Sweden, and the Black Sea in the south was dominated by Turkey. And so Peter had a vision of a new, magnificent, essentially European capital where a great navy could be based.

When Catherine arrived in Russia in 1703 work on St Petersburg, as it was to be called, was just beginning – canals were being dug, marshes drained and roads laid out. Of houses there were no more than log cabins, and Peter and Catherine lived in one such and were perfectly happy there. Peter was indifferent to discomfort and hardship and Catherine had been brought up to it. Certainly conditions were very rough. It seemed that the encampment, for it was then no more, was regularly either being swamped by floods or devastated by fire. Only someone of massive willpower could keep the project alive, but Peter never lost faith in it, bringing in armies of skilled and unskilled workers, firing everyone with his enthusiasm and then putting pressure on the well-to-do to come and live there.

In 1707 Catherine's love and loyalty were rewarded when she and Peter secretly went through a form of marriage. It was felt necessary to keep this low-key as Peter's wife was still alive and undivorced, so that in the eyes of the Church he was a bigamist. Catherine's past life had been far from virginal and she too had a lawful spouse, the trumpeter in the dragoons, although what had happened to him nobody knew. Constraint, however, did not come naturally to Peter. As his powers became more autocratic and his love for Catherine deepened, he determined that she should have official recognition. And so in 1711 he summoned all his family and told them that for eight years she had been as good as his wife, that she and she alone was his consort, and that he would have a formal marriage ceremony 'when he had time'. And such was his power that this was accepted.

Soon afterwards war with Turkey broke out again and Peter had to dash off to take command. This time he allowed Catherine to accompany him and she was to find herself in the thick of a bloody battle during which she gave what help she could to the wounded, and when the Russian army became hard-pressed she was said to have had a part in agreeing terms of peace. It is probable that her part in this was exaggerated, as on their return to St Petersburg Peter planned to have a grand public wedding in which Catherine would be officially proclaimed Tsarina. This elevation, which occurred on 9 February 1712, may have enhanced Catherine's standing but not everyone was happy about it. To some she was still 'the Lithuanian whore' and a disreputable interloper. Foreign governments were particularly sceptical. Typical of their attitude was that of the English Ambassador who wrote to his Secretary of State: 'I suppose you will have already heard that the Tsar has married his mistress and declared her empress; it is one of the surprising events in this wonderful age.'

Tsarina though she might be, life for Catherine went on much as before. Peter was as preoccupied as ever with his various projects and constantly away, leaving her behind to give birth to more children and to worry about him; as well she might, for his life was often in danger – sometimes from the enemy, sometimes from illness and sometimes from an assassin, as there were many who abhorred him and his 'ungodly foreign ways' and would be glad to see him dead. In the event of his death his heir-apparent, Alexei, was a very different character – mild and ineffective and obsessed by the doctrines and practices of the Orthodox Church. If he were to become Tsar there was a danger that he might undo much of Peter's work, and he would certainly be strongly averse to Catherine and her family. There had long been bitter hostility between father and son and this came to a head in 1716 when Alexei, fearing for his life, fled abroad and took refuge in Italy. He was hunted down by his father's agents and brought back to Russia where he was condemned to death, but in 1718, before the official execution took place, he died in mysterious circumstances in prison.

This seemed to remove the main threat to Catherine and to open the way for her baby son Peter, known as Petrushka, who might become Tsar in due course; but Alexei had left behind a son, also called Peter and of the same age, whom many were to regard as the true heir of the Romanov dynasty. Petrushka was to die a few years later.

In 1716 Catherine had had some relief from monotony when Peter had taken her with him on a tour of Europe; but this had not altogether gone smoothly as most European royalty were reluctant to receive a lady of such shady reputation as Catherine. One consequence of Catherine's European tour was an enlivening of her interest in the development of St Petersburg. This came about mainly during a visit to the city of Amsterdam with its orderly well-maintained roads and canals and fertile lands reclaimed from the sea, which opened her eyes to what the new Russian capital might become, and on her return she became closely involved in new plans, especially for the building of palaces and assembly rooms.

Already by then St Petersburg was taking on a new look. The old shanty town of log cabins, rough tracks and seas of mud were being replaced by a city of stone-built houses and churches and paved boulevards. It was, however, still liable to flooding and in winter especially the atmosphere was bleak and inhospitable, so well-to-do Russians were unwilling to move there. Peter therefore coerced them. What is more, he laid down rules of acceptable behaviour in an attempt, as he put it, to 'turn Russian beasts into human beings'. Western styles and manners were de rigueur; crude old Russian ways, including the growing of beards, were banned; and fierce punishments were meted out to those who picked their noses or spoke with their mouths full or spat on the floor. In this Peter did not always set a good example: he drank heavily and could become boisterous, not to say violent, while his choice of company was eclectic, so that stately ambassadors might find themselves carousing with boozy sailors or amorous craftsmen.

In 1722 Peter reached the age of 50 and from then on his health declined. He was laid low by one affliction after another, but he could not be persuaded to ease up; his workload remained as heavy as ever, as did his bouts of drinking. He seemed to sense that the end might not be far off and he started to make provisions for the future. He was determined that he should be succeeded by a child of Catherine rather than by the son of Alexei. To make his intention clear he decided to bestow a special honour on Catherine: she should be crowned with the Imperial Crown so that she became Empress in her own right. He prepared the way for this by proclaiming her great virtues – her valour and heroism in the war against the Turks as well as her 'endowments of mind' and 'transcendent virtues'. But not everyone was enthusiastic. There were those who were aghast that such honours should be invested on a foreigner of peasant origin and a common courtesan. But Peter's word was law and in a magnificent ceremony in the Uspensky cathedral in Moscow, which all the grandest in the land were commanded to attend, Catherine was solemnly inaugurated as Empress of all the Russias. Only ten years before, she had been a serving wench in the army baggage train.

Peter's end came in 1725 when, as a result of diving into icy waters to rescue stranded sailors, he became fatally ill with convulsions, fever and then gangrene. He died on 28 January 1725 at the age of 53. As she had always feared, Catherine's position was then indeterminate, as Peter had died without making a will nominating his successor. It was expected by most that this would be Prince Peter, son of Alexei, of impeccable legitimacy and Romanov descent. The chances for Catherine seemed slim; no woman had ever ruled Russia as Empress before, and besides, she was a foreigner of peasant origins and murky reputation. Nevertheless, she had powerful forces behind her. The governing clique, led by Alexander Menshikov, saw in her a docile creature with themselves in command. They maintained that Peter had made his intentions clear when he had had her crowned with the Imperial Crown. Whether or not that was so, the deciding factor was the loyalty of the Palace Guard and this Menshikov, with bribes and promises, succeeded in mobilising, whereupon many waverers and supporters of Prince Peter rallied behind him as did others who saw which way the wind was blowing. Catherine was proclaimed Her Imperial Majesty the Sovereign Empress with little opposition.

Her position, however, was not secure. There was a strong feeling, especially among the old nobility, in favour of a Romanov with rights of primogeniture, and Catherine was aware of this and did what she could to pander to it, cosseting Peter and treating him as her heir; but at the same time making sure of retaining the loyalty of the Palace Guard.

Catherine was soon to find that life as Tsarina was not all that could be desired. She had never been power-hungry and would have been content with a nominal role, but this proved impossible. She was always being called on to settle disputes among ministers, and petitioners crowded in on all sides. The business of government she found very burdensome; her intelligence was lively but not profound and there were many decisions she had to make which were beyond her, and in council she was often out of her depth. To relieve her responsibility, on the advice of Menshikov she set up a Supreme Privy Council which would bear the brunt of government. For a time she attended their meetings but soon became bored by them and readily delegated all powers to the ever-grasping Menshikov. She did, of course, owe everything to him; she would never have attained her present position without him, and she was not ungrateful: every conceivable title was bestowed on him and he was laden with yet more estates, serfs and riches of all sorts.

Although little interested in the workings of government and the exercise of power, Catherine had a lively concern for its trappings. She enjoyed the honours accorded to her and the life of luxury she was able to afford. But this soon palled. Her life had revolved around Peter and without him it seemed dull and pointless. She became restless and ill at ease, unable to live a well-ordered life and taking comfort in excessive eating and drinking so that she became obese and depressed. In 1726 at the age of 43 it was evident that her health was breaking down and she did not have long to live.

This was soon realised by Menshikov who lost no time in making approaches to the supporters of Prince Peter. When Catherine was on her deathbed and hardly conscious he extracted from her a signature to a will leaving the crown to Peter, and after him to her two surviving daughters. During the last 20 years Menshikov had become an extremely rich man, but there was no end to his rapacity. He had dreams of even greater wealth as well as a plan for a marriage between Peter and his daughter. But here he overstepped the mark; his enemies, of which there were many, rose against him and without Catherine to protect him he was sent into exile in Siberia where he died in 1729.

Catherine died in 1727 and was much mourned. She had not been one of the great tsarinas but was loved for her simplicity and generosity. She left behind no great achievements of her own but can surely be allowed a share in the monumental ones of her husband.

7

MARIA THERESA, ARCHDUCHESS OF AUSTRIA AND QUEEN OF HUNGARY (1717–1780)

Maria Theresa, Archduchess of Austria, Queen of Hungary and Bohemia, daughter of one Holy Roman Emperor and wife of another, was a predominant figure in the history of Europe for 40 years. Her Habsburg dominions included parts of Central Europe, Italy, the Low Countries and the Balkans. During her reign she endeavoured to modernise and consolidate her empire and was a leading combatant in two major European wars. She was also the mother of five sons and eleven daughters.

The birth of Maria Theresa on 13 May 1717 caused great disappointment to her father, the Emperor Charles VI, who was desperate for a son to succeed him in his far-flung Habsburg Empire. He was not a strong ruler and during his reign of 30 years his realms had been greatly weakened by unsuccessful foreign wars; but he was determined that his empire should be preserved undivided and that he should be succeeded by Maria Theresa. He knew there would be opposition to this as there had never before been an empress in her own right, and so he drew up a plan which he thought would ensure her succession. By this, which was known as the Pragmatic Sanction, he sought to obtain assurances from the crowned heads of Europe that on his death they would recognise Maria Theresa as Empress. This was not easily achieved as some rulers held back and could only be persuaded into agreement by bribery in the form of either money or lands. A more sophisticated man than Charles would have been doubtful of the validity of their pledges. The great military commander, Prince Eugene, told him bluntly that it would be more to the point to leave behind him a full treasury and 200,000 fighting men, but these were not available and Charles put his trust in the plighted word of his fellow monarchs.

Charles's death was to come sooner than expected, induced

perhaps by overindulgence in a pot of mushrooms.[1] And so it came about that Maria Theresa at the age of 23, with little experience of the world and none of government, came into the inheritance of an empire sprawling across most of Western Europe with races as diverse as Germans, Magyars, Italians, Flemings and Slavs. It has been written that: 'no princess ever ascended a throne under circumstances of greater peril, or in a situation that demanded more energy, fortitude and judgment'. Danger and disaster loomed on every side. At home there was widespread discontent among those who doubted that Maria was capable of fulfilling the role which had come to her, and abroad it soon became evident that few of the signatories to the Pragmatic Sanction were going to abide by their word. If ever a monarch needed strong and wise support it was Maria Theresa, and in this she was ill-served. The ministers she inherited from her father were elderly and inactive; as she herself put it later: 'too prejudiced to give useful advice, but too respectable to be dismissed'.

Maria's main prop and support should have been her husband, but he was to prove inadequate. She had first met Francis Stephen, Duke of Lorraine, when she was six and he was 14; they were greatly attracted to each other and there was talk of a possible betrothal in years to come. For a time they were parted, but when they met again nine years later their love had deepened and they were ready for marriage. Charles VI, however, whose decision it was, at first held back, hoping to find a more prestigious match for his daughter; but Maria, showing signs of the strength of will for which she later become famous, insisted that there was no one else she could think of marrying, and her father had to relent. But he drove a hard bargain: at the time he was trying to gain the assent of France to the Pragmatic Sanction, but her rulers were prevaricating and the only way they could be persuaded was by the offer of Lorraine, the dukedom of which Francis had just inherited; this he was most unwilling to give up, but it was made clear to him that only by doing so would he be allowed to marry Maria Theresa. Reluctantly and resentfully, he agreed; as compensation he received the dukedom of Tuscany, but this was largely an honorary title and gave him little joy. Francis had some amiable

---

[1] Causing Voltaire to wonder that a pot of mushrooms was to change the course of European history.

qualities – he was charming, good-natured and self-effacing – but he had no natural authority and was too inert and easy-going. When, at Maria's instigation, he was given a military command, he was a disastrous failure, after which, although officially co-Regent with Maria, he was content to have a secondary role in affairs of state and devoted most of his time to the pursuit of pleasure. His eldest son Joseph's description of him as 'an idler surrounded by flatterers' is harsh but not wide of the mark. As a husband he was dutiful and affectionate but unfaithful, which was a great sadness to Maria although she bore with it. Her advice to another lady in similar circumstances was: 'Avoid reproaches, long explanations and, above all, disputes.' In spite of his weaknesses, she was to remain completely devoted to him and in 19 years bore him 16 children.

When Maria came into her inheritance she had little idea of the corruption of European statesmen. Incapable of duplicity herself, she assumed that others were the same. She was soon to be disillusioned. All the signatories of the Pragmatic Sanction should have acknowledged her accession at once, but the rulers of France prevaricated, sensing an opportunity to do down their great rival. And within only a few months came an act of blatant aggression.

Frederick II (later known as 'The Great') had become King of Prussia, then a minor European state, a few months before the accession of Maria Theresa. At the time he was posing as a peace-loving and enlightened prince with musical and literary tastes and a passionate admiration for the French philosopher and wit Voltaire, with whom he had a close association. He also proclaimed himself a strong protagonist of Maria Theresa whom he had lost no time acknowledging as the successor to the Habsburg Empire. But beneath the surface lurked a character of a different sort. Hardened by a harsh and brutal childhood at the hands of a semi-insane father, he saw himself as a ruthless, all-powerful monarch dedicated to the expansion of his kingdom by whatever means came to hand; and he saw opportunities for this in the unstable Austrian Empire headed by a youthful and what seemed to be a faltering empress. The prize he coveted was the fertile and prosperous Austrian province of Silesia, for which he could make out some form of ancient claim. And so within six months of his accession he sent in an army which at first met with little opposition; he then informed Maria that if she accepted this occupation he would protect her from her other enemies and would give his support to the election of her husband as Holy Roman Emperor. But he had misjudged his victim, for Maria Theresa would have none of this, declaring stoutly: 'For my part not for the Imperial Crown nor even the whole world will I sacrifice one right or one inch of the Queen's lawful possessions.'

It was not until four months after the invasion of Silesia that Austrian and Prussian armies confronted each other in battle. Mollwitz was a hard-fought fight but resulted in a Prussian victory which had far-reaching consequences: not only did it consolidate Frederick's seizure of Silesia, but it marked the emergence of Prussia as a major force in the European power struggle, and it gave encouragement to others who had designs on Austrian territory – to Louis XV of France in the Netherlands, to the Queen of Spain in Italy and, most particularly, to Charles Albert, Elector of Bavaria, who sought not only Austrian Bohemia but the entire Habsburg Empire on the grounds that his wife, a cousin of Maria Theresa, had a superior claim by birth. Three months after the Battle of Mollwitz, Charles Albert invaded Austrian territory and two months later had occupied Prague and with French support had been crowned King of Bohemia; soon after he was elected Holy Roman Emperor as Charles VII. The position of Maria Theresa then at the end of 1741 was desperate: she had lost Silesia to Frederick and Bohemia to Charles Albert, and for the first time for 300 years a non-Austrian had been elected to the imperial throne. It seemed that the Habsburg Empire was disintegrating.

But Maria Theresa did not lose heart. While her ministers quivered and her husband urged appeasement, she remained firm. 'Though I am only a queen,' she told them 'yet I have the heart of a king.'[2] And the tide did then turn. Help came from an unexpected source. The loyalty of Hungary to the Habsburgs had always been strained. The proud Magyars were fiercely jealous of their independence and were doubtful about accepting Maria as Queen, but when she came for her coronation her 'youth, beauty and extreme distress' (and perhaps too her pregnancy) won all hearts, and they rallied to her cause.

---

[2] Echoing the words of Elizabeth of England at the time of the Spanish Armada: 'I know I have the body of a weak and feeble woman, but I have the heart and stomach of a king, and of a king of England too, and think foul scorn that Parma or Spain or any prince of Europe should dare to invade the borders of my realm.'

The War of the Austrian succession, as it came to be called, was to drag on for eight years. It was a wretched, inglorious affair which brought credit to no one. The morality of European leaders has seldom sunk so low. In pursuing their selfish ends they were ready to stoop to any means, however dishonourable: duplicity was common currency, allies were stabbed in the back and treaties looked on as scraps of paper. Frederick the Great set the tone, and other countries followed suit.

In June of 1742 Frederick, thinking he had a firm hold of Silesia, patched up an agreement with Maria Theresa and withdrew from the war, leaving his French and Bavarian allies to fend for themselves. For a time then Austrian armies were successful, recapturing Prague, overrunning Bavaria and embarking on an invasion of Lorraine. But then Frederick took fright that his occupation of Silesia might be endangered, and struck first. In 1744 he re-entered the war, invading Bohemia, capturing Prague and threatening Vienna; but then, following dissent with France and Bavaria, he was forced to withdraw.

At times Maria Theresa had support from England, but this was intermittent and of little effect. There was no need for England to have been drawn into the conflict apart from chronic hostility to France, but there were also the fears of George II for the safety of his kingdom of Hanover for which he always had a stronger feeling than for England. At first English help came mainly in the form of cash subsidies, but then an army was despatched to the Netherlands where it had little success except for the Battle of Dettingen in which George II himself took command – the last time an English sovereign was to do such a thing. But although the battle was accounted a victory it achieved little, and England was soon seeking peace and putting pressure on Maria Theresa to do the same. In 1745, following a Jacobite rebellion in Scotland, England went so far as to come to an agreement with Frederick (for what it was worth) to ensure the security of Hanover.

The war eventually came to an end in 1748 when a treaty was hammered out in Aix-la-Chapelle. In this Maria Theresa was the only loser, Silesia being retained by Frederick. She was strongly resentful of the pressure that was put on her by England and others to agree to this, remarking bitterly that, 'my enemies will give me better terms than my friends'. And when congratulated on the coming of peace, she retorted that, 'compliments of condolence would be more proper than compliments of congratulation'. The only gain for her had been the election of her husband as Holy Roman Emperor in 1745. Otherwise she achieved nothing; but the struggle for her was not yet over.

Maria Theresa is sometimes regarded as a pathetic character, the helpless victim of predatory neighbours, but this is misleading. When she acceded to her inheritance at the age of 23 she may have been naive and unworldly, but she was soon to learn the ways of international statesmanship – how to dissemble and deceive and evade probing questions – and she was to develop into a ruler of intelligence and determination and to become a potent force in European politics not without aggressive tendencies of her own. During her reign of 40 years her country was at war for 15, during which time she was the main driving force.

She was also actively engaged in domestic matters. At heart she was conservative but she saw clearly that far-reaching reforms were needed if her widespread heterogeneous empire was to be preserved. For Austria was still basically feudal, with local magnates exercising despotic powers, laying down their own laws and administering them in their own courts of justice. Maria attempted to centralise these and set up one legal system for all her domains but, predictably, this met with strong local opposition. She also saw that great expansion was needed in education. At that time it was almost completely in the hands of the Jesuits and, devoted Catholic though she might be, she saw that this resulted in a restricted and narrow regime in which branches of learning likely to stimulate independent thought, notably philosophy and science, were excluded. She also saw that she had to take on the monasteries, whose wealth and privileges had grown out of all proportion; and here too there was vehement opposition.

A field in which she also strove to introduce reform was that of public health, where the record was deplorable. Hospitals were responsible for more deaths than they saved. The deadly disease at that time which killed and disfigured so many was smallpox, from which several members of Maria's family died, and in 1767 she herself was to suffer a severe attack. The Austrian medical profession was helpless in face of it, relying on ancient non-scientific cures and opposing inoculation which was then becoming prevalent in England; but Maria Theresa insisted on it being introduced.

In the arts Maria Theresa was not one of the great patronesses. Her reign saw no flourishing of painting, literature or architecture, but it has been described as 'a Golden Age of Music'. Some of the new-style operas of Christoph Gluck, son of a Bohemian forester, were performed in her court; and Joseph Haydn, son of a wagon builder, was taken under her wing and given encouragement. 'He has good ideas', she wrote at the time, 'and is just beginning to be known.'[3] She was particularly entranced by the infant Wolfgang Mozart who performed wonders on the piano and a tiny violin, and then uninhibitedly sprang into her lap, 'kissing her very heartily'.

Maria Theresa's reforms were for the most part benign but not always so. She was no believer in religious toleration and her treatment of Protestants and, more especially, Jews was remorseless, brutal and included torture. Her Catholicism was rigid, looking on all unorthodoxy as mortally sinful. She not only observed strictly the rites of the Church herself, but insisted on all around her doing the same; failure to hear Mass daily or attend the confessional regularly would be noticed and held against one.

She also took a strong line on sexual immorality. At that time this was rife in Vienna, which became known as 'the city of free adultery'. Lady Mary Wortley Montagu, that ubiquitous English traveller, noted: 'Everybody seems to have two husbands, one who bears the name, the other who performs the duties'. Infidelity was taken for granted so that a husband coming across his wife in flagrante delicto would be as likely to apologise to the lover for disturbing him as to challenge him to a duel. Religion was not allowed to interfere with pleasure. 'They sin, pray and confess', it was said at the time. This licentiousness Maria Theresa attempted to curb. She may have been tolerant of her own husband but she was zealously intolerant of others. For a time she even instituted a Chastity Commission to expunge immorality and vice. Secret police kept a watch on people's behaviour and there were severe punishments for overstepping the mark. Loose ladies were locked up in convents and men were arrested on suspicion of consorting with such improper characters as actresses, dancers or singers. But Maria soon had to realise the hopelessness of such action: instead of preventing illicit sex it merely drove it underground; the Chastity

---

[3] There is a story that her care for him included a sound beating when he was a choir boy and in disobedience of an order went clambering over some scaffolding.

Commission came in for a great deal of derision and had to be abandoned. But the Empress was not to be knocked off her high moral perch completely: she remained sententious, and particularly in the theatre and all forms of entertainment, insisted on a high moral tone.

Maria Theresa did not regard Aix-la-Chapelle as the final settlement between herself and Frederick of Prussia. She never lost the determination to regain Silesia. She was confident that at some time an opportunity for this would occur. The first sign of this came with the rise of an exceptionally able minister, Wenzel Kaunitz, who had the revolutionary idea that the way forward lay in an alliance between Austria and France, the country's traditional enemy. On the surface Kaunitz appeared to be an elegant fop,[4] but underneath had a hard calculating brain which Maria Theresa came to rely on completely.

At first she was sceptical of his ideas, but then came round to them, and in 1750 appointed him Ambassador at Versailles where with brilliant diplomatic skill he aroused wide interest and enthusiasm. He saw at once that the person to be convinced was Louis XV's voluptuous mistress, the Marquise de Pompadour, who had pervasive influence.[5] Once her backing had been obtained, support for his ideas became general and led to two treaties of Versailles which stipulated in effect for joint action against Prussia and the partition of that country including the return to Austria of Silesia. In return for this France would be compensated with concessions in the Netherlands. In 1753 Kaunitz was appointed Chancellor and from then until the death of the Empress he was in control of Austria's foreign policy.

Austria's alliance with France meant the end of her alliance with England, whose rivalry with France for colonial territory in America and India was intensifying and leading to war. Maria Theresa was not unduly worried about this as she had been strongly resentful of English pressure at Aix-la-Chapelle, and besides she had no interest in India or America. It did, however, mean that George II, ever fearful about the security of Hanover, came to an understanding

---

[4] He was said to take three hours to dress with the help of four mirrors, and his favourite occupation was collecting bric-a-brac (referred to scornfully by the English ambassador as 'unconsidered trifles').

[5] To the disapproval of Maria Theresa who did not like dealing with concubines.

with Frederick, and in the Seven Years War that followed England was to be Prussia's only ally.

It was unlikely that Frederick would sit idly by while Austria and France conspired against him, especially as they seemed to be having support from the Czarina of Russia. And so he struck first. 'The lady wants war. She shall have it', he declared before sending an army into Saxony, then into Bohemia to lay siege to Prague and then to threaten Vienna. For a time the danger was acute and Maria Theresa was urged to flee, but she stoutly refused. 'The court shall remain until the last extremity', she proclaimed. 'We will meet the Prussians as we can. And if we have no army here we will arm ourselves with axes and bows and arrows, all women, as well as men, to force them out.'

The outcome of the Seven Years War should never have been in doubt. Frederick, with only insubstantial support from England,[6] was assailed on every side by all the main powers of Europe – Austria, France, Russia, Saxony and Sweden – but somehow he managed to survive. After defeat in one battle in 1759 he was to write: 'My coat is riddled with bullets, two horses have been killed under me. It is my misfortune to be still alive.' But disaster saw him at his best. He always rallied his forces and fought again; and he was helped by disunity and ineptitude among his enemies. He would almost certainly have been defeated if Maria Theresa had not appointed as commander-in-chief her brother-in-law, Prince Charles of Lorraine, once described as 'the incarnation of indecision and undue caution'. Even so by the end of 1761 Frederick was again at his last gasp – his enemies were closing in and all seemed lost; but then he was saved not by a victory in battle but by the death of the Czarina Elizabeth and the accession of Peter III, who was an ardent admirer of his and immediately made peace.[7]

He was saved. But by 1763 everyone was ready for peace and the war in Europe came to an end with the Treaty of Hubertsburg in February of that year. The terms of the treaty were daunting: after a war of seven years in which 1 million lives had been lost, no territory had changed hands and the European situation was as it had been before. The war was, nevertheless, of historic importance.

---

[6] Not so insubstantial as long as William Pitt was in office, but this came to an end in 1761, and the new ministry was opposed to the war.

[7] He was only Czar for a few months, but his successor, Catherine ('The Great') maintained neutrality.

Prussia was to become the leading power in Germany, the Austrian Empire was beginning to disintegrate, and England, the country to gain most, was established as the leading European colonial power.

As with Aix-la-Chapelle, Hubertsburg was a bitter pill for Maria Theresa to swallow. She had to face it that she would never now recover Silesia and that her arch-enemy, Frederick the Great, was not to be brought down. Everything for which she had fought so bravely and so stubbornly in the last 23 years had come to nothing.

In the years that followed troubles were to crowd in on Maria Theresa. In 1765 her husband, Francis Stephen, died suddenly from an apoplectic fit. Foolish and faithless as he had been as a husband (at the time of his death he was in the throes of a serious love affair with a princess of Auersperg, some 30 years his junior), Maria Theresa was devastated by his death. Her mourning for him was unconstrained: not only did she deck herself in widow's garb for the rest of her life but she had her rooms draped in black crepe. On anniversaries she would shut herself up alone in a room hung with pictures of 'our beloved master' who was 'the thought and purpose of my deeds ... My heart is withered ... I feel old, weak and discouraged'. And she longed for her own death 'with more impatience than fear'. In the 15 years of widowhood that lay ahead of her Maria Theresa at times had ideas of abdicating and withdrawing into a convent away from worldly affairs, but this she was prevented from doing by what an ambassador at the time called 'her natural taste for domination'.

After the death of Francis she appointed her eldest son, Joseph, co-Regent with her. At the same time he became Holy Roman Emperor. But the partnership between mother and son was not to run smoothly: they were two strong and differing characters. Maria Theresa was warm-hearted, outgoing and essentially traditionalist. Joseph was cold, introverted and a free thinker. His upbringing had been unbalanced: indulged by a weak, amiable father; but disciplined by an exacting and at times severe mother (who did not always spare the rod). As a child he had shown signs of obstinacy and had grown into a graceless, morose youth with despotic tendencies and a mind of his own, and to the dismay of his mother seemed to care little for the formalities of court life; his installation as King of the Romans he described as 'an unpleasant and needless function', and he wrote despairingly afterwards: 'My life is one long, violent effort. I have to appear delighted with a position of which I feel all the responsibility and none of the pleasure.'

Solitary and nonconformist, he looked on marriage with revulsion – 'far more frightening than going into battle'. Only a compelling sense of duty led him into it. His first wife, Isabella of Parma, a granddaughter of Louis XV of France, was a beautiful and intelligent lady but unconventional and unbalanced. Unloved by Joseph at first, she became enamoured of his sister, the Archduchess Maria Christine with whom she entered into an emotional correspondence. She also became obsessed with death: 'Death is beneficent', she wrote: 'Everything arouses in me the desire to die soon.' Her wish was to be granted after only three years of marriage. Strangely, Joseph was deeply upset by this, writing to his father-in-law: 'I have lost everything. My adored wife, my love, my only friend is gone … I hardly know if I am still alive. Shall I survive this terrible separation?' In spite of her eccentricities Isabella was also loved by Maria Theresa who wrote of her 'charming and unparalleled daughter'.

A prince of royal blood and heir to the throne, Joseph at once came under pressure from Maria Theresa and others to marry again. As before, this dismayed him, but as before, he deemed it his duty and, feeling that a love match was out of the question, was ready to marry whomsoever was wished on him by his mother. He was presented with an awesome choice: the singularly unattractive Princess Cunigunda of Saxony and the hardly less repulsive Josepha of Bavaria. 'I prefer not marry either,' he told his mother, 'but since you are holding a knife to my throat I will take Josepha because from what I hear she at least has a fine bosom.' But the marriage was to prove a torment. To Isabella's father he wrote piteously: 'Her figure is short, thick-set and without a vestige of youthful charm. Her face is covered with spots and pimples and her teeth are horrible.' Nevertheless, he was not to be put off and did what was expected of him, although any kind of contact with her was repugnant. After two years, however, he was redeemed when the unfortunate Josepha died from smallpox.

On no subject did Maria and Joseph differ more strongly than on the partition of Poland. It was to cause her deep shame and sorrow to blight her old age. The Seven Years War was not long over before Frederick scented an opportunity for the further aggrandisement of Prussia. In 1763 there occurred the death of the

119

Elector of Saxony who was also King Augustus III of Poland. The Polish constitution required that the new King be elected, and it was expected that this would be his son, but Catherine the Great of Russia had other ideas. She had a special interest in Poland and contrived that the next King should be Stanislaus Poniatowski: of noble Polish birth and an ex-lover of hers, but weak and irresolute. The result of this was that Poland lapsed into anarchy and Catherine sent in an army to restore order.

Frederick the Great too saw an opportunity for fishing in troubled waters and became set on annexing part of western Poland on the border of Silesia. For this partition much would depend on the attitude of Austria. Catherine and Frederick hoped that Maria Theresa would join in and help herself to bordering Polish territory; but at first she held aloof. She did not like the idea of such unprovoked aggression and had a strong objection to any dealings with either Frederick or Catherine: the former she still regarded as her arch-enemy and the latter as an unscrupulous and untrustworthy woman of loose morals. Joseph, however, thought differently. He saw it as a golden opportunity for territorial gains and had no reluctance in cooperating with Frederick for whom he had always had an admiration, and so in 1769 Joseph entered into negotiations with him about the division of Polish lands.

Maria was thus drawn in, but with an uneasy conscience, knowing she was doing wrong but unable to withstand the pressure put on her by Joseph and Kaunitz, it being impressed on her that Austria could not be left out in the cold while Prussia and Russia expanded. To survive she had to stake Austria's claims, but it caused her agonies. 'With what right', she exclaimed, 'can we rob an innocent nation that it has hitherto been our boast to support and protect?' Most bitter of all were the taunts of her collaborators. 'As far as dear worthy Lady Prayerful is concerned', wrote Catherine the Great, 'I can say nothing more than that she suffers from severe attacks of covetousness and imperiousness.' And from Frederick: 'She is always in tears, yet she is always ready to take her share.' And it is true that she did, indeed, join in the partition, but she was always to be unhappy about it. 'It weighs on my heart', she wrote, 'and tortures my brain and embitters my days.' Nothing was more humiliating than the thought that she had been brought down to the level of 'the monster' Frederick of Prussia and the depraved Catherine.

Cleopatra

By Michelangelo Buonarroti. Photograph: Bridgeman Art Library.

Queen Victoria of England
By Alexander Bassano.
© National Portrait Gallery, London.

Queen Victoria and Prince Albert
with their five eldest children
By Franz Xavier Winterhalter. Victoria and Albert
Museum, London/The Stapleton Collection.
Photograph: Bridgeman Art Library.

And further humiliation was in store for her when in 1777 Joseph involved her in another discreditable affair. In that year Maximilian Elector of Bavaria died without issue, upon which Joseph dug up some claims to the Electorate from the past and sent an army into the country. The legal heir by birth, the Elector Palatine, acquiesced in this and came to an agreement with Joseph, but other countries had serious objections to such a move. Frederick the Great in particular could not sit by and see such aggrandisement of Austria. Loudly he inveighed against Joseph's 'fraudulent policies' and likened them to 'highway robbery' – words which could have exactly described his invasion of Silesia 37 years before. He then prepared to give battle and for this had some support from Catherine of Russia.

It seemed that another European war was imminent, but then Maria Theresa intervened. She had always disapproved of what Joseph had done. 'In God's name', she pleaded, 'take only what we have a right to demand ... My wish is to end my days in peace.' And so without reference to Joseph she sent an envoy to Frederick asking for a peace conference to which he agreed, but insisted that the Czarina should act as moderator. Nothing could be more disagreeable to Maria Theresa than this, but for the sake of the peace of Europe she felt bound to agree. At the peace conference Bavaria was awarded to the Elector Palatine and only a small strip of territory to Austria. Joseph, who had been made to look weak and foolish, said of the settlement that 'nothing more dishonourable, more injurious, more destructive could have happened'.

Certainly it was a fatal blow to Austria, marking as it did the further rise of Prussia as the leading state of Germany, and as well the further encroachment of Russia into Western Europe. But Maria Theresa had no regrets. 'For me', she later wrote, 'it is an inexpressible happiness to have prevented a great effusion of blood.'

Maria Theresa was to have a harrowing old age. After a severe bout of smallpox at the age of 50 she lost her looks, and her health deteriorated seriously. Because of a form of dropsy she became obese even though eating comparatively little. Her eyesight also began to fade and she had difficulty in breathing so that she was always opening windows, and the rooms she used were bitterly cold to the great discomfort of her family and friends. Sadly she remarked, when still in her fifties, that she was 'getting old at a furious rate'. She remained in deepest mourning for her husband, regularly visiting the vault where his coffin was lodged with a sarcophagus next to it in readiness for her. Increasingly she brooded on death; and her religious practices became more intensive, hearing Mass twice daily and spending four hours in prayer.

She was still to have comfort from her family: from Joseph in spite of their differences and from her two eldest daughters who had been found places in convents. Her three youngest daughters were a source of anxiety. Heartlessly, it seemed, they had been married off regardless of their wishes when hardly more than children to foreign princes with unhappy results. Her sixth daughter Caroline was wedded to the King of the Two Sicilies and Naples where she described her life at first as 'hell on earth'; and her fourth daughter Amalia found herself married tumultuously to a near imbecile, Prince Ferdinand of Parma. Most tragic of all was the marriage of her youngest daughter Marie Antoinette to the Dauphin, the future Louis XVI of France; when she was barely 14 she was launched into the sophisticated, glittering court of Versailles, rapidly becoming doomed, and which was to lead in time to screaming revolutionary mobs and the guillotine. Maria Theresa kept in touch with them all, writing them long letters full of advice, warnings and reproach.[8] She never lost her love for them, but was never to see them again and must have wondered if she had been justified in making 'political sacrifices' of them.

Maria Theresa's long-drawn-out death came to an end in November 1780. She was widely mourned. In spite of costly and unsuccessful wars and severe impositions inflicted on her subjects she was greatly loved, more so than the reformist, liberal Joseph, or than the brutally victorious Frederick the Great by his subjects. When she died the empire she had inherited 40 years before was more stable and less reactionary, but it was in decline. The graceful, honourable court over which she had presided was giving way to a new power in Germany, one based on discipline and the unscrupulous use of power. She detested it bitterly and lived long enough to see that it was not to be resisted.

---

[8] In this she resembled Queen Victoria as in other ways. Both gave way to prolific mourning for their husbands and both could be described as 'the grandmother of Europe' with descendants in many royal courts. The similarity was not, however, exact. Queen Victoria would never have attended Mass twice daily and she delegated no powers to her eldest son.

8

MARIE ANTOINETTE, QUEEN OF FRANCE
(1755–1793)

Few figures in history have aroused such controversy as Marie Antoinette, Queen of France from 1774 to 1793. To some, then as now, she was 'an unparalleled princess, beautiful, warm hearted, cruelly maligned and woefully misunderstood'. To others she was, and remains, 'an extravagant foolish woman without a thought in her head except for lust'.

Certainly she was dealt a rough hand: married at the age of 14 to an eccentric and (almost) impotent husband, plunged into a degenerate court heading for disaster, and confronted always by spiteful hostility. It was no wonder that her life ended in catastrophe. It could hardly have been avoided.

Maria Antonia Josephina Johanna (Marie Antoinette) was born on 2 November 1755, an inauspicious day, the Feast of All Saints, also known as the Day of the Dead; it also coincided with a catastrophic earthquake in Lisbon which killed some 30,000 people. She was the daughter of Maria Theresa, Empress of Austria, and Francis Stephen, Duke of Lorraine, so she was half German and half French. Her mother, then aged 38, had already given birth to four sons and ten daughters; as she once said of herself: 'insatiable on the subject of children'. She was too an exceptionally conscientious and hard-working monarch to whom time was sacred, and as soon as Madam Antoine (as Marie Antoinette was first known) was born she was handed over to a wet nurse and from then on saw her mother only at intervals, often long ones. She was a caring but strict mother who saw to it that Antoine was not mollycoddled or given special privileges, but did not see to it that she had an adequate education, and it soon transpired that she had little aptitude for book learning.

In her childhood she saw more of her father, Duke Francis, a weak, ineffective character but kindly and sympathetic, whom his children regarded more as a friend than a father. He died when Antoine was ten, leaving behind for her a long treatise on how she should properly conduct her life (little of which advice he himself had practised), but Antoine treasured it and kept it by her.

Loving and caring though Maria Theresa might be as a mother, she was nevertheless clear that the prime purpose of her children was as pawns in the European marriage market. Of the betrothals she arranged the most momentous – and the most tragic – was that of Antoine to the Dauphin. Prince Louis Auguste was one year older than Antoine and had been heir to the French throne since the age of eleven. It was a union of great significance as it sealed the new-found alliance between France and Austria, for long rival hostile powers. While they were still children, statesmen of both countries had been working for it, and in 1769 after much disputation as to detail, an agreement was reached, and in the following year Louis and Antoine were married by proxy. He was 16 and she was 15.

The prospect before Marie Antoinette, as she then became known, was indeed dazzling – Queen of France and mistress of Versailles, the most glittering court in Europe. But preparatory work was necessary first. She was charming and pretty, although not a classic beauty, and her appearance had to be improved. So a *friseur* from Paris was summoned to attend to her hairline, as was a dentist to adjust her teeth. She also had coaching in poise and dancing and, most important of all, something was done to fill the extensive gaps in her education. Her teachers so far had failed to arouse much interest in any subject except music – she played attractively on the harp – but otherwise she was illiterate: she read little and could hardly write. A specially recommended French tutor, the Abbé Vermond, was appointed to widen her horizons, but he soon became aware of the magnitude of his task. He was, however, astute enough to see that something might be achieved if he could win her confidence and affection; and in this he was to have some success: her mind began to expand. She became devoted to him and he was to serve her in various capacities for many years.

Marie Antoinette and Louis Auguste were married by proxy in Vienna on 19 April 1770, she thus becoming the Dauphine. Two days later she set out on the journey across Europe to Versailles, accompanied by a cortège of 370 carriages and some 5,000 people. She had many misgivings: she hated leaving her family and their country home of Schönbrun of which she had many happy memories. She also had a dread of marriage. Her sister, Caroline, had recently wedded the violent and uncouth King Ferdinand of Naples, and it had been a horrific experience; her first week she described as 'hell on earth', and Marie Antoinette could not but wonder if the same fate was not in store for her.[1]

It took two and a half weeks to reach the Austro-French border where an official ceremony was to be held in which she renounced her Austrian nationality and adopted that of France. It had to be that in a union between an Austrian archduchess and the Dauphin there should be arguments about pernickety matters of protocol. Great importance was attached to who should sign the marriage contract first, to be settled eventually by having two contracts, one signed first by Austria and the other signed first by France. The same was to happen with the document of renunciation, with the same solution. Before that it had to be settled in which country the ceremony should take place – in France or in Austria – it being agreed finally that it should be on an island in the Rhine which was neutral territory.

A week later on 14 May Antoinette met the Dauphin for the first time. He was hardly a romantic figure: shy, graceless, overweight and clearly not interested in women and dreading marriage. Yet she was not repelled by him – she pitied him and wanted to help him – but their relationship was to be complicated. Also present at the meeting was the Dauphin's grandfather, King Louis XV, gross and debauched, but still having about him 'the remains of manly beautifulness', at times amiable and kindly, especially towards pretty young women, and he was well pleased with Marie Antoinette.

Two days later she faced the ordeal of the wedding service in the chapel at Versailles. Some 5,000 guests had been invited and many more tried to force their way in so that the police had difficulty in containing them. All eyes were on Marie Antoinette, in a not too well-fitting wedding gown weighed down with diamonds, shy and nervous but with a freshness and warmth that won all hearts. Less beguiling was the Dauphin, a shambling timorous figure looking painfully self-conscious in an uncharacteristic suit of cloth of gold.

---

[1] Caroline received little sympathy from her mother who wrote: 'Although an ugly prince, he is not absolutely repulsive … at least he does not stink'.

That evening came the stressful ceremony of the ritual bedding of bride and bridegroom: first the nuptial bed was blessed by an archbishop, then the King in ribald mood handed his grandson his nightshirt, while a royal duchess prepared Marie Antoinette. At last the onlookers withdrew and the royal couple were left to it; but nothing happened. The marriage was unconsummated, and was to remain so for several years.

Next day Marie Antoinette, still not 15, was introduced into the tumult of life at Versailles. And tumultuous indeed it was. It was described by Count Mercy, the Austrian Ambassador, as a 'horrible confusion, the abode of treachery, hatred and revenge. Everything is worked by intrigues and inspired by personal ambition, and it seems as if the world had renounced even the semblance of uprightness.'

The tone was set by Louis XV, who made little pretence of a virtuous life. He had been on the throne for the last 50 years since the age of five, and at first had been a popular king and a reasonably faithful husband to his wife, Marie Leczynska, daughter of the deposed king of Poland, who had borne him seven children. Later, however, he had let himself go and taken up with a string of mistresses of whom Madame de Pompadour was the most famous and the most powerful. She had died in 1764 and since then he had been in thrall to Jeanne du Barry, one-time shop assistant and daughter of a prostitute, whose charms he was quite unable to resist and whose influence was all-pervasive. In theory Marie Antoinette as Dauphine and future Queen should have been the leading lady of the court, but the du Barry with the King behind her brooked no rivals and she and Antoinette were to clash acrimoniously. She said of Antoinette: 'I see nothing attractive in red hair, thick lips, sandy complexion and eyes without eyelashes.' And Antoinette said of her: 'She is the most stupid and impertinent creature imaginable.' The du Barry had many enemies at court, but the King was not to be moved: 'She has given me delights', he said, 'I did not know existed.'

It did not take Antoinette long to become aware of the various vendettas and discords at Versailles. Among the many factions one of the most animated was that of Louis XV's three middle-aged unmarried daughters – Adelaide, Victoire and Sophie, 'Mesdames Tantes', as they were known. They were not greatly loved and were constantly mocked, not least by their father who gave them the uncomplimentary nicknames of 'Rag', 'Piggy' and 'Snip'. The waspish Horace Walpole on a visit to Versailles wrote of them: 'Clumsy, plump old wenches with a bad likeness to their father, stand in a row with black cloaks and knitting bags, looking good-humoured, not knowing what to say and wriggling as if they wanted to make water.' They were, nevertheless, a power in the land. The Dauphin was devoted to them and Marie Antoinette was to spend much time in their company when she was lonely; and they shared a common hatred of the du Barry.

Other frequent troublemakers at Versailles were the Dauphin's two younger brothers, Louis Xavier Comte de Provence (future Louis XVIII) and Charles Comte d'Artois (future Charles X). Like their elder brother they were overweight but they had sharper minds and more self-confidence. In childhood they had been accustomed to make fun of him and bully him and this continued into adulthood so that on occasions they came to blows, although in this the Dauphin, no physical weakling, was able to look after himself.

There can have been little joy for Antoinette in the first years of her marriage. She must have known of the hostility towards her in certain quarters, some of it personal, some of it as a daughter of the house of Austria, France's traditional enemy. She was to become known as 'L'Autrichienne' which means 'the Austrian woman', but the last syllable (*chienne*) means 'bitch', and there were those who emphasised it. Inevitably her marital problems became a matter of gossip, and she was surrounded by whispering and prying eyes. Her periods were noted and her bedclothes examined for signs of conjugal activity. Jokers and ill-wishers left aphrodisiacs for her and forced on her attention scurrilous lampoons which she tried to treat as a joke.

Each day her life was bound by rigid protocol and the mistress of her household, the Comtesse Noailles, a starchy humourless woman, was there to see that she did not deviate from it. It was laid down who should attend her dressing and undressing, her toilette and the serving of her meals, and the parts they had to play. She was attended by a staff of nearly 500, ranging from aristocratic ladies-in-waiting, chaplains and equerries to grooms, scullions and bath attendants. Each had prescribed tasks and would have been in trouble if they did not perform them, but they would have been in as much trouble if they strayed into the domains of others, who guarded their jobs jealously and liked to think themselves indispensable. In consequence, there was much overstaffing and inefficiency. Versailles, usually regarded as the epitome of grandeur and eloquence, was not all it was reputed to be. Foreign visitors were surprised by the dirt and disorder in some rooms and the neglect of fine furniture and works of art. They were also aware of a pervasive stench due to the absence of basic sanitary facilities. People relieved themselves indiscriminately and un-house-trained dogs and cats wandered about at random.

The impotence of the Dauphin and the apparent failure of his marriage were of concern to others besides Antoinette; her mother, Maria Theresa, was acutely anxious. Count Mercy, her Ambassador in Versailles, had an efficient intelligence service and sent her detailed reports of the state of play. These prompted a stream of letters from the Empress to her daughter giving advice and exhortation on a wide range of subjects from her religious practices to the necessity of wearing corsets. She was determined that the marriage should prevail and did not pull her punches. She could be brutally frank. In one letter she wrote: 'You owe your popularity to neither your beauty (which in fact is not so great), nor to your talents or culture (you know very well you have neither); it is to your kind heart, your frankness, your amiability, all exerted with your good judgement.' Other daughters of Maria Theresa felt oppressed by this flow of admonition, but not Antoinette. She delighted in it. She was desperately homesick and the letters reminded her of the family life she had once loved so dearly. 'I swear to you', she wrote, 'that I have not received one of your dear letters without having tears coming to my eyes.'

In his first report to Maria Theresa, Count Mercy wrote darkly: 'Since their first interview he [the Dauphin] has not shown the slightest sign of predilection for the Dauphine or anxiety to please her in public or private.' In time the situation was to improve, but at first they had no interests in common: the Dauphin's tastes were simple and rustic – hunting, carpentry and metal work, particularly the making of locks; and these were not shared by Antoinette whose main delights were music and theatricals. The Dauphin did have some academic leanings, notably in history and geography, and Antoinette was beginning to read more, although her tastes were mainly for light literature (*livres de boudoir* as they were known). Nevertheless, they grew to be fond of each other, even a little in love. Louis was touched by Antoinette's gentleness and forbearance in face of his inadequacy, and she responded and continued to hope that all would come right in the end. It was always evident, however, that she was not the right wife for him: a weak and indeterminate character, his need was for a strong and sophisticated partner who would guide him and buttress him, something beyond the capacity of a naive 14-year-old.

Amid her life of tedium and routine at Versailles, Antoinette did have one happy break. In 1773, after three years, she and her husband made a state visit to Paris where they had a rapturous reception which came to be known as The Joyous Entry. Crowds poured into the city, making the streets even more filthy and adding to the already powerful stench. But no matter. People were delighted with the Dauphine and she with them. 'How fortunate we are,' she wrote to her mother, 'given our rank, to have gained the love of a whole people with such ease.' She was soon to learn how ephemeral is the love of the people.

It was to be expected that King Louis XV would be anxious about the non-appearance of an heir to the throne. Impotence was not something he had experienced. After three years he ordered that his grandson be examined by a doctor, who reported that the Dauphin was 'well made and his failure was due to clumsiness and ignorance, and what was needed was patience'. But this was doubtfully a correct diagnosis, it never being clear whether Louis Auguste's disability was of a physical or psychological nature. He was aware of what was expected of him in marriage, and told his grandfather that he needed to overcome his timidity, but he did not seem to treat the matter as one of immediacy, and this might have resulted in the marriage breaking down, or even divorce (non-consummation being one of the few grounds allowed by the Church). But this did not happen and eventually (after seven years) the matter did come right in a fashion.

The great dread of Louis Auguste was the early death of his grandfather. He had no wish to become king ever, but certainly not when he was young and unsure of himself and unready for heavy responsibilities. But Louis XV's days were numbered: his dissolute life was catching up on him. In April 1774 he went into a torpor and soon afterwards red spots appeared, betokening smallpox; the end could not then be far off. Aware of this, he called for the last sacrament and a priest to whom he could confess his sins; something he had not done for 38 years, so the catalogue was a long one. But before it could happen it was felt necessary to send away the du Barry, as no confession could be considered genuine with her still in the offing. His last days were agonising: he was in great pain and his decaying body gave off a fearful odour. Few dared to go near him because of the danger of infection, but his daughters, the Mesdames Tantes, showed great devotion and courage in insisting on nursing him to the end.

When he died there was little lamentation. His unsavoury lifestyle and apparent indifference to the sufferings of the poor had made him unloved. When his corpse, tightly sealed in a coffin, was driven through the streets of Paris at full speed because of its noxious properties, people lining the streets were not silent and respectful but boisterous and jocular with cheers and cries of 'Tally Ho!' as if at a race meeting or on the hunting field.

It was with a heavy heart that Louis Auguste became King Louis XVI. His inheritance was frightening. The country had been tottering towards bankruptcy for some time and was now on the brink. There was an urgent need for drastic economies, but these could not easily be achieved. Louis XVI was not strong enough to enforce them; the funeral of his grandfather was extravagant, as also was his coronation; and when he proposed to cut the enormous expenses of the court at Versailles he incurred strong opposition from those noblemen who would be displaced. It was unfortunate that at the time of the old King's death there should have been an acute shortage of grain due to a bad harvest, and this gave rise to riots in Paris known as the 'Flour War' which boosted revolutionary ideas then circulating about liberty, equality and the rights of man.

For Marie Antoinette the transformation from Dauphine to Queen brought changes to her way of life: she became more enmeshed in protocol and ceremony, and the numerous sycophants seeking favours intruded more and more. But there were some benefits: she had greater freedom, which allowed her more opportunities to enjoy herself. Her extravagances on clothes, jewellery and interior decoration knew no bounds, and her husband did not attempt to restrict them. She also became addicted to reckless gambling in which she lost a lot of money. Her main extravagance, though, was Le Petit Trianon, a small estate 1 mile from Versailles where she tried to create a rural paradise. This included a picturesque hamlet complete with thatched-roof cottages, exotic gardens, aviaries, dovecots and windmills. There was too a model farm with rare breeds of sheep and goats, and cows more renowned for their good looks than their milk yields.[2] It was all an attempt to recapture the simple rusticity of her childhood and at the same time to create a refuge from the formal, benumbing life at court. But it was an expensive hobby, and vastly inflated estimates were to be spread abroad, doing further damage to her reputation.

Even more dangerous were her escapades to masked balls in Paris and her flirtations in the Trianon. Contrary to what came to be believed she was not sexually promiscuous – compared to some Queens she was abstemious – and she shared her mother's distaste for illicit liaisons. As will be seen, she did almost certainly have one serious extramarital affair, and had a liking for occasional coquetry, particularly with older men. It is likely that these were harmless and evanescent but, inevitably, they gave rise to gossip and exaggeration. She also invited scandal by the intimate relationships she had with other women, notably with Yolande Comtesse de Polignac, a lady of great beauty and charm and blessed with a sublime calmness. Certainly Antoinette was deeply devoted to her and lavished on her and her relations honours and riches; but the charge of a lesbian relationship is unsubstantiated.

It was always likely that Antoinette's position as both a daughter of the house of Austria and Queen of France would come into conflict. There were times when the alliance of the two countries came under strain, and both would expect Antoinette to act on their behalf. Maria Theresa in all her letters made it clear that she expected her daughter's first loyalties to be to the land of her birth; and her brother, Joseph, pressed the point just as strongly when he was granted equal imperial rights with his mother.[3] For much of the time relations between the two countries were on an even keel, but when Joseph embarked on expansionist policies (in Poland, Bavaria and Holland) critical situations arose as these were contrary to French interests.

In 1777 (three years after Antoinette became Queen) Joseph decided that he should visit Versailles in order to strengthen his sister's resolve and to save her precarious marriage. He was not altogether an attractive character – he was hard-headed, bluff and

---

[2] Contrary to legend Antoinette did not milk these in milkmaid's attire. She did adopt this but only for the purposes of theatricals.

[3] See the chapter on Maria Theresa.

aggressive, but also conscientious and ascetic. Antoinette had mixed feelings about his visit: she was delighted to see a member of her family, but apprehensive that he might be severe and scolding. Typically, Joseph insisted on coming incognito, as Count Frankenstein. Wishing to avoid all the palaver of life at court, he spurned the offer of accommodation there and took up residence in a modest hotel where he slept on a camp bed and a wolf skin, attended by only one servant.

Then he got to work. He lost no time in making a mockery of Antoinette's way of life – the amount of rouge on her face, her towering head dresses surmounted with multicoloured feathers and her constant seeking after pleasure, devoting herself to frivolous pursuits when she should be coming to grips with affairs of state. She had, he told her 'the opportunity of the finest and greatest role that any woman ever played'. But Antoinette was incapable of fulfilling it. At that time she had little interest in politics and found that when she attempted to influence her husband on foreign affairs she met with rebuttal. Louis was normally only too ready to give way to her, but on matters concerning Austria he was unusually firm; he seemed to have an innate distrust of the country. And here Joseph had to admit failure, lamenting that his sister 'thought only of enjoying herself and not doing her job as queen or woman'.

He was to have more success, however, in vitalising her marriage. Always in favour of the direct approach, he confronted both parties head on and questioned them closely about their sexual habits, coming to the conclusion that they were 'two complete blunderers, ignorant of the facts of life'. On these he proceeded to enlighten them, and this seemed to have an effect: Antoinette was made to realise that she needed to be more alluring, and Louis, mild and sheepish as always, while still regarding intercourse as a duty rather than a pleasure, determined to try harder. And in the following year Antoinette, after seven and a half years of marriage, became pregnant.

In the same year (1788) there occurred the severest test of Antoinette's loyalty to the land of her birth. Following the death of the Elector of Bavaria without a direct heir, Joseph put forward a claim to succeed him and sent an army to occupy the country. Predictably this upset King Frederick II of Prussia who threatened war, whereupon Joseph appealed to the French government to

132

honour its obligation under its treaty of alliance with Austria to come to his support. But there was strong opposition in France to Joseph's move, and although Antoinette made efforts on his behalf, they were unavailing. The threat of a European war was avoided in the end mainly by the intervention of the elderly Empress Maria Theresa; but Antoinette was made to feel that she had let Austria down, while at the same time her pro-Austrian stance added to her growing unpopularity in France.

This should have abated somewhat with the birth of her first child at the end of 1778; it was a disappointment that this was a daughter rather than a son but there was still great rejoicing. Not in all quarters, however, as there were some who had mocked at the sterility of the King for so long that they could not bring themselves to acknowledge him as the father, and there was malicious speculation as to who this might be.[4] But the legitimacy of Princess Marie Thérèse (Madame Royale as she came to be known) was not generally doubted.

The year 1778 was a critical one in French history: partly because of the Bavarian crisis, partly because of the birth of Madame Royale, but principally because it saw what many regard as the most fatal mistake of Louis XVI's reign – the decision to declare war on England in the American War of Independence. Although successful, not only did this add parlously to France's mountainous debt but it also spread enthusiasm for revolutionary ideas. When people saw that the American colonists, with French help, had rid themselves of what they regarded as a despotic power and put in its place a new enlightened form of government, they wondered whether the same should not happen in France. For this Antoinette cannot be blamed: she had always been opposed to intervention, but had been unable to prevent it.

The birth of Madame Royale came as a relief to the Empress Maria Theresa who was beginning to fear that her daughter's marriage would be childless. Her anxiety was not at an end, as there was still a great need for a son, but she was optimistic that the marital problems had now been resolved, and one was likely

---

[4] Everyone whispers

Can the King or can't he?
The sad queen is in despair.
(popular doggerel)

to follow. As indeed one, Louis Joseph, did three years later in 1781; but she was not to live to know of him. She had been in dreadful health for some years and in 1780 she died, greatly mourned and respected, especially by Marie Antoinette. She had not seen her mother for ten years but she felt her loss deeply; her life seemed incomplete without the steady stream of her trenchant, imperious letters.

The birth of the long-awaited Dauphin caused great excitement, but it was noticeable that when Antoinette went on a thanksgiving visit to Paris her reception by the crowds was cool. The times were bad, with the price of bread high and the national debt for ever increasing, and it was believed by many that Antoinette was mainly responsible for this. Hence the sour pseudonym of 'Madame Deficit'. But this was palpably unjust: certainly she had her extravagances, but these were not the main cause of the country's near bankruptcy, and they were as nothing compared with the cost of the war in America; but wild stories were spread abroad of Le Petit Trianon being studded with diamonds and huge sums being lavished on worthless favourites, even of enormous amounts being sent out of the country to her brother in Austria.

It is surprising that in spite of her undoubted charm and warmth Antoinette should have attracted so much ill will; she seems to have had a streak of insensitivity which blinded her to the offence she was giving, and there were many, including Mesdames Tantes, her brother-in-law the Comte de Provence, and especially the King's ambitious and treacherous cousin, Philippe Duc d'Orleans, who gave a ready ear to any breath of scandal and were all too prone to pass it on. There was, too, another streak in her, noticeable at times, of unforgiving obstinacy, a refusal to reconcile and make amends.

It was the case that her private life was not irreproachable, but it was not the wanton licentiousness sometimes portrayed. Her only serious extramarital love affair was with Axel Fersen, a roaming Swedish count – charming, good-looking and ambitious. He first met Antoinette at a masked ball when she was Dauphine and they made an impression on each other but no more. At the time Axel had two main objectives: a rich wife and military glory. In search of the latter he obtained a military appointment in the French army in America, and on his way there had a romantic interlude with Antoinette, ending, so it was said, in a tearful farewell on her part. But it was not until his return three years later in 1783 that they fell seriously in love. That it was a physical relationships seems certain. The Swedish Ambassador wrote to the Swedish King, Gustave II: 'I have seen signs too unmistakeable to doubt it'. And in a letter to his father Axel wrote that since he could not belong to the only person he would wish for, he did not wish to belong to anyone else: a clear reference to Antoinette. In the following years he spent much time in France, where Antoinette provided him with accommodation in Versailles. He became commander of the Royal Swedish Regiment in the French army and acted as liaison between the Swedish King and Louis XVI, who must have known of his love affair with Antoinette and had no objection to it. In the troubled times that lay ahead he was to serve the King and Queen devotedly.

In 1783 Antoinette was 27 (as was Axel), past her first bloom and inclining to stoutness, but she still had unique grace and charm, and she was in dire need of a deep emotional relationship. She and Louis had become fond of each other, but there was no close union, no meeting of minds, and their sex life was still minimal. He had never been sparkling company and with increasing obesity he was slowing down, 'shambling along', so it was said at the time, 'like some peasant behind his plough', seemingly apathetic and unaware of the disasters closing in on him.

How unpopular the Queen had become became especially marked in 1785 when, in all innocence, she was caught up in a scandalous con trick known as the Diamond Necklace Affair. But for its tragic consequences this fantastic episode could be treated lightheartedly, for it had all the ingredients of Opera Bouffe: a loose-living libidinous nobleman (also a cardinal), a scheming duplicitous seductress, a patently fraudulent necromancer and a prostitute masquerading as the Queen. The plot was exceedingly complex but it centred on an attempt to make the Queen buy a magnificent diamond necklace which she was resisting as an undue extravagance. It ended in fiasco with the necklace falling into the wrong hands, the nobleman being put on trial for fraud before a court of 64 judges, and the Queen's enemies putting it about without a shred of evidence that she was really to blame. When the nobleman was acquitted (by a narrow majority) the Queen was outraged and called it 'an atrocious insult to her reputation'. She had suffered many insults lately but such a public one as this was more than she could bear. So embittered was she that she withdrew from the public eye and became moody and depressive. It was a turning point in her life.

In the years after the Diamond Necklace Affair Antoinette's life persisted on a downward slope. She was still a hate figure, 'L'Autrichienne' (the Austrian bitch) despite her declaration that she was the wife of the French King and mother of the Dauphin and 'French to her fingertips' (she might have added she herself was half French by birth). Of this hatred she could not but be aware. Whenever she appeared in public it was either to a deafening silence or to coarse jeers. 'What have I done to them? What have I done to them?' she once cried out despairingly. Her relations with Louis remained warm but formal, and her only joy was in her children. A second son, Louis Charles, was born in 1785, healthy and strong; but a daughter, Sophia, born in 1786 was frail and died a year later; and the health of her eldest son, Louis Joseph, was causing increasing anxiety.

In these years too France continued to slide remorselessly towards the Deluge. The national debt mounted inexorably, conditions of life for the poor were grim, while at Versailles courtiers, 'buried in pleasure and dissipation', led idle useless lives, only becoming active when their privileges were threatened. The King and Queen were aware of the country's chaotic finances and attempted to economise – dismissing staff, laying off extravagant occasions and giving up serious gambling – but these made little impression. What was needed was a strong, determined ruler who would bring in a new system of government, but this Louis, timid and irresolute, was incapable of doing. Something desperate, however, had to be done and in 1788 the King gave way to persistent calls for a meeting of the States General (national parliament), and summoned one for the following year. This body had not been convened for 175 years; its composition and procedures were outdated and it would be a formidable task to establish its rights and gear it into action. But in May 1789, 1200 delegates arrived in Versailles and set about instituting a new constitution.

Predictably there was much disagreement. During the first meetings it was desirable that Louis and Antoinette should take a leading part in the deliberations, but they were unable to do so; their eldest son, Louis Joseph, had always been a delicate malformed child and was dying, and naturally most of their attention was focused on him. When he died in June, leaders of the Third Estate were insensitive in pressing business matters on the King. 'Are there no fathers among you?' he asked piteously.

While the King and the States General were arguing at Versailles, the situation in Paris was coming to the boil. People were in an angry mood and revolutionary fervour was spreading, stirred up by street orators who contrasted their wretched existence with the luxury at Versailles, as typified by Marie Antoinette who, as always, was the main target. On 14 July there was a sudden upsurge of fury and a demented mob descended on the Bastille, a gruesome semi-derelict fortress believed to contain arms and to be full of political prisoners. It was weakly defended and was overrun and the guards were slaughtered. It was found to contain few arms and no more than seven prisoners. But the storming of the Bastille rang round Europe. It marked the outbreak of revolution on an unprecedented scale.

At Versailles news of the Bastille was heard with shock and terror and many made plans for an immediate exodus abroad. The crucial question was whether the King and Queen would also leave, if not for abroad then at least to somewhere at a safe distance from Paris near the frontier. The Queen was in favour of this, but the King was persuaded that to run away would be cowardly and would make matters worse so he would stay – but it was open to Marie Antoinette to go with the children if she wished. She affirmed bravely: 'My duty is to be with the King and to die at his feet in the arms of my children.'

With many of her close friends having fled abroad, the Queen's life became ever more bereft. Her husband was of little comfort and she was still beset by a barrage of popular insults. Wild stories continued to be spread about her: that she had contrived the shortage of bread in Paris in revenge on the people she detested, and she had tried to persuade the King to bombard the city into submission, as well as the infamous *canard* that when told of the people's shortage of bread she had retorted: 'Then let them eat cake'; words which over the years have been attributed to several different people.

Meanwhile the Revolution advanced on its way. The Third Estate turned itself into the National Assembly and became the chief executive power in the country, passing some revolutionary measures to which the King tamely agreed, hoping that with compliance the present madness would die down and normal times would return. However there were few signs of this happening in Paris, which was becoming ungovernable. At the beginning of October 1789 the cry went up that the King and Queen should be brought to Paris where they could be kept under observation. This led to an assembly of market women, fishwives, some men in disguise and a bevy of prostitutes to swell the numbers setting out on the 12-mile trek to Versailles to fetch back the royal family. Never can there have been a more grisly cavalcade: ravenous, maddened women in rags and tatters, soaked to the skin by heavy rain and brandishing any weapon they could lay their hands on – knives, skewers, fire irons, broomsticks – and screaming obscene threats as to what they would do to the hated Queen.

That night the Queen came close to death when mobs broke into the palace, and she only escaped by taking refuge with the King in a strongly barricaded room. At this moment of crisis she was at her best – calm and dignified. Next day the cry went up: 'Back to Paris', and the King had to comply. And so the royal family, to shouts of 'The baker, the baker's wife and the baker's boy', in hopes that they would bring bread, preceded by the severed heads of murdered guardsmen stuck on spikes, embarked on the seven-hour journey to Paris. There they were lodged in The Tuileries – dark, damp and dilapidated from long disuse, but in time efforts were made to make it more habitable. Furniture was brought from Versailles and they were granted a reasonably generous allowance by the National Assembly. For a time their lives settled into a more or less orderly routine, but the King and Queen were aware that they were existing on a minefield, and explosions were always liable to occur.

The poet Wordsworth wrote of the French Revolution: 'Bliss was it at that time to be alive. But to be young was very heaven.' But there was little bliss in Paris at that time. The hopes of the idealists for a new, enlightened age of goodwill, justice and freedom had not been fulfilled. To the contrary, the Revolution had brought out the worst in people – cruelty, greed and hatred. The law had become unenforceable, as murderers, robbers and rapists roamed through the city looking for victims.

People sought hate figures on whom to lay the blame for these appalling conditions, and Marie Antoinette was still foremost. Odious images of her were always being paraded, the vilest abuse screamed at her, and there were also incessant plots and rumours of plots to assassinate her; one would-be assassin was able to penetrate into the interior of the palace and came near to achieving his aim. In the midst of this barbarity the Queen was outwardly calm, but to intimates she poured out piteously: 'My heart is wounded as never before, and I bring bad luck to all. What you suffer is my fault.'

Life for Marie Antoinette would have been unbearable but for the love she had for her two surviving children (Marie-Thérèse and Louis Charles, now the Dauphin), who were an infinite source of joy to her; for their sake there was nothing she would not endure. Her other great support was the loyalty and love of Axel Fersen, whose care for her was unremitting. 'All is confusion, disorder and consternation', he wrote to the King of Sweden, but there was no hardship or danger he would not confront for the sake of the Queen he idealised and who was always to him 'an angel of goodness'. From an early stage he had been urging Marie Antoinette to escape abroad with her children, and this she was convinced she should do, but she would not go without her husband, and he for the time being would not consider the idea, persisting obstinately in his policy of appeasement and 'turning the other cheek' which, he was convinced, would bear fruit in time.

But then came a change of heart. In 1791 the National Assembly came into conflict with the Pope (Pius V) about the appointment and authority of the clergy: all French prelates were required to take an oath of loyalty to the government, which the Pope forbade them to do. This brought about a schism in the Church between the clergy who took the oath (jurors) and those who refused (non-jurors). In this division the King, a deeply religious man, strongly supported the latter. He attached great importance to taking his communion from one of their number, but this he was prevented from doing, which had a profound effect on him. 'How strange', he said, 'that he who had granted freedom to the nation should not be allowed it himself.'

From then on, plans for an escape from Paris went ahead. These were spearheaded by Axel Fersen who took it upon himself to organise the whole operation including providing and paying for a Berlin carriage, large enough to accommodate six people and strong enough to stand up to a journey of 180 miles on rough and hazardous roads.

At first everything went according to plan; the royal family was smuggled out of the Tuileries and then, in the guise of a Russian noblewoman and her attendants, met up with the Berlin carriage and set out on the long journey. Their objective was the border town of Montmédy where loyalist forces were awaiting them. Whether or not they would then cross into Austria was left open. The mood of the party was lighthearted and optimistic. Their appurtenances included such diverse objects as mirrors, wine glasses, toothpicks and a gilded chamber pot. It was a serious disadvantage that the King would not allow Count Fersen to accompany them, which meant there would be no strong guiding hand, something the King himself was incapable of providing.

For a time the flight continued to go well: supporting troops and fresh horses awaited them at appointed staging posts, and they were at least ten hours ahead of any pursuit that might be mounted. But then delays occurred and they became behind schedule so that those expecting them thought that the operation had been called off and abandoned their posts. The crisis came at the town of Sainte Ménéhould where the postmaster of the town, a staunch republican named Jean-Baptiste Drouet, thought he recognised the King (from his portrait on banknotes) and raised an alarm, so that at the next staging post at Varennes a contingent of the National Guard was awaiting them. Their passports were examined and found to be in order, and it was then up to the Procurator of the town to decide whether or not they should be allowed to proceed. At this juncture the future of the royal family, and indeed of France, rested in the hands of this minor official, a candle chandler of the name of Sauce. He took the fateful decision that the party should be delayed for 34 hours while their circumstances were further examined.

Much was to happen during that time. Further units of the National Guard arrived on the scene, as did a crowd of local inhabitants, stirred up by wild and inflammatory reports. And then there came two horsemen from Paris with a decree from the National Assembly ordering the arrest of the King, who by then had become positively identified, and Louis had had to own up to who he was. Sauce then felt bound to order the return of the King and his family to Paris.

As was to be expected, the return journey was a nightmare. Coming from Paris to Varennes took 22 hours; going back took nearly four days. The heat was intense, the roads bumpy and dusty, and two extra people – the emissaries from Paris – had to be squashed into the Berlin carriage. And for nearly all the way there were hysterical crowds, sneering and spitting, poking their heads through the open windows and reaching out to touch the King and Queen. It could have been felt that the unsuccessful flight to Varennes would mean the end of the monarchy. Certainly it played into the hands of the extremists, who were loud in their demands for the deposition of Louis, but this was not to happen yet.

The National Assembly was in the process of drawing up a new constitution which was completed in September 1791. It provided for the continuation of a hereditary monarchy but with the King's powers reduced and much of the mystique and protocol of monarchy swept away: it was no longer necessary to bow to him and to be always standing in his presence. Essentially he was a representative of the people. Much against his will, but persisting in his policy of conciliation, Louis gave his consent to all of this which infuriated Marie Antoinette who described the new measures as 'monstrous' and 'out to demolish the monarchy stone by stone'. She also described the members of the new Legislative Assembly, as it was now called, as 'a collection of scoundrels, lunatics and beasts'. And this attitude was not entirely concealed.

At the age of 36 Marie Antoinette was a different person to the young, beautiful, happy-go-lucky queen of ten years before. Now white-haired, stooping and drawn, she was weighed down by cares. Surrounded by hatred and conspiracy and separated from Fersen, her great love, who had become a marked man unable to return safely to France, she spent much time writing elaborately ciphered letters to him which caused her great mental fatigue. And always she was haunted by the flight to Varennes which had so nearly succeeded; if it had, her situation would have been so very different.

At the end of 1791 the atmosphere in Paris became more fraught, with the threat of foreign invasion. So far the major powers of Europe had held aloof from the Revolution; their rulers had disliked it but were not disposed to become involved. After the flight to Varennes, however, and the subsequent humiliation of the King and Queen, and under pressure from the increasing number of émigré French noblemen and others who had fled the country, they were becoming more concerned. In August 1791 the Emperor of Austria came to an agreement with the King of Prussia and together they issued a declaration to the effect that: 'the present situation of the King of France is a subject of common interest to all the sovereigns of Europe'. They pledged themselves to act promptly with all the force necessary to restore the kingly rights of Louis XVI.

Such a threat to the internal affairs of their country drove Frenchmen into a fury of revolutionary zeal and patriotism, and the danger to the remaining aristocrats, non-juror priests and anyone showing counter-revolutionary tendencies became intense. Summary executions by hanging from a lamppost (to cries of '*A la lanterne*') were not unusual, and public executions increased after April 1792 when a new beheading apparatus, the guillotine, was tried out and found to be 'prompt and expeditious'.

With the massing of Austrian troops along the French frontier ready for invasion, the National Assembly on 20 April 1792 decided on a pre-emptive strike, and Louis was compelled to agree, to the dismay of Marie Antoinette who found herself torn between her country of birth and that of her adoption. More and more she became an object of hatred and suspicion, and this came to the boil in June 1792 when a mob, screaming abuse and armed with anything they could lay their hands on, broke into the Tuileries and ran amok. They were confronted by the King who calmly and courageously tried to reason with them, as also did the Queen, although seething with rage, until the National Guard arrived to turn the intruders out.

Soon afterwards the Austrian army made headway into France. The French army – ill equipped, outgunned and undisciplined – had been unable to repel them. On 25 July 1792 the commander of the Austrian army, the Duke of Brunswick, issued a manifesto declaring that if the Palace of the Tuileries were assaulted or invaded and if the least violence or insult were directed at their Majesties, the King and Queen, an exemplary and memorable vengeance would follow and the city of Paris would undergo a military execution. But this threat, instead of intimidating the Parisians, only infuriated them the more. There was a call to arms and appeals for help were sent to the rest of France, in response to which came, among others, 600 men from Marseilles who 'knew how to die', bringing with them a thrilling new anthem, *The Marseillaise*.

At the beginning of August there were rumours of a major assault on the Tuileries by a large crowd, armed not only with knives and hammers this time but with several cannons in tow. Forewarned, the King was ready to go into safety with his family in the hall of the National Assembly. Both he and the Queen were unwilling to do this and were only persuaded by the danger to their children. With a resolute leader the attack on the Tuileries could have been withstood, but as always the King wavered and forbade the opening of fire, and the result was catastrophic. The Swiss Guards and other defenders were overrun and massacred. By the end of the day The Tuileries were a wreck.

In the following days, the National Assembly pronounced the monarchy to be dissolved and all executive powers to be invested in a new assembly to be known as the National Convention. For the time being the King and his family were lodged in a medieval fortress known as The Temple – bleak and uncomfortable but secure – where they would await the decree of the National Convention as to their future.

In the meanwhile the war against the allied invaders – Austria had now been joined by Prussia, Holland and Spain – was going badly. With the capture of Verdun on 3 September 1792 the way to Paris seemed open but the news of this drove the Parisians into even greater frenzy and provoked the most terrible mob violence of all when on 3 September a maddened crowd, yelling for blood, broke into the prisons of Paris and slaughtered the inmates – men, women and children – perhaps some 1300 in all.

During the time Louis spent in The Temple he behaved with exemplary piety and restraint; he remained calm in spite of all insults and maltreatment. To Marie Antoinette he showed special tenderness, saying that he had never doubted the warmth of her maternal feelings and begging her forgiveness for 'all the ills she has suffered for my sake and for any grief I may have caused her in the course of our marriage'.

He seems, however, to have had little doubt as to his impending fate, and it can have been no great surprise when on 11 December the Mayor of Paris and other officials arrived at The Temple to bear him off to the bar of the National Convention to be put on trial for treason. It was a foregone conclusion that he would be found guilty, but his calmness and dignity, while all the trumped-up charges against him were read out, amazed the spectators. One of them, the American Ambassador, Gouverneur Morris, recorded his disbelief that 'the mildest of monarchs to have ascended the throne of France should be denounced as a monstrous tyrant'. The verdict against him was almost unanimous, but it was only by the narrowest of margins that he was sentenced to death.

On the scaffold Louis was again calm and composed, but his execution on 21 January 1793 was woefully fouled: roughly and unnecessarily he was hustled by the guards who tried to bind his arms and cut off his hair, and when he attempted some last words they were drowned by a roll of drums. Then the guillotine malfunctioned so that it was neither 'prompt nor expeditious' and caused Louis to cry out in pain. The scene afterwards was ghastly, in marked contrast to that at the execution of the English King Charles I, 144 years before. There, according to one present, 'the dignity and courage of the King struck awe into all who witnessed it, and when his severed head was held up there was such a groan as I never heard before and desire I may never hear again'. But when Louis's head was held up there was an outburst of savagery with maniacs dancing wildly round the scaffold, screaming and yelling and trying to grab hold of strands of Louis's hair or bits of his clothes, until his corpse was unceremoniously bundled into a basket and driven off to an unmarked grave. The English Prime Minister, William Pitt, described the execution of Louis as 'the foulest and most atrocious deed which the history of the world has yet had occasion to attest'. Not many would disagree. But worse was to come.

In Marie Antoinette's marriage contract it was stipulated that on the death of her husband she would have the right either to remain in France or return to Austria. But in 1793 with the two countries at war there was little chance of her being allowed the latter option, although it was thought that a deal might be negotiated at a price – either in the form of money or in exchange for eminent French prisoners held by the Austrians. But Francis II (Austrian Emperor since March 1972) made no serious attempt to obtain the release of his aunt. It may be that he thought that his armies would soon be in Paris and she would then be freed.

By September 1793, however, the war had taken a new turn: French forces were rallying, the invading armies were shilly-shallying and the immediate danger to Paris had receded, which made the position of Marie Antoinette much more dangerous. Until then she had been of more value to the Revolutionary Tribunal (the country's new ruler) alive than dead as a possible hostage; but this was becoming a lesser consideration and at the same time pressure was mounting from left-wing extremists[5] to bring 'the woman Capet',[6] as she was then known, to trial. She was still a hate figure, and Jacobins vied with each other in denouncing her. Incredibly, in a civilised country there were those who could demand that she be driven in an iron cage through the streets of Paris, or that she should suffer the same fate as Jezebel, Queen of Israel, who was trampled to death by horses and her body then devoured by wild dogs (II Kings Chapter 9).

Of the cruelties and humiliations inflicted on Antoinette at this time by far the worst was the separation from her son, Louis Charles (regarded by royalists as Louis XVII), then aged eight. It was decided that he needed a more democratic upbringing, which meant that he was handed over to an odious thug, one Antoine Simon, a cobbler by trade, who bullied and brutalised him and coerced him into blaspheming and cursing his own family. Later, as will be seen, an even more monstrous crime was to be perpetrated on him.

By July 1793 the Jacobins had gained control of the National Convention and the so-called Reign of Terror was raging. At the beginning of August the Committee of Public Safety, which had taken over the government, ordered Marie Antoinette to be removed from The Temple and transferred to the prison known as La Conciergerie where her treatment was more harsh. The Temple, though bleak and inhospitable, was at least a royal residence and some royal rights were accorded her there; but in La Conciergerie she was just prisoner 280, locked up in a dark, damp, insalubrious cell with all privileges withheld and cast among prisoners who might be, like her, political offenders but might also be common criminals – thieves, prostitutes, murderers. Nevertheless, grim though conditions might be, there were possibilities of escape, and several plans were hatched. Her nephew, the Emperor, might have failed her but there were lesser people (including a band of smugglers) who were ready to help; but their plans always miscarried and when one of them became known to the authorities security surrounding her was tightened up: a coarse, burly gendarme was permanently in her cell and watched over her every movement (even undressing and calls of nature).

---

[5] Known as Jacobins or 'The Mountain' from the fact that they occupied the highest seats in the assembly of the Convention.

[6] Name of French dynasty.

The next stage in the abasement of the ex-Queen came at the beginning of October by when the government had decided that she had to die, and the Public Prosecutor, the egregious Antoine Fouquier-Tinville, out for as many deaths as possible, set about drawing up an indictment – which he did zealously, knowing that his life depended on it.[7]

On the night of 12 October, just after Antoinette had gone to bed, an armed guard arrived at La Conciergerie to bear her off for a preliminary interrogation by the Revolutionary Tribunal. This proved to be a long, gruelling affair, lasting 16 hours, in which all manner of insults and accusations were thrust at her. But in spite of sleeplessness, malnutrition and illness she survived courageously, never losing her calm and making no damaging admissions. At the end of it, as had been prearranged, she was committed for trial, but some semblance of legality was to be maintained: a show trial was set up with a president of the court and a suitably democratic jury (including a cobbler, a carpenter and a hat maker), and two young lawyers were co-opted for the defence – an impossible task as they were given no time to prepare their brief, and in any case the verdict was preordained.

Long before the trial began on 14 October there had been an inrush of spectators into the courtroom, including the ghoulish market women with their knitting (*tricoteuses*), expecting (and no doubt hoping) to witness a dramatic collapse of the ex-Queen. But they were to be disappointed: pallid and emaciated though she might be, Marie Antoinette held her own. For two long days she was subjected to intensive questioning and accused of all manner of crimes – licentious debauchery, conspiracy with foreign powers to overthrow the Revolution, riotous extravagance leading to national bankruptcy, and prompting the King, her husband, in all his misdeeds. These charges, although distorted and exaggerated, were not without some validity, although of hard evidence there was none.

But there were others that were outrageous, notably one that she and her sister-in-law, Madame Elisabeth, had led her son, Louis Charles, into lubricious sex acts and committed incest with him, and the wretched child, dazed and uncomprehending, was brought into court to testify to it. This was the only occasion when the

---

[7] Ultimately, however, it was not to save him. He was guillotined in 1795 soon after the fall of Robespierre.

Queen showed signs of agitation and she made an emotional appeal to all mothers present to reject such vile and unnatural accusations. And this had an effect: usually her enemies were ready to believe anything of her, however dreadful, but this was going too far; for once there was a wave of sympathy in her favour, and the prosecution made little further mention of the matter. In spite of this, and the fact that all the charges against her were based on rumour and hearsay, the jury, as was expected of them, found her guilty and she was condemned to death. Even then, to the dismay of her enemies, her composure did not falter. They had greatly underestimated her toughness and courage.

In her last days most of Marie Antoinette's requests had been rejected out of hand, but on the day before her death she was allowed writing materials for a last letter to her sister-in-law, Madame Elisabeth. In this she committed her two children to her care; her only sadness in dying was being separated from them, and she begged forgiveness for her son for having betrayed them at her trial, saying that an eight-year-old child could be made to say anything. The tone of the letter was calm and benevolent, urging that no vengeance be taken for the deaths of herself and her husband. In moving terms she bade farewell to her family and friends and regretted any offence she had caused them. She also attested her firm belief in the Catholic Apostolic and Roman faith and her determination to have last rites only from a non-juror priest. It was a beautiful letter and should surely have laid to rest the notion, held then and to this day, that she was essentially shallow and light-headed.

Marie Antoinette met her death with the unflinching courage she had shown during her trial. Everything was done to humiliate and distress her: her hair was shorn off, her hands were bound and she was dragged off to the guillotine in a rough cart with her back to the horses, mocked and jostled all the way, and (unlike her husband) to be allowed no ministrations from a non-juror priest. But at no time did she lose her composure; she even managed an apology to the executioner for treading on his foot. Like the Thane of Cawdor, 'nothing in her life became her like the leaving of it ... to throw away the dearest thing she ow'd as t'were a careless trifle'.[8]

---

[8] *Macbeth*, Act I, scene 4.

Such, then, was the tragic and tumultuous life of Marie Antoinette. It remains hard to understand why she stirred up so much hatred and mistrust. Tactless, lightheaded and extravagant she might have been, but she was not a truly wicked woman. She was not cold-hearted and cruel, nor was she vicious and vindictive. And no woman, however villainous, deserved the gruesome fate endured by her. Her role in the French Revolution, though not insignificant, has surely been overrated. To say, as Thomas Jefferson[9] did, that 'had there been no queen, there would have been no revolution' is out of proportion.

---

[9] One of the founding fathers of the United States and third President.

9

CATHERINE THE GREAT (1729–1796)

The legendary reputation of Catherine II, Empress of Russia, known as 'The Great', rests on the way that she, a princess from a lesser German state, was able to seize the Imperial Russian crown unlawfully and reign for 34 years during which time Russia's frontiers expanded and the country became a major European power. She is remembered today too for her awe-inspiring love life.

Catherine, or Sophia as she was first known, came from the German state of Anhalt-Zerbst. Her father, Christian August, was a minor princeling under the sway of Frederick the Great and was content to remain as such; but her mother, Johanna Elizabeth, was more ambitious and sought a leading role on the European stage. She had close ties with Elizabeth Petrovna, Tsarina of Russia, who had once been engaged to her brother and who was looking for a bride for her nephew, Archduke Peter Ulrich, whom she had nominated her successor. To Johanna it seemed that her daughter Sophia would make an ideal marriage partner. She was no beauty but had a strong character, which a wife of Peter Ulrich would need as he was lamentably weak, ill-graced and pathologically retarded, spending much time with puppets and model soldiers. He could not be less suited to be Tsar of all the Russias for, as well as other failings, he had a strong dislike of the country and greatly preferred all things Germanic, notably his father's dukedom of Holstein,[1] and for Frederick the Great he had a passionate admiration. As heir to the throne of Russia, however, he was the most sought-after husband in Europe, and when the Tsarina invited Johanna and Sophia to Russia with matrimony in mind, they accepted eagerly.

On arrival in St Petersburg Sophia could not but be shocked at the prospect of marriage to the Archduke Peter; his weaknesses

---

[1] His father was married to Tsarina Elizabeth's sister Anne.

were all too apparent, and these were enhanced when he became pockmarked by smallpox. He also lost no time in letting her know that he was in love with another woman and was only marrying her at the behest of his aunt, who dominated him. Sophia, however, was determined that she had to go through with the marriage and did everything required of her including abjuring the Protestant Lutheran faith in which she had been brought up and being received into the Russian Orthodox Church, after which she became known as the Archduchess Catherine.

Peter and Catherine were married in 1745 and for the next 16 years life for the latter was to be an ordeal. As well as the quirks of her husband she also had to put up with the treatment meted out to her by the Tsarina – at times affectionate and considerate, at others cold-hearted and brutal, and always unpredictable. The daughter of Peter the Great, she combined his forcefulness and ruthlessness with the warmth and earthiness of her mother, a peasant from Lithuania whom Peter had raised to be Tsarina.[2] Voluminous and uninhibitedly sensual, Elizabeth never married but took as lovers whomsoever she fancied; it might be a courtier, a guardsman or a shepherd boy from the Ukraine. To all impulses she gave full rein, at times kneeling in superstitious reverence at holy shrines, at others disporting herself in transvestite orgies where she made a splendid figure of a man while more diminutive women looked like 'scrubby little boys', and grave statesmen and prestigious military men tripped around in whalebone corsets and petticoats. In spite of her excesses, however, and perhaps because of them, she was always popular and kept a firm grip on power all her life.

Catherine was of course in great awe of her. Her future depended on her. If she so decided, her marriage to Peter could be terminated and she could be either relegated to a nunnery or sent back to Anhalt-Zerbst as a disgraced and impoverished relic. Catherine knew that the security of her position depended on her giving birth to an heir. The Tsarina was desperate for this in order to perpetuate the Romanov dynasty, but at first it could not be achieved as, owing to a physical disability, the Archduke Peter was impotent, so that for nine years his marriage to Catherine was unconsummated. In time, however, the disability was overcome and in 1754 Catherine gave birth to a son, Paul Petrovitch, the future Tsar Paul I. It has

---

[2] See the chapter in this book on Catherine I Tsarina of Russia.

never been certain, however, whether he was the son of the Archduke or of Catherine's current lover, Serge Saltykof, a chronic philanderer who set his sights on beautiful and seemingly unattainable ladies, and when they succumbed lost interest in them, especially if, as was the case with Catherine, they became overzealous and too demanding. After an affair of less than two years he went off on a mission abroad and made no move to keep in contact with her. Whoever was the father of Paul Petrovitch, the Tsarina was delighted by him. She had the lowest opinion of her nephew, once describing him as 'a little monster', and so long as there was a male heir who could be accepted as a Romanov she felt no need to enquire into his paternity. As soon as the baby was born she lost no time in taking complete charge of him, leaving Catherine alone and neglected.

Catherine's bleak existence was relieved temporarily when in 1755 there arrived in St Petersburg an English ambassador with orders to gain Russian support for England in any European war, especially one in the defence of Hanover, the English King's other realm. Suave, cynical and worldly-wise, Sir Charles Hanbury-Williams came prepared for this task with not only diplomatic skills but also plenty of money which he was ready to disburse freely, having no doubt that in Russia, as in England, 'all men have their price'. He was aware too that there were other inducements besides money. Seeing that in St Petersburg there was a tsarina reputed for her licentiousness and an archduchess unhappily married to the heir to the throne and apparently not inaccessible, he had included in his retinue a young Polish courtier renowned widely for his charm and good looks.

Stanislaus Poniatowski was very different from Saltykof; he was no roving Don Juan. Sensitive and romantic, he looked on love as something sacred. At first he regarded Catherine with awe and kept his distance, but she took the initiative and they fell in love. Their romance lasted for less than two years, during which there were secret trysts and blissful moments of love-making. It seems certain that the daughter born to Catherine in 1757 (to die in infancy) was fathered by Poniatowski. Certainly Catherine's husband thought as much, as he was heard to exclaim in typically facetious manner: 'Heaven knows how it is that my wife becomes pregnant, though I suppose I shall have to accept the child as my own.'

It was at this time that Catherine became initiated into the world of intrigue, not only in love but also in politics. Hanbury-Williams was anxious to gain her support for English interests and was ready to pay for it, and she, always in financial straits, was ready to receive. By coming onto the payroll of England, Catherine was playing a dangerous game, since if this became known it could be construed as treason, especially after 1756 when the Seven Years War broke out and Russia was aligned with France and Austria against Prussia, supported by England.

The first years of the war were the unhappiest of Catherine's life. Everything went wrong for her. Poniatowski had to leave the country and Catherine was aware that he was not sorry to go. Later she was to write: 'I sensed that he was bored and it nearly broke my heart.' But it was perhaps more likely that he was worn out rather than bored, as Catherine's demands on her lovers were extortionate. Hanbury-Williams also had to go, which meant that his funds dried up and Catherine's financial problems became acute. At the same time her strongest supporter in the Russian government, Count Bestuzhev, was dismissed and replaced by Count Mikhail Vorontsov who was less friendly. As she later testified, she had never felt so alone and insecure, so much so that she determined on desperate action: she would go to the Tsarina, confess faults of error and judgement and ask to be sent back to her homeland of Anhalt-Zerbst. This was in fact impracticable as this state had ceased to exist, having been incorporated into Prussia; and Catherine must have been confident that so long as her son Paul was heir to the throne she had to be maintained in her present state and could not be allowed to leave. And so it proved. The Tsarina showed some sympathy but was insistent that she stayed put. Catherine felt some reassurance at this, but her years of rejection and frustration were to continue for some time yet.

Catherine was to declare several times during her life that she could not exist for a single day without love, and by this she meant not just physical satisfaction but sympathy and intimacy as well. For a long time she had been without these, but in 1760 there came into her life someone who was to provide love abundantly. He was also to have a fateful role in her destiny. Gregory Orlov was a junior army officer of enormous physical strength, dauntless courage and inexhaustible virility: in war at the forefront of the battle, and in peace leading the band in roystering, whoring and gambling. Catherine was overwhelmed by him. He could hardly have been a greater contrast to the amorous but faltering Poniatowski. But although physically unmatched, he had little brain. Basically he was a simple, affable, plain-spoken man who gave free rein to his impulses, with little thought to their consequences.[3] He may have lived dangerously, but he survived as Catherine's lover for ten years.

Catherine had long been hoping for the death of the Tsarina. Until that happened her life would remain empty and purposeless. Elizabeth had several times come near to dying but had always recovered, sometimes it seemed miraculously. But at the end of 1761 her condition became desperate and on Christmas Day she died. She was widely lamented; for most of her reign the country had been at peace and, as Russian autocrats go, she had shed little blood, fulfilling the pledge made at the beginning of her reign that she would sign no death warrants. She was not, as it might have seemed, just an outsize voluptuary. Catherine had laid plans for what should happen on her demise but it came inopportunely, when she was six months pregnant (by Orlov), so she had to keep in the background. But in the public eye her behaviour was impeccable – spending long hours on her knees by the dead body of Elizabeth and prostrating herself in homage before Tsar Peter III, her despised husband.

The behaviour of Peter, on the other hand, could not have been more foolish and shameful. His frivolity and lack of respect at his aunt's funeral caused outrage, as did his open contempt for the rites of the Orthodox Church. But the greatest offence of all was given to the army, when he immediately made a humiliating peace with Prussia. At the time Frederick the Great was at his last gasp: Russian armies had won great victories and were closing in on him and he seemed doomed, but then suddenly with the accession of Peter III came salvation. To make matters worse, Peter then declared war with Denmark over a quarrel with his native Holstein in which Russia was not involved. It was becoming increasingly evident that he was out of place as Tsar. His unconcealed dislike of Russia and preference for Germany and his growing mental instability made his position impossible.

But who then was to take his place? By rights it should have

---

[3] When he was on a visit to London Horace Walpole wrote that, 'he dances gigantic dances and makes gigantic love'.

been his son Paul, then aged eight, and there were those who thought that his mother should act as Regent until he came of age. But this was not Catherine's intention. She would not be satisfied with temporary power. She aimed to be Tsarina in her own right. There was no law of primogeniture in Russia at that time; recent tsars and tsarinas had come to the throne either because they had been nominated by their predecessors or because of a palace revolution. She might be a German princess with no trace of Romanov blood, but during the 15 hard years since her marriage she had worked assiduously to become 'Russianised', mastering the language, adapting to the Orthodox Church and acquainting herself with Russian traditions and ways of life. She felt that she now had a right to the tsardom and was entirely confident in her ability to carry out its duties. Action became urgently necessary when it became known that Peter was planning to have her deposed and the infant Paul declared illegitimate; then he would marry Elisabeth Vorontsov and their issue would be heirs to the throne.

The coup when it came was engineered mainly by Gregory Orlov and his four brothers who, like him, were men of action and great physique. Their standing in the Palace Guard was decisive. Early in the morning of 28 June 1762 Catherine was roused from sleep by Gregory's brother Alexis who told her that she had to come instantly as the action had begun. And so, dressed hastily and after an incomplete toilet she then drove with him into the centre of St Petersburg, where in the cathedral the Archbishop gave her his blessing and proclaimed her Autocrat of all the Russias. When Peter heard of this he was overcome with fear and presented a pitiful spectacle. He still had troops loyal to him and could have made a fight of it; instead of which he became paralysed into inactivity and tamely signed an instrument of abdication and was led off into imprisonment, as Frederick the Great put it, 'like a child who had been sent off to bed'.

The question then arose as to what should happen to him next. Catherine would have liked to spare his life and send him into exile, but she knew that as long as he was alive there would always be conspiracies to reinstate him. Yet she did not want to be held responsible for his death. Within a week he had died, allegedly of natural causes; but what actually happened was that he was murdered by or on the order of Alexis Orlov, the most ruthless and ambitious of the brothers. Years later a letter of his to Catherine came to light in which he explained somewhat incoherently that Peter's death had been accidental, and he implored her forgiveness. To what extent Catherine was involved cannot be known, but it is certain that she took no steps to investigate the death or to bring to justice those responsible. At the least she was an accessory.

Even after her husband's death Catherine's position was not secure. She was widely suspected of having had a part in it and there were bound to be strong feelings about the foreign princess who had 'usurped' the crown which should have gone to her son. Separated from him since his birth, there was little love between them. To the contrary, there was strong dislike and mistrust. Paul always suspected that his mother was responsible for his father's death and feared he might suffer the same fate, while Catherine regarded him as the main threat to her throne. Her treatment of him showed the hard and ruthless side of her character: she paid him little respect in public and when he came of age would not allow him any part in government. She even had thoughts of disinheriting him and nominating his eldest son, Alexander, as her successor, but this she did not do.

Even more ruthless was her behaviour towards the ex-Tsar Ivan VI, a great-nephew of Peter the Great who had been proclaimed tsar in babyhood but had soon been dethroned and had spent the rest of his life, more than 20 years, in solitary confinement. On becoming Empress Catherine might have ordered some relief to his dreadful conditions but instead she ordered them to be intensified so that he might die a natural death. She also gave instructions that in the event of a rescue attempt he was to be put to death instantly, and when this occurred the order was carried out and Catherine showed her approbation.

For the first ten years of her reign Catherine colluded closely with Gregory Orlov to whom (with his brothers) she owed her throne. There was a strong love between them and Gregory was able to satisfy her ever more insistent sexual needs. For the time being he was the most powerful man in Russia, 'emperor in all but name' as one diplomat described him. It seems that Catherine did consider marrying him, but was dissuaded by an elder statesman who told her that the Russian people would never accept 'Mrs Orlov' as Empress. Their liaison was only ever a physical one; there was no meeting of minds. At the time, Catherine's intellect had been awakened by reading the works of Voltaire, with whom she had entered into a regular correspondence. Later she was to declare that everything she did 'had to pass the test of whether it would please Voltaire'.

After 12 years there were signs that Catherine and Orlov were falling out of love. His behaviour towards her in public was often rude and peremptory and it was no secret that he was having other lovers on the side. He was also wearying of the staid and superficial life at court and longing for activity and danger. In 1770 he asked permission to go and restore order in Moscow, then in a state of turmoil following an outbreak of cholera, and to this Catherine consented which she would have been unlikely to have done a few years earlier. This mission he achieved successfully, but two years later he was sent south to conduct peace talks with the Turks which resulted in deadlock, and while he was there Catherine took another lover, one Alexander Vassilchikov, a fine figure of a guardsman but otherwise undistinguished. When Orlov heard of this he was enraged and returned immediately to St Petersburg, seemingly bent on trouble, but he was persuaded to accept the situation, partly because of the great riches and honours with which he was bought off and partly because he had become besotted with a young girl of 13 whom he was later to marry. He died ten years afterwards of apoplexy.

Catherine had come to the throne with many enlightened ideas which she hoped to be able to realise, but she was to find that most of them could not be attained. She spent long hours in drawing up proposals for a new legal code to be applied to the whole country, unlike previous ones, but these met with little enthusiasm and were found to be unenforceable. Of greater moment were plans for bringing relief to the country's millions of serfs (90 per cent of the population) who were virtual slaves, but here too she was unable to overcome vested interests; at the end of her reign there were more serfs than there had been before and the power of their masters over them was greater than ever.

She did have some success, however, in bringing Western European culture into the country. Peter the Great had worked wonders in creating the new capital of St Petersburg on the bleak marshlands of the estuary of the river Neva as well as bringing into being a Russian navy and many new crafts and industries, but he was short on the arts, and this Catherine set out to rectify: she bought up art collections and libraries from all over Europe and attracted into the country foreign painters, architects and writers; she also encouraged music and the ballet in spite of the fact that she herself was tone deaf. By the end of her reign she had done much to dispel Western European ideas that Russia was a dark land mass – semi-barbaric and more Asian than European.

Catherine's principal achievements, however, lay in foreign affairs: during her reign Russia's frontiers were extended and the country came to be regarded as a major European power. But in achieving this, she was guilty of great crimes, committing the country to costly and unnecessary wars and, in particular, of being mainly responsible for the partition of Poland.

Poland at that time was a large sprawling country stretching from the Black Sea to the Baltic. It covered nearly the whole of Russia's western frontier and if there was to be Russian expansion into Europe, which was Catherine's hope, it would have to be at the expense of Poland. In 1763 on the death of Augustus VIII Catherine managed to obtain the election of Stanislav Poniatowski, her ex-lover, as the new King of Poland. Poniatowski was of Polish nobility, a man of charm and erudition but weak and malleable, an ideal puppet king. In the chaos that ensued Catherine sent in a Russian army to restore order and this resulted in the first partition of Poland in 1772, in which Russia, Prussia and Austria took over all the Polish lands they wanted without any justifiable claim to them, so that Poland was deprived of one-third of her territory and some 5 million inhabitants. Surely this was one of the most shameful events in European history, and it was not the end of the story.[4]

Catherine did not linger long with Alexander Vassilchikov. He was no more than a stopgap between the mighty Orlov and the all-powerful Potemkin. He was amiable enough and physically satisfying, but nothing more. Mentally, he was negligible. Catherine described him as 'an excellent but very boring citizen', and later as 'a nuisance who complains of pains in the chest'. And so he was pensioned off.

Waiting in the wings was the most illustrious and most talented of all Catherine's lovers, indeed thought by some to be the greatest statesman of his age. As a young man Gregory Potemkin had been in doubt as to whether to make his career in the army or the Church. In deciding eventually on the former he retained a leaning

---

[4] For a fuller account of the partition of Poland see the chapter on Maria Theresa.

towards a monastic life and a deep interest in theology. Certainly he was no ordinary soldier. He first attracted Catherine's attention when she was proclaimed Empress in 1762: and as a junior officer in the serried ranks he noticed that her military uniform was incomplete, lacking a sword knot, and he came forward to present her with one. It was a bold thing to do, but it paid off: Catherine recalled the incident, and promotion came his way. In 1773 at the age of 34, when he was serving in the war against the Turks, he received a letter from his Empress, expressing concern for his safety and welfare. Knowing her penchant for young army officers, Potemkin took this as an invitation into her favours and lost no time in returning to St Petersburg where he confidently expected an invitation into either her government or her bed; but this did not materialise at once. He was given no special responsibilities and Vassilchikov remained *amant-en-titre*. It seems that he was expected to be no more than a presence at court, which did not satisfy him, and his reaction was to take himself off to a monastery and a life of devotion.

What his motives were cannot be known, but the result was that Catherine soon took steps to attract him back to court, for which he made certain conditions including his appointment as Adjutant-General, well known to be a stepping stone to greater favours. From then on honours and riches poured in on him. No favourite ever made such rapid progress. Catherine became enamoured of him in a way she had never been before. He was quite different to his predecessors. Unlike the brawny Orlov or the vacuous Vassilchikov he was an intellectual and he and Catherine were well matched. He was also a superb entertainer and could make Catherine laugh not only by his wit but also by his mimicry of others, including Catherine herself. Beautiful he was not: he was gross, ungainly, unkempt and (often) unwashed. The English Ambassador of the time wrote of him: 'His figure is gigantic and disproportioned and his countenance is far from engaging.' His behaviour was unpredictable: he might be charming and dynamic, he might be silent and withdrawn. But there was always something compelling about him, and his power over Catherine was dominating. A foreign diplomat was to write: 'Prince Gregory Potemkin rules her with an absolute sway – thoroughly acquainted with her weaknesses, her desires and her passions, he operates on them as he pleases.' Almost always he could make her do what he wanted, even to the extent of a secret marriage; there is no written record of this and it cannot be proved, but Catherine's frequent references to him in her letters in such terms as 'dear husband' and to herself as 'loving wife' must make it virtually certain.

When Potemkin came to power in 1774 the country was in a dire state: the war with the Turks was dragging on indefinitely; a rebellion of the serfs led by a charismatic character, Emelian Pugachev, was gaining strength; and the country was nearly bankrupt. Catherine's personal position too was precarious: her son Paul had just come of age and there were those who thought he should now enter into his kingdom as the heir of the Romanovs, while there was an underlying threat from the Orlov brothers who had already dethroned one tsar and might dethrone another. But in the following year these dangers were receding: Turkey was induced to make peace, the serf rebellion was crushed – brutally and mercilessly – the Orlovs were paid off, and it was becoming increasingly apparent that Paul was not the stuff of which tsars are made. As was said of him at the time: 'His soul was noble but his head was confused.'

Certainly Catherine and Potemkin were a powerful combination and not only in politics: their personal relations were of a special nature; their love for each other was profound but volatile; quarrels quite often occurred but were seldom long-lasting and with reconciliation came even greater love and understanding. At heart they were both united by a devotion to the interests and aggrandisement of Russia.

Their political partnership was to last for 17 years, but their love life for only two; at the end of that time Potemkin's physical love began to wane; he could not keep pace with Catherine's insistent sexuality and besides, he had found other attractions. But he was determined not to lose the power base he had established. He dreaded being sent off into retirement like Orlov with a golden handshake, so he set out to create a new relationship; but in this Catherine had anticipated him: she had sensed a diminishing in his attentions and while he was away on a journey to central Russia had taken another lover, one Peter Zavadowski, an army officer on her secretariat – dark, good-looking and respectable, who conceived a passionate love for her and a strong jealousy of Potemkin. On his return the latter tried to make the Empress get rid of her new love but she was not to be parted from him, so that for a time they coexisted in an uneasy *ménage-à-trois*.

In the end Zavadowski was pensioned off, but Potemkin had come to realise that the new set-up at which he was aiming would have to include a third party to contain Catherine's sexual needs which were imperative; her tremendous energy and drive depended on them being satisfied. When she declared: 'If in my youth I had been allotted a husband I could love I would have remained eternally loyal to him', it is hard to believe. Certainly he would have had to have great stamina. Potemkin contrived to see to it that her lovers were of his choosing, but he was not always successful in this.

Whether or not Catherine and Potemkin were married, neither made any pretence at marital fidelity. Potemkin was to spend some time in the south of the country, acting as viceroy and commander-in-chief in the war against the Turks, where he lived in oriental splendour with a well-filled harem. His behaviour there was, as always, unpredictable – sometimes dynamic, sometimes inert. Visiting foreign potentates were seldom given much respect; they might be ushered into his presence where they would find him sprawling on a divan half-dressed, his 'naked frailties unhidden',[5] and his attitude offhand. But in spite of all hostility he maintained his authority, and he did have success in his war with the Turks, notably in the absorption of the Crimea in 1783 and the establishment of a Russian fleet in the Black Sea.

At the same time in St Petersburg there was no let-up in Catherine's prurience as youthful favourites came and went. A system had been evolved by which before being admitted to favour these were vetted – first a medical examination to see they were free of venereal disease and then a test of virility, carried out usually by the Empress's closest female confidante, Countess Bruce, a lady of loose principles. One of these candidates, Nicolai Korsakov, seemed to have had all the qualities including a pleasant singing voice to which Catherine loved to listen in spite of being unmusical; but he could not recover from his introduction with Countess Bruce, and they became lovers, but were caught by the Empress in flagrante delicto and were banished from court.

Korsakov was succeeded by Alexander Lanskoi, 30 years younger than Catherine and one of her most dearly loved favourites. Charming, handsome, self-effacing and with no political inclinations, he appealed

---

[5] *Macbeth*, Act II, scene 1.

not only to Catherine's lust but also to her maternal instincts. She loved to teach and he was ready to learn. Their partnership might have lasted permanently but after four years he died, allegedly of diphtheria but, according to some, from taking too many aphrodisiacs to keep pace with Catherine (then aged 55). His death caused Catherine extravagant grief: 'I have never been so unhappy as now', she exclaimed, 'that my best and kindest friend has abandoned me.' She was unable to take another lover for seven months.

During these vagaries Catherine's relationship with Potemkin remained intact. She was deeply appreciative of what he had achieved and every Russian honour – prince, field marshal, admiral – was piled on him; she was also able to obtain for him the highest honours from abroad, notably from a reluctant Maria Theresa that of Prince of the Holy Roman Empire which carried with it the title of His Serene Highness, so that he became known thereafter as 'Serenissimus'.

To mark the extension of Russian frontiers in the south, Catherine agreed that in 1787 she should make a stately visit to the newly incorporated lands. This was a formidable undertaking, involving thousands of miles of travel over rough, frozen roads in coaches mounted on sleighs. The hardship and boredom of this might have been intolerable, but Potemkin saw to it that everything possible was done to make the journey as comfortable and splendid as possible. Entertainments of all sorts were laid on along the route – dancing, music, gala dinners, military displays and fireworks. Triumphal arches, garlands and newly planted gardens greeted the Empress everywhere as also did cheering crowds of peasants, specially dressed up for the occasion, scattering flowers in her way. Never has there been such a royal progress. But it ended in anti-climax. One of the objects of the exercise had been to impress and intimidate foreign countries, especially the Turks; but soon after it ended the Turks declared war, catching the Russian army off-guard, as also did the Swedes who were able to bring their cannon within range of St Petersburg. And the expense of the operation had been prodigious, only made possible by an almost unlimited supply of slave (or serf) labour.

In the following year the French Revolution broke out and with it came a profound change of heart in Catherine. In the early years of her reign, as has been seen, she liked to present a liberal image, projecting the works of such writers as Voltaire and Montesquieu, and encouraging advanced ideas in education. But with the storming of the Bastille and the execution of King Louis XVI and Queen Marie Antoinette, her attitude changed abruptly. Liberal ideas became taboo and she became rigorously repressive. Freedom of speech was banned and people with advanced views, once tolerated as harmless intellectuals, were then treated as dangerous revolutionaries. French ways and French literature, even Voltaire, were pushed out of sight.

At the age of 60 and heavily overweight, Catherine was still active and retained much of her dignity and charm, but there were signs of decline. A foreign diplomat wrote of her at the time: 'Her worst enemies are flattery and her own passions. She never turns a deaf ear to the first, be it ever so gross, and her inclination for gratifying the latter appears to grow upon her with age.' In 1789, she took a new lover, Plato Zoubov, some 40 years younger, handsome and potent, but a malign influence. Potemkin tried to displace him but to no avail; his hold over Catherine was absolute. The history of Eastern Europe might have been different but for the priapic powers of this youth in his twenties.

Catherine did not, as might have been expected, send an army to join forces with Austria and Prussia in an invasion of revolutionary France. She was content that they should become occupied there while she directed her attention to neighbouring Poland which, she became convinced, was 'a nest of Jacobins'.[6] In 1791 there had been an uprising which brought in a new and more viable constitution, and which was accepted by King Stanislaus, but this did not suit the Empress who stirred up trouble in the country, and malcontents were induced to appeal for Russian intervention which was readily forthcoming. This led to the second partition of Poland by which Russia and Prussia annexed lands to which they had no justifiable claims. For the time being Stanislaus remained King, a compliant and humiliated figure; but in 1794 after another rebellion he was dethroned and there was yet another partition, as a result of which Poland was reduced to one-third of the size she had once been.

Potemkin died in 1791. His partnership with Catherine over 17 years had been unique, a blending of two larger-than-life personalities. It had not always run smoothly and at the end had come under particular strain: Potemkin had heartily detested Zoubov and

[6] Extreme French revolutionaries.

disapproved of the carving-up of Poland, which he regarded as an essential buffer between Russia and the Western powers; while Catherine, although certainly no prude, could not but disapprove of the flagrancy of Potemkin's personal life and his relations with three beautiful nieces. Her own personal life was far from chaste but she always covered it with a veil of decorum: no allusions to it were made and risqué stories and bawdy behaviour were not tolerated at court. Nevertheless, on Potemkin's death she was grief-stricken and poured out praise for 'the greatness of his mind and the soul which set him apart from the rest of humanity'.

Catherine outlived Potemkin by five years. During that time she remained dominated by Zoubov, a mean, avaricious character out only for his own ends, particularly in Poland where he enriched himself inordinately. Catherine died suddenly from apoplexy in 1796. Her reign of 34 years had seen Russia become larger and more powerful and more civilised, but this had been achieved on the basis of millions of serfs whose numbers had increased rather than diminished while she was Empress. She bequeathed to her successors the day of reckoning.

10

JOSEPHINE EMPRESS OF FRANCE (1763–1814)

The Empress Josephine was the wife of one French emperor (Napoleon I) and the grandmother of another (Napoleon III). For 13 years she was married to the most powerful man in Europe. By him she had no children, but by her former husband her descendants were to occupy the thrones of Norway, Sweden, Belgium, Denmark and Greece. She came from a minor aristocratic family living in the French colony of Martinique, and was not a classical beauty nor particularly clever, but she had grace and charm which few could resist and warmth and generosity which made her greatly loved. Her turbulent and heart-rending life story led to her becoming a legendary figure.

Marie-Joseph-Rose Tascher was born on 23 June 1763 on a sugar plantation in Martinique. During her childhood she was known by her pet name of Yeyette. Her father, Joseph-Gaspard Tascher (known hereafter as Joseph) had some ability as a military commander but little as the manager of a sugar plantation. Naturally lethargic, he was further weakened by bouts of tropical fever which left him bereft of the energy necessary to run his business. He was of minor nobility and had once served as a page at Versailles to the Dauphine, Marie-Joseph de Saxe. In his youth he had been pushed into a loveless marriage with Rose-Claire des Vergers de Sanois, of similar nobility but more wealthy. Soon afterwards he moved onto the de Sanois plantation at Trois-Ilets, and it was there that Yeyette was born. Two more daughters followed but not the longed-for son. The family atmosphere was discordant, Joseph spending too little time on the plantation and too much in Port Royal, the main city of Martinique, in search of the fleshpots. He was not well thought of on the island.

The trade of Martinique had been badly affected by the English blockade during the Seven Years War, and then in 1766 came a great natural disaster in the shape of the mightiest hurricane in living memory. Yeyette was three at the time and she and her family had to dash for safety into the sugar refinery, one of the few buildings capable of standing up to the hurricane's force; and there they and many others, including slaves, huddled for hours until it subsided. When they emerged there was a scene of desolation: the family house, all other buildings and all the shacks of the slaves had been flattened and the crops of sugar cane were devastated. For several years the family of Joseph and Rose-Claire had to make do on the first floor of the sugar mill amid cranking machinery and the odour of crushed cane.

In spite of hardships and tensions Yeyette's childhood was not altogether unhappy. Martinique was a beautiful island with its profusion of wild flowers and animal life which she loved. She loved the people too, and not least the slaves with whom she had an affectionate relationship. Nevertheless she was obsessed with a dream of one day visiting France. She was fascinated by the stories told by her father of the delights of Paris and Versailles and longed to be among them. But for the time being the dream seemed unattainable. Shortage of money and the dangers of the Atlantic crossing during the Seven Years War were the main reasons, and it might have been that she would have married a fellow Creole[1] and settled down to a pastoral uncomplicated life on one of the Caribbean islands. That she did not do so and became instead Empress of France was due in the main to her aunt, Marie Euphémie-Désirée (known generally as Edmée).

Aunt Edmée was a lady of strong character and remorseless ambition. In Martinique she had become the mistress of the Governor, François Marquis de Beauharnais. She had also acquired a husband, Alexis Renaudin, for whom she had no love and from whom she was soon separated. At the time of Yeyette's birth Edmée was living in France in a *ménage-à-trois* with the Marquis and his wife the Marquise. Four years later, on the death of the latter, Edmée and the Marquis might have married but this was not possible as Edmée could not be divorced from Renaudin. However, she took charge not only of the Marquis's household but also of his children, with one of whom she had a special relationship. Alexandre, her godson, had been born in Martinique just before his parents returned

---

[1] A native-born person of European origin.

to France, and because of the dangers of a transatlantic crossing in wartime he had been left behind in the care of the Tascher family with whom he had remained until he was five when it was considered safe for him to travel to France.

On the death of his mother two years later it was found that she had left most of her estate to him with the stipulation that he should not have access to it until he married. There was therefore a strong incentive for him to marry early, and Edmée was determined that it should be to one of the daughters of her brother, Joseph Tascher. In this she was, no doubt, looking to the future, reckoning that the Marquis de Beauharnais was much older than her and when he died his pension would die with him and she would be left out in the cold, and so her future welfare might depend on a godson married to a niece. The Marquis and Alexandre were agreeable to this idea, and their preference was for one of the younger daughters as the age gap between them and Alexandre would be greater so they might be more amenable, and there would be time to give them a smattering of Parisian polish; but owing to the death of one and the illness of the other this proved impossible, so it had to be Yeyette, still three years Alexandre's junior.

The problem then arose as to the cost of the journey which was beyond the means of Joseph, but Edmée undertook to pay for part of it so that in 1779 Yeyette (aged 16) accompanied by her father, her Aunt Rosette and her maid Euphémie set out on a voyage that was to be of exceptional rigour and danger; rigorous because they were all confined in a tiny cabin with minimal facilities and existing on foul food and water, and dangerous because France was again at war with England, giving support to the American colonists, and their ship might be intercepted.

They were, however, to arrive safely in Brest, but owing to a failure in communications there was no one there to meet them, and for two weeks they were stranded, unattended, and with Joseph in serious ill-health. When Alexandre did arrive with Edmée he busied himself at once with providing for the needs of the travellers and rented a cabriolet to take them to Paris. But he could not but be dismayed by Yeyette. She had warmth and a compelling personality, but her manners and general demeanour were, to say the least, unsophisticated, which was not what he had become accustomed to. He had been educated for some years in a ducal household, and at the age of 19 was a smart, aspiring officer in an eminent regiment, good-looking, full-blooded and with more than a touch of arrogance. His ambitions were limitless and he expected a wife who would keep pace with him. A callow girl from the colonies, gauche and with little education, was not to his taste.

He must have had thoughts of calling the marriage off, but under pressure from Edmée and his father he decided to go through with it, thinking Yeyette might be moulded into something presentable. He was also in a hurry to be married so that he could lay his hands on his inheritance. Guardedly he wrote to his father: 'Mlle Tascher will perhaps appear to you less pretty than you had expected but I think I may assure you that the frankness and sweetness of her nature will surpass what you have been told.' The situation was not made easier in that at the time he was deeply enamoured of a married lady eleven years his senior, beautiful, sensuous and worldly, who had just borne him a son. Her name was Laure de Girardin.

If Alexandre's impressions of Yeyette were doubtful, hers of him were enthusiastic: the handsome young officer, so polished and self-assured, was all she had hoped for; disillusion was not to set in for some time. What her first impressions were of Paris, the city of her dreams, cannot be known, but it can hardly have delighted her. The house occupied by Edmée and the Marquis in the rue Thévenot was damp and depressing and in none too salubrious a district: open drains ran in the street so that pedestrians were liable to be splashed by mud and other filth, and there was a powerful stench made worse by a local tannery.

Alexandre and Yeyette were married in December of 1779, from which time she was to be known as Marie-Rose (until she became Josephine). It was not likely that life in the house in the rue Thévenot would be agreeable to her. In the first place it was overcrowded, housing not only Edmée and the Marquis but also, for the time being, Joseph and Aunt Rosette. It should also have housed Alexandre, but he was hardly ever there. It soon became apparent that the marriage was not running smoothly. Alexandre had been accustomed to a loose and free-ranging lifestyle which he was not prepared to give up – rather, with the access to funds following his marriage, he expanded it. It was necessary for him to spend six months of the year with his regiment, and of the other six precious little of them found him at home. There were interludes of domesticity and he was delighted when in 1781 Marie-Rose gave birth to a son whom he named Eugène-Rose,[2] but for the most part he occupied himself in what Marie-Rose later described as 'a life of dissipation'. And she did not take kindly to this. She was not prepared to be a submissive, accommodating wife; rather, she became resentful and suspicious.

Nor was she prepared to be educated. Alexandre set great store by this and appointed a tutor for her, but she had no aptitude for book learning and resisted it. Relations became increasingly strained. Alexandre was dismayed that Marie-Rose remained as graceless and ignorant as ever, hardly able to write him a literate letter, while she became sullen and jealous, having at some stage found out about him and Laure. Edmée did her best to keep them together and in 1782 she persuaded Alexandre to go on a classical tour of Italy so that he could get away and reflect calmly; and this he did without Marie-Rose. On his return he seemed to be in a more reasonable frame of mind and seemed well pleased to hear that Marie-Rose was again pregnant, but this was deceptive; for he had in mind a far-reaching plan.

He had always thirsted for military glory and in 1783 this was to be most readily gained in America, where France was giving support to the colonists rebelling against England. His efforts to reach America directly, however, were unavailing; it was apparently necessary for him to go first to Martinique, and this he was secretly planning to do. In 1783 he crept out of the house at the dead of night and set off for Brest where he would take ship. From there he wrote Marie-Rose long, rambling letters, mostly of self-pity and complaints, but also containing extravagant and insincere words of love. These did not deceive her: before he left she learned that he was being accompanied to Martinique by Laure de Girardin, who had business to attend to there. For Marie-Rose this was intolerable, and while he was away she maintained a frigid silence, leaving all his letters unanswered.

When Alexandre reached Martinique he found that the war in America was nearly over and peace terms were being negotiated. So he spent some time visiting the haunts of his childhood and the Tascher family who had cared for him. But he then embarked on a vicious campaign to blacken the character of Marie-Rose.

---

[2] Later to be Viceroy of Italy, and three of whose children were to occupy royal thrones (Sweden, Portugal and Brazil).

Urged on by the malignant Laure de Girardin and maddened by Marie-Rose's epistolary silence – he had to learn all news from home including the birth of his daughter from letters to the Tascher family – he set about digging up every scandal he could find about Marie-Rose's past life in Martinique. No holds were barred, even slaves were bribed to make up stories. He also became obsessed with the idea that the daughter to whom Marie-Rose had just given birth, Hortense,[3] had to be illegitimate because her pregnancy had not lasted a full nine months since his return from Italy. At the same time he wrote letters of hysterical abuse to Marie-Rose, calling her 'the vilest of creatures' and 'beneath all the sluts in the world'. Finally he ordered her to go into a convent. Such outrageous behaviour appalled the people of Martinique, especially the Tascher family. Before he left, Joseph shouted at him angrily: 'So this is the outcome of your illustrious military campaign against the enemy! You have done nothing but declare war on your wife's reputation and dishonour us all!'

When Alexandre returned to France he gave his family a wide berth, perhaps feeling embarrassed about his behaviour in Martinique. But he did not relent about evicting Marie-Rose, who had to put Hortense into the care of a wet nurse while she with Eugène went into the convent of Penthémont. Life in this convent was not unduly austere; it was not so much a convent as a retreat for well-to-do ladies like Marie-Rose who found themselves in distressed circumstances. Comfortable, indeed luxurious, apartments were available; one could come and go as one pleased and religious obligations were minimal. Marie-Rose's residence in Penthémont was to be something of an eye-opener, as it brought her into close contact with high-born, worldly ladies who had a profound influence on her. She adapted to their manners and attitudes, coming to the realisation that marital fidelity was not to be expected, that most husbands behaved badly, and that wives should avail themselves of such opportunities as came their way.

While she was in the convent Edmée and the Marquis had been forced because of financial straits to give up their house in Paris and go into lodgings in Fontainebleau where Marie-Rose joined them, and it was noticeable how much her way of life by then

---

[3] Hortense-Eugénie, destined to become Queen of Holland and mother of the future Emperor Napoleon III.

had changed. When in the autumn King Louis XVI came to hunt in Fontainebleau many noblemen came too, and some of these Marie-Rose entertained intimately.

By then with help from Edmée, she had managed to extract from Alexandre a legal deed of separation with provisions for finance and care of the children. This had become urgently necessary after Alexandre had arrived at the convent one day while Marie-Rose was out, and abducted Eugène. Marie-Rose had then invoked the law, and an official laid it down that Eugène should be returned to his mother, but that after the age of five he should be in the care of his father. Hortense should for the time being remain in the care of her mother.

In 1788 Marie-Rose with Hortense went on a visit to Martinique. It is not clear why she went, or whether she intended it to be a short visit or a permanent one. In the event this was decided for her. It was nine years since she had left the island and her return was not altogether a happy one. Her family, still living in the sugar mill, was in a parlous state. Her father Joseph was at death's door, her sister Manette was seriously ill, and her Aunt Rosette was as embittered as ever. Only her mother, Rose-Claire, seemed to be surviving steadfastly, remarkable in one who had had so much to put up with. However, they welcomed her warmly and urged her to stay, but Marie-Rose had greatly changed since she left. She was no longer a callow young Creole, she was a woman of the world, liberated, about whom there hung a whiff of scandal, and old friends and relations held back from her.

Soon after her arrival in August 1788 alarming news started coming in from France. In desperation at the state of his finances King Louis XVI had summoned a parliament (States-General), the first for 175 years, and the spirit of revolution was intensifying, culminating in the storming of the Bastille on 14 July 1789. This spirit, blazoning liberty and equality, was soon to reach Martinique where the situation could become exceedingly dangerous: of the population four out of five were slaves and of the rest there were ex-slaves, mulattos and poor whites only too ready to respond to revolutionary clamour. Marie-Rose soon decided that she had to go back to France, but this was not easily done. With help from the Governor she was able to board a ship, but under a hail of bullets and without her luggage, so her voyage to France was again one of exceptional discomfort and hardship.

Back in France Marie-Rose found that Alexandre had embarked on a political career. He had been elected to the States-General and had made his name by long, eloquent speeches extolling liberty and equality; he had attached himself to the party of the far left that came to be known as the Jacobins. He was to go far. In 1791, when the States-General had become the National Assembly, he was appointed President for a term of two weeks, crucial ones as they proved to be, as they coincided with King Louis's ill-fated attempt to flee the country,[4] and briefly he was one of France's rulers. But disaster lay in store for him.

There was to be no reconciliation between Marie-Rose and Alexandre, although their relationship became more accommodating. They had a mutual interest in the welfare of their children, Alexandre now accepting the legitimacy of Hortense, but in 1791 he intervened unfortunately when he prevented Marie-Rose from sending them to safety out of the country, as this would jeopardise his reputation as a genuine revolutionary.

Marie-Rose soon realised how much France had been transformed while she had been away, and she was quick to adapt to the new spirit that was abroad, flaunting revolutionary colours and mouthing revolutionary slogans. No longer was she the Vicomtesse de Beauharnais, but Citoyenne Beauharnais, and it was necessary for her children to be attached to some trade – Eugène to a cabinet maker and Hortense to a seamstress. Being of aristocratic origins, she herself was liable to come under suspicion from the fanatics running the country. Her best hope was to lie low and keep out of the limelight, but this she did not do.

When her sister-in-law, Marie-Francoise do Beauharnais (wife of Alexandre's elder brother Francois, a staunch conservative who had emigrated) was in danger, she pleaded on her behalf; and then, more significantly, she pleaded the cause of her husband. For in the rapidly changing political scene in Paris Alexandre had had to relinquish his seat in the Convention (as the National Assembly had become), and had taken a senior military command, first as Chief of Staff to the Army of the Rhine and then as its commander-in-chief. But this was beyond his capability. For a time all was well: because of his extravagantly expressed political views he was held in high esteem by his political bosses, but his position was

---

[4] Known as the 'Flight to Varennes'. See the chapter on Marie Antoinette.

precarious; should he encounter defeat or even setback there were those who would be at his throat, denouncing him as a half-hearted ex-aristocrat, dragging his heels and failing in his duty. And this is what happened.

At the end of 1792 the Revolution which had begun with noble ideals descended into fanaticism and butchery. In September mob rule ran wild: prisons were ransacked and 1,300 prisoners massacred in cold blood, as were 117 priests who refused to take an oath of loyalty to the new constitution. The moderate Girondin party was ousted and replaced by the Jacobins who set up a Reign of Terror in which anyone upon whom the least suspicion fell was imprisoned, given a mock trial and then sent off to the guillotine. Everyone sought to outdo everyone else in revolutionary zeal, and were ready to hound others to death to save their own skins.

In this maelstrom it was unlikely that Alexandre would survive. In spite of loud protestations of his republican beliefs and exemplary egalitarian behaviour he was arrested in March of 1794, charged with dereliction of duty and hauled off to one of Paris's 40 prisons, an ex-Carmelite monastery known as the Carmes. In spite of his past maltreatment of her, Marie-Rose lost no time in interceding for him, approaching those in authority with whom she thought she had some influence. But in vain. At that time, to show mercy was a sign of weakness, even treachery. And what she did drew attention to herself.

Earlier on she had withdrawn from Paris to the village of Croissy, some 10 miles outside, where revolutionary ardour was less intense, but this did not save her; there too there were spies and informers who reported that her house was 'a gathering place for suspected persons'. She might be the estranged wife of Alexandre, but that was enough. On 19 April (Easter Day by the old calendar) two deputies arrived in Croissy and searched her house. They found nothing incriminating but still took her back to Paris in custody. There she was put into the same prison as Alexandre but isolated from him, although they had one fraught meeting in the garden.

There then began for her three and a half months of hell on earth. Crammed into a small compartment with a dozen others, the walls bespattered with blood, everywhere the stench of ordure and unwashed bodies, and tormented with vermin, somehow she survived through the long, hot summer. Much the worst of her ordeal was seeing fellow prisoners being taken away to the guillotine every day in increasing numbers, the iniquitous Public Prosecutor, Fouquier-Tinville, declaring gleefully: 'Things are going well. Heads are falling like tiles off a roof.' Any day it might be her turn. Her only consolation was the visits of her children, Eugène aged 12 and Hortense aged eleven. With help from their governess they contrived to bring her hope and made impassioned appeals to those in authority, but no one dared to come to her rescue.

After three months Alexandre was taken off to execution. He met his end manfully, proclaiming that liberty and equality were 'engrained in his heart' and praying for forgiveness of those who had falsely denounced him. In times of revolution, he said, there were bound to be suspicions and if he was the victim of these, so be it. For his children he expressed 'tender affection'; for Marie-Rose 'brotherly love'.

In the normal course of events Marie-Rose would have followed him to the guillotine soon afterwards, but by a miracle she was spared. A prison doctor affirmed that she was so ill that she could not long survive, and there was no need for her to be executed. Then suddenly in July 1794 the whole scene changed with the downfall of the murderous tyrant Maximilien Robespierre, whose solution to every problem was more and more executions. Soon afterwards one of Marie-Rose's patrons in high places, Jean Tallien, plucked up the courage to order her release, and on 6 August she was once again free.

Free though she might be, her situation was parlous. She at first had no home of her own, precious little money and two children to support. Some finance did come through from her mother in Martinique and some from Aunt Edmée who with the Marquis (now in his eighties) had managed to survive the Revolution in Fontainebleau. But it was woefully inadequate, and it was necessary for her to live by her wits, which she did with some aplomb. Wheeling and dealing in goods and valuables – paper money having become almost valueless – and making free with her favours she somehow got by. She was still, at 32, an attractive woman with grace and charm, a shapely figure, and a sweet and seductive voice. She also had great perspicacity in her choice of contacts, particularly bankers and rich men with influence.

After the agony and tenseness of the Reign of Terror, Parisian society broke out into a riot of gaiety and uninhibited behaviour, and it was not long before Marie-Rose was taking part in it. She had taken a house in fashionable rue Chantereine with a domestic staff, had put her children into private schools and even acquired a carriage and horses. Mainly responsible for this transformation was Paul Barras, a man of wealth and power and few scruples. His achievements were significant: he had had a leading role in the downfall of Robespierre and then later in the rise of Napoleon; for a time he was the most powerful man in the country, and somehow he had kept his head on his shoulders. For about a year Marie-Rose was his mistress and hostess.

Napoleon Buonaparte arrived in Paris in the spring of 1795. He had just won distinction for himself at Toulon where, mainly owing to his efforts, the city had been recaptured from English-backed rebels. At 26 he was already a Brigadier-General and was acclaimed a hero, but he did not cut an impressive figure – he was shabbily dressed, shy and undersized. But Barras had a high opinion of him and when rebellion broke out in Paris put him in charge of subduing it, which he did ruthlessly by opening fire with grapeshot on an unarmed mob, killing some 200 people. As a result he became Commander of the Army of the Interior and one of France's leading generals.

It is not certain how he first met Marie-Rose, but it is likely to have been at a reception of Barras. At the time he affected to despise Parisian society, but secretly he admired it, and was bent on finding an elderly rich widow who would finance his military career, which was all-important to him. At first sight Marie-Rose seemed to be suitable, but on making enquiries he found that she was not wealthy and was a lady with a past. However, he found himself deeply, even passionately, in love with her, and her lack of money was overlooked as was a tarnished reputation. He became determined to marry her.

At first Marie-Rose was overwhelmed by his attentions. She was not in love with 'the Little General' as she called him, but she could not but be fascinated by his magnetism and the intensity of his devotion; and he was an up and coming young man who could give her and her children security. So in February 1796 she accepted him and they were married a month later – a bleak affair in a registry office with no relatives present. Napoleon's family was shocked that he should be marrying a Creole widow, six years older than himself, with little money and a dubious reputation, while Eugène and Hortense did not like the idea of Napoleon as a stepfather. There was time for a honeymoon of no more than two days before Napoleon had to rush off to take command of France's army in Italy. At his insistence Marie-Rose from then on became known as Josephine, while he changed the spelling of his name from Buonoparte to Bonaparte.

Napoleon would have liked Josephine to go with him to Italy, but this was forbidden by the Directory as it was feared she would distract him from his military responsibilities. And these were formidable. The condition of the French army of Italy was at a low ebb – its men were ill-fed, ill-disciplined, unpaid and mutinous. It was Napoleon's achievement – some say his greatest – that he turned this rabble into a victorious army, crossing the Alps and winning battle after battle against the Austrians and Sardinians. In view of such dramatic success the Directory decided that it could no longer withhold permission for Josephine to join her husband; but this she was unwilling to do. She had not yet learned to love 'the Little General', and was not attracted by the idea of joining his campaign trail; she preferred the social life of Paris in which she was such a bright light. And there was something else keeping her there: for perhaps the first time in her life, she had fallen deeply in love.

Only a few weeks after Napoleon's departure there arrived in Paris a lieutenant, nine years younger than she, Hippolyte Charles – suave, articulate, humorous and adept in the ways of love, all the things Napoleon was not, and she found him irresistible. She had had many lovers before but nearly all of them had been with an eye to business, so that it seemed she was incapable of disinterested love. But with Hippolyte, impecunious and of no great rank, she was helpless. However, in view of her husband's blaze of glory and the pressure put on her by the passionate love letters he had been writing, she felt she had to join him. Her sorrow was relieved when it was found that Hippolyte could accompany her in order to take up an army appointment. There also went with her two future marshals of France, Junot and Murat, a bevy of domestic servants and a bodyguard; in addition there was a snarling snappy lapdog, Fortuné, from whom she seemed to be inseparable.[5]

The journey over the Alps to Milan took two weeks; there a

---

[5] On their wedding night Napoleon had objected to his presence in the marital bed, but he was overruled and bitten in the leg.

sumptuous palace was awaiting her, but no husband, who was embroiled in military campaigning. He arrived three days later, however, for an emotional reunion. His love-making had always been rough and ready, both in private and public, with people in the same room hardly knowing which way to look – one writing of his 'conjugal liberties which embarrassed us all'.

Josephine was to be in Italy for nearly 18 months, for much of the time basking in the reflected glory of her husband, feted wherever she went and lavished with gifts and praise. But it was not a happy time for her. She was plagued by ill-health, particularly migraines, constantly anxious about Napoleon's frequent absences, and longing for Hippolyte now that he was separated from her. She wrote to Aunt Edmée at the time: 'I should prefer to be a simple nobody in France. I do not enjoy the honours of this country. I get very bored.' There were times too when she was in danger, in sight of Austrian troops and under fire from them, but Napoleon always saw her through to safety.

One of her more unpleasant experiences in Italy was when Napoleon took the large villa of Mombella, to which he invited all members of his family, and she was expected to be the gracious hostess. This was a severe strain as they were all strongly hostile, notably his mother, Letizia Bonaparte, a matriarchal figure in her late forties who had borne 12 children and had inflexible views on what was proper. Cold, upright and icily correct, she had no sympathy with a flashy Parisian socialite who had seduced her son into an unworthy and as yet childless marriage. And there was her daughter Pauline, the beauty of the family, but spiteful and vulgar, and bitterly jealous of Josephine. Most dangerous of all was Napoleon's elder brother Joseph, dark and vindictive and always out to make trouble. In the midst of all this hostility Josephine survived coolly and courteously, but it was a great relief when Napoleon was recalled to Paris, and she followed after him.

Napoleon arrived in Paris to a triumphant welcome. The French dearly love a military hero, and already there were those who were looking to him as the saviour of France. After nine years of revolution the condition of the country was as bad as ever with food shortages, precarious law and order, wrangling ineffective politicians and – still in action – the guillotine. People were longing for a strong leader who would restore stability and order, and Napoleon after his achievements in Italy seemed to be the man to do this. He was not yet ready, however, for political power; he was looking for further victories on the battlefield. He was offered the command of an invasion of England, but this he turned down as being impractical at present. He was much more interested in striking at England's trade with India and the East. The idea of an invasion of Egypt and then an advance eastwards he found very appealing, and in 1798 he was authorised to carry this out.

Josephine arrived back in Paris later than expected so that a grand ball in honour of her and Napoleon had to be postponed twice. Her condition at the time was distraught. She was exhausted after a long and hazardous journey and was still harassed by ill health; she was also deeply worried that Napoleon had been hearing about her liaison with Hippolyte Charles. In the following months her behaviour was to be highly indiscreet. It seemed that she was bent on a divorce from Napoleon and marriage to Hippolyte who, she was convinced, was the only person who could bring her happiness. She was tired of public occasions, of her husband's emotional demands and the backbiting of her in-laws. To finance her divorce and remarriage she became involved with a none-too-reputable firm of army provisioners by the name of Bodin. She also arranged for Hippolyte to join the firm and for him to live for the time being on their premises which she visited regularly; all of which was noticed by Joseph Bonaparte's spies and reported back to his brother, who had a confrontation with her about what he had heard. In desperation she denied everything and Napoleon, still in love and immersed in his Egyptian expedition, wanted to believe her; but he insisted that she should accompany him to Egypt, and to this she had to agree as she was not yet ready for a break. They set out in May of 1798, but when they reached Toulon Napoleon changed his mind and said she was to stay in France for a few weeks until the situation in Egypt had been clarified.

Soon after landing he defeated the Turks (then the nominal rulers of Egypt) at the so-called Battle of the Pyramids, but then came disaster when his invasion fleet was destroyed by Nelson at the Battle of the Nile. His army thus became stranded. At first, however, he did not despair and decided to proceed with his advance to the East. In this his army suffered terribly from scorching heat and tropical disease, and many died. Then he was unable to capture the key port of Acre, heroically defended by an English force under Admiral Sir Sidney Smith.

While Napoleon was away Josephine had resorted to the spa of

Plombières in southern France where she was taking the waters, and where she had a serious accident when the balcony on which she was standing collapsed under her. She was badly hurt and for a time it was feared that she might not be able to walk again. She was treated with great care by the local doctors who prescribed among other things compresses of boiled potatoes and a covering of the afflicted parts with the skin of a freshly slaughtered sheep. Whether or not it was because of these medicaments, she was able to walk again after a few weeks and return to Paris.

Meanwhile in Egypt, Napoleon had at last become convinced by two of his senior generals of Josephine's infidelity and her questionable dealings with Bodin. This left him stunned. 'I have nothing to live for', he declared. 'I have exhausted everything.' His reaction later was to console himself with local talent, and he ordered some Egyptian beauties to be brought to him, but these he found too graceless and obese and sent them away. He did, however, have a serious love affair with the wife of a French officer, who had smuggled herself into Egypt disguised as an ordinary soldier. Pauline Bellisle Fourès (known as Bellilotte) was ten years younger than he and very attractive. He fell in love with her at first sight and lost no time in despatching her husband on a special mission to France.[6] Under her spell he seems to have been overcome by exotic dreams in which he imagined himself an oriental despot living a rich, overflowing, uninhibited life. He was later to write: 'The time I spent in Egypt was the most beautiful of my life.'

He was soon to be brought down to earth. When his army was held up in front of Acre he decided that his oriental expedition was a write-off. At the same time came alarming news from Paris: the Directory was tottering, conditions were chaotic and rebellion was in the air. Brooding on this he came to the decision that the time had come for him to strike: he would gamble all on a return to Paris and put his fortune to the test. And so, leaving his army to its fate and somehow avoiding the English blockade he made his way to France (without Bellilotte) and set out for Paris.

There, things had been going from bad to worse for Josephine. Recklessly, with money she did not have, she bought a country

---

[6] He was intercepted by an English ship whose captain was aware of gossip from Egypt and with wry humour sent him back there when Bellilotte sued for divorce.

estate at Malmaison. Bodin had been convicted of fraud, and Hippolyte was showing signs of wanting to disentangle himself from her. When she heard that her husband was returning her immediate thought was that she must get to him before he reached Paris, where poison would be poured into his ears by the Bonaparte clan. She therefore set out for the south but missed him as he came by an unexpected route, and by the time she got back to Paris he had installed himself in their house in the rue Chantereine (since renamed rue de la Victoire), and was bent on a divorce and refusing to have anything to do with her. From this attitude he was eventually persuaded to relent by the pleas of Josephine's children. He had formed a strong attachment to Eugène, who had been his aide-de-camp in Egypt and had acquitted himself bravely and loyally; and to Hortense too he was devoted. He had come to look on both of them as adopted children. He was particularly impressed when Eugène told him that if he divorced his mother he would go with her even, if necessary, to Martinique. And so there was a reconciliation. Bellilotte was allowed to lapse and Hippolyte was relinquished.

Though reconciled, their relationship was not to be the same again. Napoleon was no longer in emotional thrall to her. His attitude was different: affectionate rather than passionate, at times kindly and good-humoured, at others scornful and mocking, still physically attracted but often blatantly unfaithful. He was capable of calculated cruelty and seemed to enjoy tormenting her, as when he boasted of his mistresses, and when she was in a fragile and nervous state forcing her to undertake duties he knew she dreaded. But for the time being they both needed each other: Josephine, bereft of her former lovers – Barras and Hippolyte, among others – was dependent on Napoleon, while he needed her to grace his court and give it class. As the former Vicomtesse de Beauharnais she brought an elegance and style which it could not have had from Nabuleone Buonaparte from Ajaccio. They were to stay together for another nine years, but harmony was fragile.

By the coup d'état of 12 December 1799 the Directory of five was overthrown and replaced by a Consulate of three, of which Napoleon was the first and dominating member. As if to emphasise this, he and Josephine moved into the royal palace of the Tuileries, still bearing scars from its invasion by a Paris mob in search of Louis XVI and Marie Antoinette. Work was put in hand to remove blood stains and bullet holes, although there were those who thought they should have been left as a memorial.

Paris at that time was gradually reverting to pre-revolutionary ways. Tricolour cockades were no longer de rigueur, people were daring to wear smart clothes and jewellery and were addressing each other as 'monsieur' and 'madame' rather than 'citizen' and 'citizeness'. In this the court in the Tuileries led the way. It was still necessary for it to have a revolutionary flavour, but it had much in common with the *ancien régime* – formal, sumptuous and well ordered. Napoleon had inherited from his mother a degree of prudishness and would not allow any taint of scandal. Ladies with dubious pasts were excluded and he particularly concerned himself with the seemliness of ladies' dresses. Josephine, although her own past was far from chaste, fell into line and set the tone. At 36 she was still lovely to look at, and was a gracious hostess and generally better liked than her husband. But she did have her critics, one remarking that she had 'a head without a brain' and another that 'she occupied her day between futile and gallant conversation and tears which the harshness of Bonaparte drew from her'.

It was no part of the new relationship between Napoleon and Josephine that the former should be a faithful husband. He made no secret of his numerous mistresses, gloating over them and regaling Josephine with erotic details about them. At first this caused her passionate jealousy so that she became almost hysterical, but when she tackled him on the subject he was unrepentant, even aggressive. 'I am not like other men', he told her. 'Laws that govern conventional behaviour do not apply to me'. He seemed genuinely puzzled by her jealousy. Could she not see that his infidelities were passing whims and had nothing to do with true love? But she was not assuaged and continued to work herself into rages about them. This came to a climax when she caught him in flagrante delicto with one of his mistresses. Great as her anger was, it was as nothing compared to his. He stormed at her that he wanted no more of her jealousy and spying on him, that their marriage was at an end and he would marry someone younger and more beautiful who would bear him children. In time he cooled down and relented, partly owing to the intervention of Eugène, but Napoleon made one condition that he would require a divorce in time, and Josephine would be obliged to agree to it.

In the meanwhile Napoleon's power and prestige continued to

grow. In 1801 a deferential Senate elected him First Consul for life and in 1804 voted him the title of Emperor. For this he planned a magnificent coronation and had to decide whether at the same time Josephine would be crowned Empress. In this, of course, the Bonaparte family did all they could to dissuade him, stressing once again the need for a more suitable and high-born consort. But after a long delay Napoleon decided in her favour. In this he was influenced by the realisation that his love for her was not dead, and that she had supported him loyally in good times and in bad. He had also become annoyed by the behaviour of his siblings on whom he had been lavish in bestowing honours and principalities (Joseph King of Naples, Louis King of Holland), but this had given rise to jealousies and complaints among them which contrasted sharply with the Beauharnais family, notably Eugène and Hortense who never asked for anything for themselves.

The coronation took place on 1 December 1804 in Notre Dame, still bearing scars from its despoliation during the Revolution when it had been relegated to a Temple of the Goddess of Reason. It was the first coronation for 30 years and attracted widespread enthusiasm, although not from the Bonaparte family who continued churlish and uncooperative, particularly Elisa and Caroline who felt it beneath their dignity to bear Josephine's large and heavy train; and Letizia, the matriarch, who was so disgusted that she boycotted the ceremony altogether.

Pope Pius VII, gentle and conciliatory, had been summoned from Rome for the occasion and arrived attended by six cardinals and no less than 100 bishops. He had expected that he would perform the actual crowning of the Emperor and Empress, but he was edged out and Napoleon took the task on himself. The long ceremony of four hours must have been a severe strain on Josephine, aged 41 and in fragile health, but she bore up marvellously well, one person there describing her as 'the personification of elegance and majesty'; in contrast, some thought, to the Emperor who looked 'short, fat and awkward'.

As Empress Josephine found the new duties that came her way burdensome, and at times she longed for a life of anonymity and seclusion, but she knew that for her own sake and that of her family she must keep going for as long as possible. She decided therefore that her role from then on had to be one of passivity, soothing Napoleon in his rages, obeying his every command and even banishing jealousy and tolerating his sexual peccadilloes. For some time their relationship continued to blow hot and cold. It was noticed that Napoleon was at his worst after he had just taken on a new mistress, when he became blustering and bullying, breaking up furniture, throwing things in all directions and striking out at servants within reach. And he was a hard taskmaster, seeing to it that Josephine performed her duties exactly as he had prescribed and taking no heed of the nervous exhaustion that occasionally overtook her; he was particularly concerned with her clothes, some of which he approved, but others drove him into a frenzy so that he threw them into the fire or poured ink over them so they could not be worn again. At other times, however, he could be forbearing and affectionate, even loving, so that people became embarrassed when he behaved in public 'with more freedom than decorum'.

In spite of some harsh treatment and multiple infidelities Josephine could write to her mother in Martinique: 'He is kind, pleasant in every way, a charming man and he truly loves your Yeyette.' And he could write to her (fresh though he might be from the arms of his latest love): 'You are still essential to my happiness.'

The year 1805 was to be momentous in European history: Nelson destroyed a Franco-Spanish fleet at Trafalgar, and six weeks later Napoleon gained a crushing victory over the Austrians at Austerlitz[7] which made him in effect the arbiter of Western Europe. The terms he imposed on the Austrians were harsh: France's dominion was extended over Holland and Belgium and most of Italy, and the centuries-old Holy Roman Empire was brought to an end. In Paris Napoleon's manner became notably more regal and despotic, giving himself airs and graces and fussing over minor points of protocol. It was noticed by many that his relationship with Josephine was becoming more distant as he aspired to a more exalted wife and one that could bear him children.

Those who hoped that Napoleon's defeat of Austria would bring a peaceful European settlement were to be disappointed. It became evident that his thirst for military glory was insatiable. In 1806 he led an army against Prussia which he defeated overwhelmingly at the Battle of Jena. But in the following year there came a setback when he confronted a Russian army at Eylau where his losses were disproportionate and he came close to defeat.

---

[7] He described it as 'the most beautiful that I have fought'.

In Paris Josephine was having a *crise de nerfs*. There was much to depress her: the pervasive talk of Napoleon's divorce and remarriage (the current favourite being a sister of the Czar of Russia), the everlasting hostility of the Bonaparte family and the long absence of her husband who, it was rumoured, was having a serious love affair with a Polish lady. This proved to be true: Maria Walenska, aged 17 and married to a husband of 70, was a beautiful lady of high principles, but she came under pressure from Polish patriots to become the mistress of Napoleon in order to influence him in restoring the independence of Poland, and this for the sake of her country she did. Most of Napoleon's liaisons were loveless, but for Maria he had a deep and lasting love.

In her distress Josephine could have had comfort from her children, but Eugène was in Italy as Viceroy, and Hortense was with her disagreeable husband as Queen of Holland. She did have a moment of joy when a son was born to Eugène (Napoleon had married him off to a princess of Bavaria), but soon after she was overwhelmed with grief when the eldest son of Hortense, Napoleon Louis Charles, died at the age of three from croup; he was an exceptionally attractive child and a great favourite of not only Josephine but also Napoleon, who had nominated him his heir. Grief-stricken and tormented though she might be, Josephine could not let up on official duties, as a stream of letters kept coming from her husband telling her what things she had to do, with precise details as to how she should do them.

When Napoleon returned to Paris in July of 1807 after an absence of nearly a year, he was a changed man. While he was away he had become acquainted with some of the royal courts of Europe and had been dazed by their grandeur, and was determined that his should be in no way inferior. For this a wife of royal birth was essential and one able to bear children. Josephine had undertaken to go when required, and Napoleon hoped that she would go calmly without making difficulties. He also hoped that she would take the initiative and ask to be allowed to leave; he did not want to appear to be putting away his much-loved wife of 12 years' standing.

But this Josephine refused to do; she would accept divorce when she had to, but in no way would she facilitate it. She came under strong pressure to do so from the dreaded Chief of Police, Joseph Fouché, who urged her that in the public interest the Emperor should have an heir and it was up to her to 'make the inevitable sacrifice'. This upset her terribly and she rushed to Napoleon to ask if Fouché was acting on his orders, which he denied. For some time longer he continued to waver. It occurred to him that there was a strong case against divorce: it would be unpopular and he would have to adapt to the ways of a new and much younger wife. He confided to his Foreign Minister, Prince de Talleyrand: 'If I separated myself from my wife, I should thereby renounce all the charm she lends to my domestic life ... Josephine adapts herself to everything and knows me perfectly. In brief, I should show myself to be ungrateful for all she has done for me. I am not liked. She is a link between me and many people.' Once again he had fallen under her spell, which was still powerful. This was noticed by one of his mistresses, who had no reason to love Josephine but who became 'strongly attracted, magnetised, aware of a mysterious influence, a charm infinitely suave which emanated from her'.

Nevertheless, divorce was inevitable. In 1808 Napoleon was called away to Germany where the Austrians were giving trouble, and when he returned in the following year (after another victory at Wagram) his mood was hard and cold. Josephine found the communicating door between his apartment and hers firmly locked; and at official functions Napoleon's sister Pauline (now Princess Borghese) was the hostess while Josephine was relegated to the sidelines and treated as if she was not there. Those last weeks were agony for her: she must have known that divorce was imminent, she was hurt by the Emperor's coldness and she became convinced that she was in danger of being poisoned. In her misery she found consolation in a riot of extravagance, buying more clothes than she could ever possibly wear and more *objets d'art* than she knew what to do with. She also resorted to the occult, consulting soothsayers and endlessly dealing out tarot cards.

Napoleon finally brought himself to tell her that their marriage was at an end on 30 November 1809. His hope that she would be calm and resigned was to be dashed. She became demented and lapsed into semi-consciousness, and had to be carried to her room and put to bed. Napoleon, whose conscience was not clear and whose love was not completely dead, did what he could to comfort her. Certainly he made her a generous financial settlement: possession of the country house at Malmaison and the Elysée Palace in Paris and an annual allowance of 3 million francs. She also retained the title of Empress and was offered the principality of an Italian state but this, perhaps wisely, she declined.

The next days were spent moving her multitudinous possessions out of the Tuileries into Malmaison. Then on 14 December there was held a formal ceremony of divorce; attended by the highest in the land in their finest array. Napoleon had made it clear that nothing was to be said in dishonour of Josephine. The tone of the proceedings should be one of sacrifice and service rather than rejection and shame. In his opening statement Napoleon declared that in seeking a divorce he was motivated only by concern for his subjects and the need to provide a successor to the throne, and it was

> with much anguish of heart that he was giving up the wife that he loved ... Far from ever finding cause for complaint I can to the contrary only congratulate myself on the devotion and tenderness of my beloved wife. She has adorned fifteen years of my life; the memory will always remain engraved on my heart.

In reply Josephine started to read a speech that had been prepared for her:

> With the permission of our august and dear husband, I must declare that, having no hope of bearing children who would fulfill the needs of his policies and the interests of France, I am pleased to offer him the greatest proof of attachment and devotion ever offered on this earth

Until then her comportment had been calm and graceful, but at this point she was overcome by tears and the rest of her speech had to be read for her. In this she declared that she would always remain the Emperor's 'best friend' and both of them 'would find satisfaction in the sacrifice they were making for the good of the Empire'. The solemnity of the occasion was marred only by members of the Bonaparte family present, who could not conceal their delight at the outcome.

The divorce was thus settled to Napoleon's satisfaction. It did not seem to concern him that by French law it was illegal, since only the Pope could dissolve a marriage, and at that time Pope

Pius VII was under house arrest on Napoleon's orders and had just excommunicated him.

For some time afterwards Napoleon went out of his way to be kindly and attentive towards Josephine; more so, it seemed, than when they were married. He visited her frequently at Malmaison and did what he could to boost her spirits, but his attentiveness diminished in 1810 when plans for his remarriage were under way. By then his hopes of marrying the 15-year-old sister of the Czar had been thwarted and he had turned his attention towards the daughter of the Austrian Emperor, the Archduchess Marie Louise. It was hardly an ideal match: the lady was not willing and only six months before she had declared that 'to see the man would be the worst form of torture'; after being coerced into acceptance by her father she still talked of 'a painful sacrifice'. There were those in France too who looked upon such a marriage as being one of ill-omen, remembering the fate of her aunt, Marie Antoinette. Plump, homely and graceless, Marie Louise was the antithesis of Josephine, but she was robust and cheerful and, as was soon to be shown, fertile; and she was determined to make the best of things. Certainly Napoleon spared no pains to please her, redecorating the Tuileries, attending in detail to all her possible needs and putting aside (albeit at the last moment) his current mistress; he even took lessons in waltzing.

Marie Louise arrived in Paris at the end of March 1810. She and Napoleon had already been married by proxy, and he lost no time in taking her to bed, the success of which can be judged by a later remark of his on St Helena; 'she asked me to do it again'. A magnificent wedding in the Louvre took place soon afterwards, but it was no more than a civil ceremony. The Church would have no part in it; to churchmen it was unlawful and adulterous.

Josephine, of course, was far away at the time. Napoleon was definite that she must be kept at a distance. Malmaison was too near, so he bestowed on her the Duchy of Navarre in Normandy (some 60 miles away) which included a beautiful garden but an almost derelict mansion in which she was to suffer great discomfort. In the first months after the divorce she was not unhappy. She was comforted by Hortense, now separated from her husband following his abdication of the throne of Holland, who told her: 'For the first time in our lives, far from the world and the court, we will lead a real family life and know our first real happiness.' But her rise in morale was not to last long. In the autumn of 1810 it became known that Marie Louise was pregnant, and this caused her great distress. It showed that it was not because of Napoleon's infertility but of hers that they had had no offspring; and besides this, an heir to the throne would pose a threat to herself and her family. Napoleon was insistent that she should continue to give Paris a wide berth, and so for the time being she had to keep away from Malmaison, her dearly loved home where she delighted in her art collection, her greenhouses with their exotic plants and her zoo of wild animals.

One reason why Napoleon had delayed in divorcing Josephine was an instinct he had that she brought him good luck. This superstitious belief was shared by others, so that she became known in some quarters as 'Our Lady of Victories', and this was to be borne out by events, as his decline coincided quite closely with the departure of Josephine from his life. Since 1807 there had been signs that his incredible run of victories was becoming less clear-cut, and his dominion over nearly all of Western Europe less complete.

This stemmed from his imposition of the so-called Continental System by which he forbade all European countries to trade with England which, he hoped, would compel 'the nation of shopkeepers' to sue for peace. But this he was finding impossible to enforce. The first country to ignore the embargo was Portugal, so that in 1807 a French army invaded the country. This led in the following year to a dispute with Spain and the deposition of the Spanish King, and his replacement by Joseph Bonaparte. This was a fateful error and gave rise to the long-drawn-out Peninsular War which Napoleon later on St Helena described as 'the running sore which brought down my Empire'.

Disregard of the Continental System was one of the reasons for Napoleon's invasion of Russia. For this he gathered from all over Europe an immense army, over 600,000 strong, which he was confident would overwhelm Russia in a few weeks. But it was to end in cataclysmic disaster. Far from giving in, the Russian armies withdrew into the seemingly limitless interior of their country, destroying or taking with them everything that could be of help to the invaders. And the Grand Army went after them, losing men by the thousand every day from disease or desertion. When at last the Russians were brought to battle at Borodino it was down to

150,000 men. There, nevertheless, it gained a victory, albeit an expensive one, and a week later was in Moscow. Then surely, Napoleon thought, the Russians would surrender, but instead they set fire to the city and retreated further, so that the Grand Army was left stranded with diminishing food supplies and the onset of the fearsome Russian winter. Too late, on 18 October, Napoleon ordered a withdrawal, of some hundreds of miles, to the nearest supply base. Then the snow began to fall and the Grand Army, starving and frozen, and harassed all the time by Russian guerrillas, struggled on, somehow clinging to life. By mid-December a bedraggled remnant reached Poland and comparative safety.

During the winter Josephine had been in a state of tense anxiety. Napoleon had told her that he did not expect the campaign to last longer than five weeks, but during that time there was an ominous silence. She had been cheered by a report of the Battle of Borodino from Eugène, who held a senior command in the army, and of the occupation of Moscow; but then there was no definite news, only disturbing rumours. Then on 19 December the full truth became known when a bulletin was issued in Paris revealing starkly the destruction of the Grand Army.

It was a relief to Josephine that Napoleon and Eugène arrived back safely, but the future of the former was very uncertain. He was no longer the invincible warrior; opposition to him was building up. Somehow, however, he managed to conjure up a new army of some 200,000 men and, showing all his old brilliance, had been able to stem the advance of the Russian armies, since joined by the Prussians. A temporary truce was agreed and, unwisely, Napoleon refused generous peace terms, restricting France to her natural frontiers – the Alps, the Pyrenees and the Rhine. When war was resumed, Austria and Sweden joined the invading forces and in October of 1813 Napoleon was heavily defeated in the three-day Battle of Leipzig. After that his fate was sealed as the Allied armies advanced inexorably into France. On 1 April 1814 they entered Paris.

Three days earlier Josephine, strongly urged by Hortense (now a lady-in-waiting to Marie Louise), made a move from Malmaison to her estate in Normandy with her most valuable jewellery sewn into her petticoats. It was a dreadful journey as the roads were clogged with refugees and there was the terror (unfounded as it proved) that they would be set on by roving Cossacks. On arrival after two days Josephine was desperate for news from Paris, as she was convinced that her fate was bound up with that of Napoleon, and she was distraught when Hortense arrived to tell of Napoleon's abdication and his exile to the island of Elba. A provisional government had been set up under Napoleon's one-time Foreign Minister, the Prince de Talleyrand, and Josephine wrote to him, throwing herself on his mercy. To this she had an encouraging reply; it seemed that she was in no danger – to the contrary, she was sought after. For Talleyrand – who was wise, cynical and far-seeing – thought she might be of use to the new government. He was intent on restoring the Bourbons, and Josephine might be able to attract supporters for this idea.

On his advice she returned to Malmaison where she found herself the focus of attention. Among her many visitors was Czar Alexander of Russia who was immediately captivated by her and promised her his full support (including a palace in St Petersburg if she wanted it). For a brief time she was once again a great hostess entertaining the grand figures then assembled in Paris. It was a strain on her as her health was failing, but in the interests of her family she felt she must keep going. In May of 1814 King Louis XVIII, younger brother of the guillotined Louis XVI, enormous and almost immobile from gout, returned from exile in England. Hardly a charismatic figure, he needed all the support he could get and invited Josephine to the Tuileries, but she was not able to go.

A few days before she had caught a cold which she made light of, but she became feverish with a cough that prevented her from sleeping and her condition grew worse. The strain had been too great. On 29 May she died in the arms of Eugène, 'going', he said, 'as gently and as sweetly to meet death as she had met life'. The official autopsy showed that she had died of pneumonia and angina, but her own doctor was perhaps nearer the mark when later he told Napoleon that she died of anxiety and grief. Her resistance to disease had collapsed, her mind had become clouded and her ex-husband had fallen from grace. Perhaps a contemporary had a point when she said in lighthearted vein: 'She had the good taste to die at the right time.'

The shy, awkward Creole from Martinique had come a long way since her arrival in France 35 years before. Her life had been a fantasy – at times joyous and triumphant, at others humiliating and traumatic.

After her death Josephine's reputation was to have many fluctuations – at times extravagantly praised, endowing her with qualities she did not have; at times harshly condemned, her warmth and munificence ignored. Napoleon himself was ambivalent: in St Helena he was apt to be disparaging, blaming her for extravagance and deceit. But perhaps his true feelings were voiced at Malmaison with Hortense during his 100 days: 'She was the most alluring, the most glamorous creature I have ever known, a woman in the true sense of the word, volatile, spirited and with the kindest heart in the world.'

11

QUEEN VICTORIA, QUEEN OF ENGLAND
(1819–1901)

Queen Victoria's reign of 63 years, the longest in British history, saw the development of the country from an aristocracy of landowners to a democracy based on industry; and Queen Victoria herself developing from a naive unworldly princess into a great Queen-Empress, sovereign of the world's most powerful country and at the head of an empire covering a quarter of the earth's surface. Her name also became associated with a new deeply respected way of life which spread worldwide.

Queen Victoria – Alexandrina Victoria as she was christened – was born on 19 May 1819. Her father, Prince Edward Duke of Kent, was the fourth son of George III. Then aged 52, his life had been ill-fated and undistinguished. The King had ordained for him a career in the army where he was known as a fanatical disciplinarian, inflicting brutal inhuman punishments (lashes by the hundred) for even minor offences. This, however, was found to be counterproductive, causing mutinies and desertions rather than smartness and efficiency, so that he had been forced into early retirement. In civilian life he was found to be a man of contrasts. Instead of the hoary reactionary that might have been expected, he proved to be a stalwart liberal and patron of numerous charities, with an interest in the socialist experiments of Robert Owen in his cotton mill in Lanarkshire. But troubles were to close in on him, particularly in the matter of finance. He had no idea of living within his means, was wantonly extravagant, and always in debt.

As the fourth son of the monarch there had for long been little likelihood of his succeeding to the throne; but this was to change. With the death in 1817 of Princess Charlotte, daughter of the Prince Regent (future George IV) the situation arose that in spite of fathering 15 children, George III had no legitimate grandchildren.

The matter was regarded as serious, so much so that there was then something of a rush among royal princes to make belated lawful marriages and so beget lawful offspring.

One of these was Edward, who for the last 27 years had been living in domestic bliss, although nuptial unorthodoxy, with a French Canadian lady, Julie Madame de St Laurent. In 1817, convinced of his duty to his country, he persuaded Julie to withdraw with a pension and a title while he looked for a wife among the minor royalty of Europe who would be permissible under the terms of the Royal Marriages Act. At his age, heavily in debt, with eccentric ways and a somewhat tarnished reputation, he was not exactly a prime catch; but he managed to find a young royal widow in the tiny German state of Leiningen who was willing to take him on. Princess Victoire, who came originally from the state of Saxe-Coburg, was lively, attractive, conscientious and of proven ability to bear children; but, as was to be found later, also apt to be wilful and quarrelsome.

She and Edward were married in 1818 and soon afterwards she became pregnant. For reasons of economy they were living abroad at the time, but Edward attached great importance to the child being born in England, as he or she might one day succeed to the throne. And so his wife, the Duchess, in an advanced state of pregnancy, was subjected to a long and harassing drive, bearing one who was to be among England's greatest sovereigns. However, they arrived in time and safety and the Duchess was delivered of a robust and healthy baby girl.

Owing to financial stringency Edward then had thoughts of returning to a life abroad, but decided to stay on for the time being in the hopes of obtaining a monetary grant from Parliament. In the meanwhile, however, it was necessary for him to go into seclusion in order to avoid his creditors, and the refuge he chose was the Devonshire seaside resort of Sidmouth where, he expected, he and his family would benefit from the healthful sea breezes. But the sea breezes, far from being healthful, proved lethal, and within a few weeks Edward had died of pneumonia, leaving the Duchess and her baby stranded. However, her brother Leopold, then King of Belgium, came to their rescue and brought them back to London to an apartment in Kensington Palace, which was to be their home until Victoria's accession to the throne 18 years later.

During those years the English monarchy was to be infiltrated by the German state of Saxe-Coburg – no larger than an average

English county. During the Napoleonic Wars it had been devastated and at the end lay downtrodden and impoverished. Yet within a generation members of its ruling family had found their way into nearly half the courts of Europe with an influence and prestige out of all proportion to its size and standing. Leading the field was Prince Leopold, who became engaged to the heiress to the throne of England, Princess Charlotte (daughter of George IV). When she died he was offered the throne of Greece, which he declined, then that of Belgium, which he accepted, while at the same time he was to maintain a strong presence in England through his influence on his niece, the future Queen Victoria. Also influential was his sister Victoire who a few months after her marriage to the Duke of Kent found herself the mother and sole guardian of the heir-presumptive to the throne of England, and so a power in the land. Later an even greater power was to appear from Saxe-Coburg in the form of her nephew Prince Albert who was to marry Queen Victoria to achieve a unique position in the country.

Victoria's childhood was not of the happiest – it was narrow, confined and joyless. Her mother took her responsibility seriously and kept her on a tight rein, allowing her no freedom and barring all access to her except for a chosen few. She had to be accompanied everywhere and could only ever be alone in a room with either her mother or governess; and until she became Queen she had to sleep in her mother's bedroom. She had little association with children of her own age and practically no male company apart from her Uncle Leopold, a paternal figure, and her cousins from Saxe-Coburg whose occasional visits were a delight to her. Generally her daily routine was monotonous and colourless with little gaiety or enjoyment; a bleak life indeed, and made worse by the friction and dissent in her mother's household.

Soon after her husband's death the Duchess of Kent had fallen under the spell of an ambitious and unscrupulous army officer, Sir John Conroy, who came from one of the wilder parts of Ireland (Connaught) and was richly endowed with Irish charm and loquacity. He had been taken onto the staff of the Duke of Kent who described him as 'a very intelligent factotum', and came to rely on him heavily. On the Duke's death Conroy set his sights on the Duchess and soon made himself indispensable to her, calling himself her 'confidential adviser'. The nature of their relationship is not entirely clear but it is probable they were not lovers, although he did come to dominate her life. He did not stop there, for looking to the future he sought to establish a hold over Princess Victoria, and it was at his instigation that a regime was instituted whereby she became totally dependent on her mother, and so on him. But Victoria was not deceived by him: instinctively she always disliked and distrusted him, although out of respect for her mother she was silent on the matter.

In spite of the pains she endured, Victoria was no rebel. She grew up demure and dutiful, fully accepting her role in life; but it must be doubtful that she could have survived without the love and support of her governess. Louise Lehzen, daughter of a German clergyman, was an inspired teacher with the ability to evoke enthusiasm and to impart knowledge. Under her tutelage Victoria not only developed wider interests and a lively mind but also came to rely on her judgement. This influence was to be profound and lasting.

The dissensions in the royal family at this time were often acute, but none more so than that between the Duchess of Kent and William IV, who became King in 1830 at the age of 56 after a totally undistinguished life in which his main achievement had been the begetting of ten illegitimate children by a well-known actress. A bluff, roisterous ex-naval man with little brain power but genial and good-natured, he had wanted to make contact with his niece and heir-apparent. But the Duchess had stood in the way, thinking (with some reason) that William, like all the sons of George III, was dissolute and debauched and her daughter should be kept at a distance from him. Some contact, however, he did have and years later the Queen wrote that he was 'kind and considerate', but that he was also 'odd, extremely odd and singular'. As a result of the Duchess's attitude, William IV took a strong dislike not only to her but to all her Coburg relations, and tried to prevent their visits to England. He also tried to steer Victoria away from marriage with one of them, to one of the grandsons of the King of Holland. But there he was unsuccessful, Victoria declaring the Dutch princes 'heavy, dull, frightened and not at all prepossessing', while the Coburg princes she found 'amiable and extremely merry'.

The hostility between the Duchess and William IV came to a head in August 1836. The King had discovered that, contrary to his orders, the Duchess had appropriated an extra suite of rooms in Kensington Palace. His anger could not then be contained and

194

came bursting forth on a most unsuitable occasion – a banquet celebrating his birthday. With the Duchess sitting beside him and Princess Victoria opposite, and in front of more than 100 guests, he launched into a furious tirade, accusing the Duchess of insulting and frustrating him, that she was surrounded by evil advisers and was quite unfit for any responsibility; and he prayed that his life would be spared until the Princess came of age and the regency of her mother would be avoided.

As it came to pass, the King's prayer was to be granted with barely a month to spare. Even then the Duchess and Conroy did not give up hope of a regency, telling Victoria that she was too young and inexperienced to rule on her own. Rumours of this reached her uncle Leopold who sent over from Belgium his most trusted adviser, Baron Stockmar,[1] to give his niece advice and support, and with his help her mother's scheme was frustrated. In gratitude Stockmar remained a close adviser to Queen Victoria, and later to Prince Albert, until just before his death in 1856.

Early in the morning of 20 June 1837 the Archbishop of Canterbury and the Lord Chamberlain arrived at Kensington Palace to break the news to Victoria that she had become Queen, and she received them in her dressing-gown, alone. Later in the day she received the Prime Minister, Lord Melbourne, alone, and presided over the Privy Council, also alone. This was significant because it marked the end of the dominance of her mother and Conroy, who from then on were increasingly relegated into the background. One of Victoria's first orders as Queen was that her bed should be moved out of her mother's room.

There was, of course, much speculation as to how the young Queen, naive and inexperienced, would make out. All eyes were upon her and all were agreed that she performed her ceremonial duties marvellously well – gracefully, confidently and with natural dignity. But how would she cope with affairs of state? With those mounting despatch boxes full of documents requiring decisions and comments? Would she not be overwhelmed by them? But here, fortunately, near at hand was someone ideally suited to help her out. Lord Melbourne, the incumbent Prime Minister, a widower of 58, a man of great charm, sympathetic understanding and good

---

[1] Stockmar, of Swedish origin and once a physician, was to be reputed in many courts of Europe for his judgement and integrity. He was consulted on many and varied subjects and always gave well-considered, if somewhat prolix advice.

humour, won her confidence and had the gift of making all public business comprehensible and absorbing. They were to form a unique partnership and did not confine themselves to public affairs. In the evenings she would listen to him, enthralled, reminiscing on a long and varied life, and they would engage in simple games like draughts or putting together 'dissected pictures' (the forerunner of jigsaw puzzles). At first everything went swimmingly, so that after a few months the Queen could report that it had been 'the pleasantest summer she had spent in her life'.

Her people delighted in their sovereign – a pure young virgin instead of gouty, debauched old men to whom they had long been accustomed. For her coronation Parliament voted an exceptionally large sum of money, and people thronged the streets to cheer and catch a glimpse of her. The coronation service itself did not go altogether smoothly. The attendant bishops and archbishops seemed unclear as to the parts they had to play and failed to prompt the Queen as to what she should do next. One forced a ring awkwardly and painfully on the wrong finger and another turned over two pages at once so that an important part of the service was left out and it was necessary to go back for it. Then an ancient and very decrepit peer stumbled on the altar steps on his way to pay homage, and the Queen impulsively came forward to help him up. But all was well in the end and there was universal euphoria.

However it was all too good to last, and it was not long before clouds began to gather. Lord Melbourne, although a splendid father figure to a young queen, was less adept at governing the country and it was becoming likely that his prime ministership might be coming to an end. At the same time the character of the Queen began to harden. The first storm, which blew up suddenly in 1839, concerned the alleged pregnancy of one of the Duchess of Kent's ladies-in-waiting, Lady Flora Hastings, an unmarried woman of no great beauty and not always of a balanced frame of mind.

At Kensington Palace she had incurred the strong dislike of Victoria partly because of her interfering ways and partly because of her association with Sir John Conroy. This dislike had persisted. In 1839 it was noticed that her figure had become suddenly swollen, giving rise to some ribaldry and the thought that she might be 'with child'. When Queen Victoria heard of this she treated the matter lightly, opining that Lady Flora should be examined by the court physician, Sir James Clarke. This was done, but cursorily

196

and roughly, so that Lady Flora's condition was left in some doubt. She was then examined by another doctor who stated positively that she was not pregnant but was suffering from a liver disease, whereupon the Queen apologised and the affair seemed to have come to an end. But it was stirred up again by Lady Flora's family who were indignant at the treatment she had received and wrote letters to the press about it; and when shortly afterwards Lady Flora died there was an outburst of popular anger directed against the court, the government and, more particularly, the Queen, who was accused of having been tactless and heartless. For a time she became unpopular and was hissed when she appeared in public, and she was thought to be in danger from popular demonstrations. In time the ill-feeling died down, but it was immediately followed by a more serious affair, the so-called Bedchamber Crisis.

In May 1839 the majority of Lord Melbourne's Whig government in the House of Commons fell so low that he felt he had to resign. This drove the Queen to distraction. She could not abide the thought of being parted from her beloved minister. The alternative was the Tory leader, Sir Robert Peel, a man of outstanding ability but cold, reserved and awkward, the antithesis of Melbourne. The thought of his replacing him so appalled the Queen that she sought ways of preventing it, and was able to do so over a disagreement about her ladies-in-waiting, more particularly the Ladies of the Bedchamber. These were all staunch Whigs, some of them the wives of prominent Whig politicians, and Peel insisted that if he was to form a government some of them should be replaced by Tory supporters. How could he expect to have the confidence of the Queen if she was surrounded intimately by members of the opposition? But at this the Queen dug in her heels and refused to make the smallest concession. The elderly and greatly revered Duke of Wellington was called in to try and settle the matter, but even the conqueror of Napoleon could not prevail on the Queen to change her mind. 'They wished to treat me like a girl,' she wrote at the time, 'but I will show them that I am Queen of England.' And so an impasse was reached and Melbourne was recalled for two years of ever more shaky government. The Queen then had got her way, but there were those who thought that she had been obstinate and unreasonable.

After two years on the throne, the Queen's character had changed noticeably. No longer demure and ingénue, she had become assertive and obstinate with a mind of her own. Baron Stockmar, a great admirer, wrote that she was 'as passionate as a small child, and that if she feels offended she throws everything overboard without exception'. The scandalmongering diarist, Thomas Creevey, put it more crudely that: 'the Queen is a resolute little tit'. Even her beloved Uncle Leopold she found too interfering, complaining that his advice was not disinterested and that he always wanted 'to rule the roast [*sic*]'. With her mother, she had a blazing row over the Lady Flora Hastings affair so that they were hardly on speaking terms.

To Lord Melbourne she remained as devoted as ever, her great dread still being that she would be parted from him. This had been avoided by the stand she had taken over the Bedchamber Crisis, but a change of government was bound to come. In the meantime a threat came from another quarter.

There was great concern in the country that Victoria should marry and bear an heir to the throne. If anything were to happen to her she would be succeeded by her uncle, the Duke of Cumberland, a man of evil repute.[2] In time she was to bear heirs abundantly, but at first she was in no hurry to marry. A husband would intrude between her and Lord Melbourne.

It had long been ordained by her Coburg relations (notably her Uncle Leopold) that Victoria should marry her first cousin Prince Albert, second son of Ernest I Duke of Saxe-Coburg-Gotha, who was almost exactly the same age as she. She had first met him in 1836 when at the age of 17 he came on a visit to England. She was impressed by him then, writing that he was 'so sensible, so kind and so good and so amiable too. He has besides too the most pleasing and most delightful exterior you could wish to see.' She accepted that one day she would marry him, but not yet.

Albert too accepted that one day he would marry Victoria, but out of a sense of duty rather than love. He was in no hurry to leave his homeland which he loved dearly and where he had had a very happy childhood, which was surprising as it had not been untroubled. When he was four years old the marriage of his parents had broken down. His mother was thought to have been too friendly with a court chamberlain and was banished, and he never saw her again. With his father, the Duke, and his elder brother, Prince

---

[2] The fifth son of George III and since the death of William IV, King of Hanover where female sovereigns were disallowed. Many scandals including murder were associated with him.

Ernest, he was on good terms, although they were of very different character – dissolute and out for pleasure while he was studious and strictly virtuous.[3]

His marriage to Victoria might have been long delayed, but in 1839 he paid another visit to England. Only a short time before, the Queen had been assuring Lord Melbourne that she had no intention of marrying for two or three years yet; indeed she was not firmly committed to marrying at all. However, when she and Albert met she had a sudden change of mind. Since their last meeting he had become outstandingly handsome and more 'sensible and amiable' than ever, and Victoria was swept off her feet. Within a few days she was telling Lord Melbourne that she was ready to marry at once, and then lost no time in inviting Albert to become her husband, which he graciously agreed to do, although he was not yet in love with her.

Although people had been longing for the Queen to be married, the engagement was not particularly popular. It was felt that the younger son of a tiny impoverished German principality was unworthy of the Queen of England, and at first the Prince had much to contend with. His uncle, Prince Leopold, had been granted £50,000 a year by Parliament when he became engaged to Princess Charlotte, then heir to the throne, and Albert could reasonably expect the same sum, but it was reduced to £30,000 mainly because of the hostility of the Tory party, smarting from the Bedchamber Crisis and the prevalence of Lord Melbourne's Whig government. It was also made clear to him that his private rights were restricted; his secretary and other personal staff were to be handpicked not by him but by the Queen and Lord Melbourne, and his request for a honeymoon period of a few days after the wedding was firmly refused. His political influence at first was non-existent; he was not present at most of the conferences between Victoria and Melbourne, and at one of the first he attended the Queen wrote that he had helped with the blotting paper. Later this was to change completely.

Actually, at that time this exclusion did not worry Albert unduly. He was not then especially politically minded; he was more interested in science and the arts. Of greater concern to him was that he was not the master in his own house. Since she had become Queen,

---

[3] Because he was so different in both character and looks it was rumoured that the Duke was not his father, but this is unsubstantiated.

Victoria's domestic affairs had been put in the charge of her ex-governess, Baroness Lehzen, to whom she felt she owed a great debt of gratitude and of whom she still stood in some awe; and the Baroness was determined that there should be no intrusion into her realm, even though there was much that needed doing. The domestic arrangements in Buckingham Palace were chaotic: there were several different authorities, vying with each other and guarding their rights and duties jealously so that some tasks were overmanned while others were not done at all. In time Albert was able to install greater order, but not until Lehzen had been eased out (in 1843) and even then it needed tact and patience as there was strong opposition from vested interests.

By 1841 the days of Lord Melbourne could no longer be prolonged. In that year the Whigs were heavily defeated in a general election and a Tory government became inevitable. This time there were no difficulties about the ladies of the bedchamber owing to a tactful negotiation between Albert and Sir Robert Peel, with whom he was to develop a strong liaison,[4] and from that time Albert's political influence was to increase rapidly. It was of course impossible that a man of his intelligence and strength of character would long be content to remain his wife's gentleman-in-waiting. He soon became in effect her secretary and confidential adviser, and then her guide and mentor. In 1845 the diarist Greville wrote: 'He is king to all intents and purposes.' Far from the Queen resenting this, she delighted in it. Over and over again in her journal she recorded her gratitude in having such a wise and wonderful counsellor. She had taken a tearful farewell of Lord Melbourne, but had soon come to realise that her attachment to him had been no more than a temporary phase which she would outgrow; and a more mature and deep-rooted partnership would take its place. It was not only in politics that Albert's influence increased: he was also to bring about a change in Victoria's way of life; partying and pleasure-making were to give way to the stolid Victorian virtues of duty, domesticity and morality.[5]

---

[4] It took a long time for the Queen to forgive the leaders of the Tory party; the Duke of Wellington and Sir Robert Peel were not invited to her wedding.

[5] By 1846 the Queen and Prince Albert had five children: Victoria Adelaide Mary Louisa (1840–1901), later Empress of Germany; Albert Edward (1841–1910), later King Edward VII; Alice Maud Mary (1843–78), later Grand Duchess of Hesse-Darmstadt; Alfred Ernest Albert (1844–1900), later Duke of Edinburgh and reigning Duke of Saxe-Coburg and Gotha; Helena Augusta Victoria (1846–1923), Princess Christian of Schleswig-Holstein.

Once Peel had gained the respect and confidence of Prince Albert it was not long before the Queen's view of him changed. Eighteen months after he came to office she was writing of him: 'He is undoubtedly a great statesman, a man who thinks but little of party and never of himself'; and she was greatly distressed when he was forced out of office following the repeal of the Corn Laws in 1846.

He was succeeded as Prime Minister by the Whig Lord John Russell, who was amiable but ineffective, and the dominant member of this government for the next five years was to be the Foreign Secretary, Henry John Temple, 3rd Viscount Palmerston. He was a political phenomenon. During his life of 81 years he had held high government office for 50 years, including nine as Prime Minister and 16 as Foreign Secretary. He had started as a Tory and ended as a Whig; but he really belonged to no party; he was a law unto himself and in relations with foreign countries went his own way, blustering and bullying and not afraid to use force. He has been described as 'the most feared, the most hated and the most admired statesman in England'. In 1846 he became Foreign Secretary for the third time and proceeded to take charge of foreign affairs with total disregard for anyone else – the Prime Minister, his Cabinet colleagues or the monarchy.

Here there was to be a clash, for Queen Victoria and Prince Albert took a close interest in European matters – to be expected as they had relations in most of the courts of Europe – and they objected strongly not only to Palmerston's principles but, more especially, to his methods. For Palmerston, although staunchly conservative in domestic affairs, gave support, sometimes irresponsibly, to revolutionary movements abroad, and seemed to delight in defying and insulting established regimes that smacked of despotism. The Queen and Prince Albert were not opposed to liberal ideas but they approached them more judiciously. They disliked despotism, but they were apprehensive of anarchy and mob violence and what Prince Albert called 'the unregulated mass of illiterate people'; and some of Palmerston's policies they thought reckless and dangerous. Albert would approach every problem studiously and meticulously before making a decision, and he was appalled by the way Palmerston seemed to act on the spur of the moment, relying on instinct rather than careful appraisal. The Queen and the Prince made their objections known, but Palmerston took little notice of them, continuing to throw his weight about and doing things his way regardless of the consequences. The Queen urged Lord John Russell to dismiss him, but this he was reluctant to do because, although he might be loathed abroad, he had great support at home where his bluff knockabout treatment of foreigners appealed to many English people.

One important point, however, that the Queen and the Prince did achieve was that all despatches to foreign countries had to be submitted to the Queen and signed by her before being sent off, and were not to be altered subsequently. It was also agreed that if the Foreign Secretary failed to do this, the Queen had the right to dismiss him. This was surely an anachronism; by the mid-nineteenth century the time had passed when the monarch could dismiss individual ministers at will. As it happened, this right was never exercised.

For five and a half years the Queen and the Prince endured Palmerston's excesses, but in 1851 he went too far when on his own authority alone he recognised the coup d'état by which Louis Napoleon made himself the Emperor Napoleon III. Then at last Lord John Russell plucked up his courage and dismissed him, which appeared to be a notable royal victory; but as will be seen, Palmerston was soon to return.

The government of Lord John Russell lasted only a few months after the dismissal of Palmerston and was followed by a coalition of Whigs and dissident Conservatives known as the Peelites, who had broken away from the main body of the party after the repeal of the Corn Laws and the downfall of Peel. The Prime Minister was Lord Aberdeen, a Peelite and a man of great honour and integrity but fatally weak, and it was while he was in office that the country was drawn into a futile and unnecessary war in the Crimea. Albert, backed by the Queen, had tried to prevent this and had become very unpopular for doing so; but once war was declared no one was more patriotic and pugnacious than they. Albert bombarded the War Office with schemes, some enlightened and some far-fetched, for winning the war while Victoria concerned herself with the sufferings of British troops during the grim Russian winter and gave enthusiastic backing to the mission of Florence Nightingale. She also instituted a new medal for gallantry open to all ranks, to be known as the Victoria Cross. She even agreed, when the war was going badly, to accept Lord Palmerston as Prime Minister, it being generally thought that he was a man strong and decisive enough to bring victory.

In the middle of the nineteenth century the wealth of Great Britain was at its zenith. Her foreign trade was more than twice that of any other country and her industrial output greater than that of the rest of the world put together. In 1851 this was splendidly reflected in the greatest Exhibition of its sort there had ever been. Many contributed to this but it was primarily the work of Prince Albert, without whose backing and inspiration it could never have got off the ground. His aim was that it should be a great festival of peace and goodwill where every country in the world would display its achievements in industry, science and the arts. It was held in Hyde Park in a gigantic glass structure known as the Crystal Palace and was a huge success. During the five months it was open it attracted millions of visitors from all over the world and made a substantial profit which was devoted to the foundation of the museums in South Kensington. For Albert it was a magnificent achievement and no one was more overjoyed than Queen Victoria, who declared that, 'Albert's dearest name is immortalised with this great conception', and 'it made my heart swell with pride and glory and thankfulness'.

With one brief interlude of Conservative government Palmerston was to remain as Prime Minister until his death in 1868. For most of the time relations between him and the Queen were comparatively smooth, the main exception being the matter of the unification of Italy (the Risorgimento). Here Palmerston and Lord John Russell, who had become Foreign Secretary, gave strong support to those aiming to set up a united kingdom of Italy, free from the domination of Austria and the Pope. 'The liberation of Italian people from a foreign yoke', Palmerston wrote, 'is an increase of freedom and happiness at which well-wishers to mankind cannot but rejoice.' This was not, however, the view of the Queen and Prince Albert who wrote: 'The state of Italy brought into being by revolution, civil war, treachery and invasion cannot prove a success.' Later when Italian unity had been achieved and the Italian hero, Giuseppe Garibaldi, visited London where he was greeted tumultuously, Queen Victoria kept her distance.

By 1860 Queen Victoria's family had grown to nine, ranging in age from three to 20. Of these the eldest, Victoria Princess Royal, was a paragon of virtue – high-minded, scholarly, self-sacrificing and a constant joy to her parents. Not so her eldest son, Albert Edward Prince of Wales, who was of a different hue. At an early age his father had drawn up a formidable programme of education for him in which he would study relentlessly all that was beautiful and of moral worth, it being impressed on him at all times that 'life is composed of duties and that in the discharge of them the true Christian, the true soldier and the true gentleman would be found'. But unfortunately the glove did not fit. Bertie, as he was known, was by nature indolent, pleasure-loving and no intellectual, and quite incapable of taking on board all the learning and morality that was thrust on him. The Queen and the Prince were to learn that 'the perfect being' at which they aimed could not be created by education.

By 1861, when the Prince was 20, they were becoming seriously worried about him and in that year there came to the ears of the Prince word that Bertie had been involved in an affair with an actress. Some fathers might have taken this philosophically but Albert was devastated. Sexual irregularity was something he regarded with horror and he told his son that what he had done had given him the greatest pain of his life. At the time Bertie seemed penitent, but he was not to mend his ways.

The year 1861 was to be an *annus horribilis* for Queen Victoria. At the beginning of the year her mother, the Duchess of Kent, died suddenly. Since coming to the throne relations with her had come under strain at times, but fences had been mended and she was dreadfully upset by her death, weeping copiously for days. Then in the summer it was found that her youngest son, Prince Leopold, then aged eight, was suffering from haemophilia and needed special treatment abroad. Soon afterwards came the thunderbolt of Bertie's imbroglio and then the greatest tragedy of her life. For some time Albert had become careless of his health, overworking persistently and allowing himself to become run down. In December he contracted flu which developed into typhoid fever. If this had been diagnosed earlier he might have survived, but on 14 December he died. It must be doubtful that this was due in any way to Bertie's affair, but Queen Victoria believed that it was and she held it against her son for the rest of her life.

The sudden death of the Prince Consort at the age of 42 brought great public mourning, greater than might have been expected as he had never been widely popular. His achievements during the 20 years he had lived in England were extraordinary. His support of a young, inexperienced, wilful queen had been of the highest order; he had relieved her of many of the more arduous and less agreeable of her duties, and his advice on political matters had always been sound and temperate. More than this, he and the Queen had established for the sovereign a new standing, one that accepted the limitations of a constitutional monarch while at the same time ensuring that he or she had a significant role and was more than just a decorative figurehead. Outside politics too his influence had been deep and far-ranging. He had been pre-eminent in promoting public appreciation of science and the arts, of which he had exceptional knowledge. And more than that: the much-acclaimed Victorian way of life with its emphasis on morality, duty and hard work was stimulated by him.

For all that, however, he was still not liked. There was about him a coldness and aloofness, often taken for arrogance, which people found unendearing. In English eyes he was lacking in exuberance and good fellowship. The aristocracy in particular could not take to him. Although he was a crack shot and rode fearlessly to hounds there was always a barrier between them. In death, however, this barrier was breached. People became more aware of his true worth. Even his old antagonist, Lord Palmerston, wept profusely when he heard that he had died and in a tribute described him as 'a perfect being'; and Lord Clarendon, Foreign Minister, said his death was 'a national calamity of far greater importance than the public dreamed of'.

For the Queen it was a calamity from which she was never to recover. She declared that life had ceased for her, that all happiness was at an end and that her dearest wish was to rejoin Albert as soon as possible. Her mourning for him was carried to extremes. His rooms and books were to be left exactly as they were, with hot water and a clean towel laid out for him every day. In the following years numerous monuments were put up in his memory, notably the Albert Hall and the prodigious memorial in Kensington Gardens near to the site of the Crystal Palace, replete with 170 life-size figures representing *inter alia* the great moral virtues, all the arts and eight branches of science. In the midst of all these Albert is to be seen seated with a catalogue of the Great Exhibition. There had to be, too, a full-scale biography, and Sir Theodore Martin toiled away at this for 14 years, omitting nothing. It was to be found, however, that such a monumental work, five volumes of unremitting adulation, was too much of a good thing. Readers were dazed by so much virtue so that the true worth of Albert was obscured rather than portrayed.

At first the Queen was overwhelmed by the immensity of the task that lay ahead of her. She had come to depend on Albert so completely. He had taken over all public business, writing letters and despatches for her, making clear to her complex political matters and guiding all her decisions. Besides this he had managed the running of the households, supervised her tastes in the arts and seen to the upbringing of their family. At first it seemed to her that she could not possibly cope with such burdens without him. But then she resolved that she must in order to make sure that his memory was preserved and his good works and saintly character made known to all. So she set herself to master the duties of the monarch, poring over piles of documents, questioning decisions, adding words of her own, and all the time ensuring that she was doing what Albert would have wished.

As might be expected, after her husband's death the Queen withdrew from public life. It was reasonable that for a time she should do so; but it began to look as if she intended her seclusion to be permanent, as she buried herself away in Osborne, Windsor or Balmoral, travelling between them by special train in closest privacy. Of Buckingham Palace she saw practically nothing – only a few weeks in the 40 years of her widowhood (causing a joker to pin a notice on the railings: 'This desirable residence to let, the owner having declined business').

Such behaviour was self-indulgent. She might work hard behind the scenes, but the British public expected more than this for their money; they wanted pomp and pageantry and grand colourful occasions. In time the press became insistent that she should appear in public more often, causing her to write a letter to *The Times* that she had 'other and higher duties' to attend to than what she called 'mere representation'. But the Editor of *The Times* held his ground and maintained that if she immured herself from the world she was unfitting herself from those 'other and higher duties' at which she worked so hard. Later she was induced to undertake certain public ceremonies, but these were always painful to her. When she opened Parliament in 1865 (four years after Albert's death) she wrote piteously: 'It was a fearful moment when I entered the carriage alone and the band played; also when the crowds cheered and I had great difficulty in repressing my tears.' In the

206

whole of her widowhood she never went to a theatre or concert or gave or attended a state ball.

There were some at the time of the Prince Consort's death who thought the Queen would abdicate, but this, in spite of the immense burden laid upon her, she had no intention of doing. Besides her mission to pay homage to the memory of Albert, she considered her eldest son unfitted for the role of monarch. Bertie was everything his father was not – he was sociable, outgoing, pleasure-loving and with no intellectual interests. And because of this and because she was haunted by the thought that he was partly to blame for his father's death, she tended to despise him and to bombard him with outspokenly critical letters.

In 1863 Bertie had married Princess Alexandra of Denmark. By then he had come of age, had his own establishment which rapidly became the centre of fashionable London, and was able to do all the things he enjoyed most – yachting, horse racing, shooting as well as other less reputable pursuits. Of such a life the Queen thoroughly disapproved, describing it as 'fast and loose' and 'a whirl of amusement'. In particular she deplored the company Bertie kept: not safe, respectable scions of ancient aristocracy but vulgar upstarts – racing types, actors and actresses, Jewish financiers, even Americans. In face of a barrage of criticism Bertie was always tactful and forbearing, listening deferentially but then going on as before, and there was never any question of his emulating his Hanoverian forbears and setting up a court of his own in opposition to the sovereign. In public he was always totally loyal to the Queen, just as she fully supported him in the various scandals in which he became involved – a divorce case and an incident of cheating at cards among others.

In private the Queen continued to voice her disapproval, but in doing so she might have realised that she was to some extent responsible for his way of life by not allowing him any position in government. For this he was well qualified, particularly in foreign affairs, as he spoke three languages fluently and was on familiar terms with most of Europe's rulers, to many of whom he was closely related. If he had been given some governmental post he might possibly have been distracted from some of his hedonistic delights. But the Queen was adamant: she would admit of no sharing of the royal prerogative.

In October 1865 Lord Palmerston died at the age of 81. The

Queen's feelings were ambivalent: she was clear that she had never liked him but he did have 'valuable qualities' and he was a link with 'the happy past'. This happy past was to recede further with the emergence of new men, in particular two men of genius – William Gladstone and Benjamin Disraeli – whose rivalry was to light up the political scene. They could not have been more different. Gladstone, the son of a wealthy Scottish merchant, had had a brilliant career at Eton and Oxford and at an early age had found a seat in Parliament where he soon made his mark as a powerful orator and an excellent man of business. He was also deeply religious and a strong High Churchman. In contrast Disraeli, of Jewish origin, had had an irregular education and had had to fight hard all the way with many setbacks. He was elected to Parliament on his fifth attempt and then had had to overcome virulent opposition. As an orator and businessman he was Gladstone's inferior, but his political skills, his intuitive understanding of men and women, and his mordant wit were unsurpassed. To Gladstone a political career was a sacred calling – an opportunity to serve some great cause. To Disraeli it was 'a colourful adventure story'.

It might have been expected that Gladstone with his background would have become leader of the Tories, the party of the landed gentry and the Church of England, while Disraeli with an unorthodox upbringing and no deeply entrenched beliefs would have gravitated towards the party of reform. But by a strange quirk of fate it was the other way round. It might also have been expected that Queen Victoria would have favoured the former and been disapproving of the latter, but again it was the other way round. This was all the more strange, as the Prince Consort had spoken highly of Gladstone and had said of Disraeli that 'he had not one single element of a gentleman in his composition'.

In 1868 both men became prime minister for the first time. Gladstone pronounced at the time: 'I ascend a steepening path with a burden ever gathering weight. The Almighty seems to sustain and spare me for some purpose of his own, deeply unworthy as I know myself to be.' Disraeli said simply: 'I have climbed to the top of the greasy pole.'

It did not take Disraeli long to get the measure of the Queen: he saw that the way to her heart was by adulation of Albert, and this he laid on lavishly. 'The Prince, he wrote, 'is the only person he has ever known who realised the Ideal. No one with whom he is acquainted has ever approached it. There was in him a union of the manly grace and sublime simplicity of chivalry with the intellectual splendour of the Attic Academe.' And more in the same vein. Queen Victoria lapped it up, writing that: 'he was the only man who really appreciated her husband in his spotless and unequalled character'. There was something else about Disraeli which delighted her: his charm, lightness of touch and lucidity made the business of government not only easy but a pleasure; under his aegis the most complicated matters became clear and of interest. Unfortunately his first tenure of the premiership only lasted a few months; at the general election at the end of 1868 the Conservatives were defeated by the emerging Liberal Party led by Gladstone, which the Queen did not welcome.

Certainly Gladstone was a very different cup of tea. Public business to him was a grave and serious matter, not to be treated lightly. He had great gifts of intellect and strength of mind, but he lacked sensitivity and imagination, and he was entirely unable to understand Queen Victoria and to connect with her. When they were together he declaimed at her formally and rhetorically as if she was a public meeting. He always treated her with the greatest veneration, but could not understand that she preferred to be treated as a woman rather than an institution; and she had great difficulty in understanding the long convoluted letters he wrote to her, so that business became tedious and burdensome. Not surprisingly she wrote that: 'Disraeli's mind was so much greater, larger and apprehensive of things great and small and so much quicker than that of Gladstone.' As well as disliking Gladstone personally she was also shocked by his politics and his determination to make so many changes; and she strongly disapproved of the way he stomped the country, making impassioned speeches to massed audiences. Posterity has judged Gladstone's first ministry to have been of historic importance, pushing through urgently needed reforms in the army, the civil service, education and the legal system. But the Queen was unappreciative and relations between them were always uneasy, and when the Liberals were defeated in the general election of 1874 she welcomed Disraeli back jubilantly.

Disraeli was to be Prime Minister for the next six years and during that time he managed the Queen artfully and assiduously. He had had much experience in currying favour with elderly ladies – his whole career had been brought about by it – and he knew that they were susceptible to flattery; and with the Queen he laid it on with a trowel. He wrote:

> Mr Disraeli wonders that he should be the servant of one so great, and whose infinite kindness, the brightness of whose intelligence and the firmness of whose will have enabled him to undertake labours to which he otherwise would be quite unequal, and supported him in all things by a condescending sympathy which in the hour of difficulty alike charms and inspires.

The Queen loved it, allowing herself to be led by him and sending him bunches of primroses (his favourite flower) picked by herself, for which he thanked her ecstatically in terms of wildest hyperbole, saying 'they were more precious than rubies, a Faery gift, and came from another monarch: Queen Titania gathering flowers with her court in a soft and sea-girt isle and sending magic blossoms which, they say, turn the heads of those who receive them'.

In the course of this fanciful flirtation, however, there was at times some tension. The Queen was subject to spasms of emotion which were not easily contained. In 1875 on her insistence Disraeli proclaimed her Empress of India, although he was doubtful about the wisdom of this.[6] Her feelings were more tumultuous when Russia and Turkey went to war in 1877. The Eastern Question, as it was known, was one on which she had passionate views, despising and mistrusting the Russians who always seemed to be attempting to spread into Western Europe at the expense of the Turkish Empire, which at that time stretched over most of the Balkans. As at the time of the Crimean War she became very bellicose. 'If the Queen were a man', she wrote, 'she would like to go and give those Russians, whose words we cannot believe, such a beating.' She demanded insistently that the country go to war, and when the government held back, she uttered a dire threat:

> This delay, this uncertainty by which, abroad, we are losing our prestige and our position, while Russia is advancing and will be before Constantinople in no time! Then the government will be fearfully blamed and the Queen so humiliated that she thinks she would abdicate at once. Be bold!

---

[6] Gladstone called it 'theatrical bombast and folly'.

210

Lord Beaconsfield (as Disraeli had by then become) could not but have been shaken by such words, but he did, with difficulty, manage to pacify her until a meeting of the great powers at the Congress of Berlin where he had a notable triumph by wringing concessions out of the Russians, so that the peace of Europe was maintained.

By the time of the Congress of Berlin a new Victoria had emerged from the shadows. Gone was the mournful recluse; in its place had come a more buoyant figure. In the early 1990s she had suffered a number of misfortunes: the Prince of Wales had been cited as co-respondent in a divorce case and a year later had nearly died of typhoid fever (the same disease as had killed his father). The Queen too had been in poor health with pains in her arms and feet, and her nervous system was in a sorry state. At the same time, the country had been swept by a wave of republicanism. This had been prompted by the downfall of the French Emperor Napoleon III and his replacement by a republic in 1871, but the main cause of it was Queen Victoria herself. For ten years she had hardly appeared in public at all, and it was being said that the cost of the monarchy was out of all proportion. As one newspaper put it: 'the monarchy was forty times as much as a president would cost and for a queen they never saw'. In 1871 grants were made to two of the Queen's children, Princess Louise and Prince Arthur, and there had been some strongly worded opposition in Parliament. The Queen's finances too had come under attack. What had happened, it was asked, to the large sums of money she had been voted when nothing was spent on public ceremonies?

The Queen bitterly resented these calumnies. She wrote that she was 'a cruelly misunderstood woman', and that 'ministers, public and press were all against her. Did they not realise how she had been worn down by anxiety and hard work?' But on all sides people were urging that this work should be, in the words of Gladstone, 'more visible and more palpable'.

Republican sentiment had been significant, and extended to the well-to-do as well as the poor, but it was to vanish almost completely. This disappearance, rather strangely, began with the miraculous recovery of the Prince of Wales from typhoid which caused a surge of emotion, heightened when the Queen emerged from privacy and drove in state to a thanksgiving service in St Paul's. From then on the reaction in favour of the monarchy increased steadily as the Queen was seen more often in public, and entered a new phase when in the general election of 1874 the Conservatives were returned to power and the Queen was reunited with her beloved Beaconsfield.

Once again affairs of state became a pleasure rather than a burden; and with his encouragement she went about her duties with confidence and enjoyed being Queen again, visiting hospitals, laying foundation stones, reviewing troops and exulting in being the head of an ever-growing, multiracial empire. And it was not only in politics that her life changed: her interests expanded; her reading spread into biography and works of fiction instead of tomes on constitutional law. She even became liberated to some extent from the all-encompassing memory of Albert. Of course he was always to remain the fount of all wisdom and virtue, but she brooded on him less intently and became less bound by what he might have thought and done, and had more ideas of her own.

After the electoral defeat of the Conservatives in 1880 the Queen did all she could to prevent Gladstone from becoming prime minister again. She had been appalled by his behaviour during the Eastern Crisis when he had burst out of retirement and embarked on a tempestuous tour in Scotland known as the Midlothian Campaign, in which he had furiously denounced the Turks as 'the one great anti-human species of humanity' and attacked Beaconsfield's (and the Queen's) policy of supporting them. In her outrage the Queen declared that she would 'sooner abdicate than send for or have any communication with that half-mad firebrand who would soon ruin everything and be dictator'. But it could not be avoided. He was too mighty a political force. No one could lead the Liberal government but he. As a constitutional monarch Queen Victoria should have held the balance impartially between the political parties, but this she made no pretence at doing. When Gladstone became prime minister for the second time her treatment of him was cold and formal and she continued to communicate with Beaconsfield, writing that: 'I never write except on formal matters to the prime minister. I look always to you for ultimate help.' But this was to be available no longer after the death of Beaconsfield in 1881.

Gladstone's second ministry was to be beset by difficulties and misfortunes. Strongly opposed as he might be to colonial wars, he became involved in conflict with Egypt, mainly concerning the renunciation of the country's foreign debts; and this led to the invasion of Egypt's southern province of the Sudan and a notorious incident when General Charles Gordon, a mystic and eccentric soldier, became stranded in the Sudanese capital of Khartoum and Gladstone failed to send help in time to rescue him – to the fury of the Queen, who sent Gladstone and members of his government angry telegrams, uncoded and for all to see, expressing her outrage.

The greatest problem to afflict Gladstone, however, was the insoluble problem of Ireland, where hatred and violence were raging unabated and law and order had virtually broken down. The Queen and Gladstone were not at one in dealing with the situation. The Queen insisted that top priority be given to overcoming lawlessness by strong measures of coercion, after which some concessions might be made, while Gladstone maintained that concessions should come first and then coercion might not be necessary. Gladstone's ministry came to an end in 1886 when his bill for Irish Home Rule was defeated in Parliament– to the great satisfaction of the Queen who deplored it. From then, with two short breaks, there were to be Conservative governments for the rest of her reign, headed by Lord Salisbury, solid and wise, to whom she became almost as devoted as she had been to Beaconsfield.

In 1887 came the Queen's Golden Jubilee. It was to be an occasion of tremendous rejoicing. By then relations between Queen and people had been mended and there was a great outpouring of love and devotion. The Queen was deeply moved by it, so that her outlook on life changed. In the 1870s from the seclusion of Osborne or Balmoral she had written gloomily: 'The things of this world are of no interest to the Queen; her thoughts are fixed above.' In the 1880s her tone had changed: 'May God enable me to become worthier, less full of weakness and failings, and may he preserve me yet for some years.'

Although for most of her reign Queen Victoria was to prefer Conservative to Liberal governments, she was no hidebound reactionary. She liked to claim that no one could be 'more truly liberal at heart than herself'. But it was a cautious liberalism. She had been in favour of the Reform Bills extending the franchise so that nearly all male Britons had the right to vote, but she had reservations about universal compulsory education as this would lead to the masses becoming restless and discontented. She supported all measures aimed at promoting the welfare of women and relieving them of the drudgery and pain of their lives, but was vehemently opposed to them being given the right to vote. She wrote:

The Queen is most anxious to enlist everyone who can speak or write to join in checking this mad, wild folly of 'Women's Rights' with all its attendant horrors on which her poor feeble sex is bent, forgetting every sense of womanly feeling and propriety. Lady Amberley [a leading suffragette] ought to get a good whipping.

In matters of religion the Queen was subjective and Low Church. She disliked too much ritual and dogma and was opposed to the 'Romanising' of the Church of England. She felt more at ease in the humble parish church of Crathie in Deeside than in St Paul's or Westminster Abbey. She took to heart the dictum passed on to her by her husband that 'people should show their religion by leading moral lives not in slavishly attending services in church'.

The Queen's liberal ways were evident too in her relationship with humble folk, particularly Scottish humble folk. She felt more at ease with the crofters and ghillies[7] of Balmoral than in the well-to-do smart society favoured by the Prince of Wales. To one ghillie she became closely attached. No one could have been more different from fawning, flattering politicians than John Brown – rugged, blunt, treating the Queen as an equal and peremptorily ordering her about. There were those in her entourage who were appalled at such treatment of the great Queen-Empress, but she seemed not to mind it, even to relish it. Certainly she made no attempt to conceal her special relationship with him, taking him with her everywhere, not only on Highland picnics but even to ceremonies of state. Inevitably this gave rise to ribaldry in some quarters and there were crude jokes about 'Mrs Brown'. But to the more imaginative it was inconceivable that there was anything improper in their relationship and it was understandable that the Queen should delight in the company of a simple, straightforward character, totally loyal and unpretentious and giving himself no airs and graces. She let it be known that Brown was her 'confidential servant' because of his particular gift of insight and understanding, and to those who suggested that their relationship was 'inexpedient' she replied that she saw things in black and white and 'expediency' was a word unknown to her. Later, after the death of Brown, she was to show similar favour to one of her Indian servants, Abdul Karim

---

[7] A ghillie is one in attendance on fishing and shooting parties.

known as 'The Munshi'. Once again tongues wagged and once again the Queen took no notice.

In 1896 Queen Victoria became the longest-reigning monarch in English history, and in the following year came her Diamond Jubilee, by when she had become a legend. People marvelled that a little old lady of 78 in widow's weeds and bonnet and shawl with simple domestic tastes should be at the head of the world's greatest empire and should wield such widespread influence. By then she had descendants in most of the courts of Europe, all of whom regarded her with awe and treated her every word as oracular.

During the last years of her life, however, clouds were to gather. In her vast empire minor troubles were always liable to break out, but at the end of the century there was a serious disaster in South Africa. War between Boers and Britons had been brewing there for some time. At the heart of the matter lay the ambition of Cecil Rhodes and other imperialists to extend British rule in South Africa as far north as possible, stretching eventually from the Cape to Cairo. But in the way of this dream lay the Boer republics of the Transvaal and the Orange Free State, which wanted to have nothing to do with Rhodes and his empire building.

War finally broke out at the end of 1899, and at first the Boers carried all before them, invading the British colonies of Natal and Cape Colony and threatening to drive the British out of South Africa altogether. This caused surprise and dismay in England, and there was some talk of making a conciliatory peace. But such ideas were put aside, it being insisted that anything smacking of defeat at the hands of a small insignificant country would be a calamitous blow to British prestige.

Foremost among the hawks was the Queen, who whatever the rights and wrongs of the case might be, would not hear of anything but complete victory. We are not interested in the possibilities of defeat,' she declared. 'They do not exist.' At the time she was 81, racked with rheumatism and with failing eyesight, but she spared herself no pains, reviewing troops about to set out and giving them heart and comforting their families left behind. She even visited Ireland, where she had not been for nearly 40 years, as a mark of gratitude to the numerous volunteers who had joined the army. Thus exhorted, the government bent to its task and despatched massive reinforcements (which included troops from the newly self-governing colonies of Canada, Australia and New Zealand). This proved decisive and the Boers were overwhelmed by such mighty forces.

By the summer of 1900 their armies had been defeated and their territories occupied; but the war was to drag on for two more years as the Boers resorted to guerrilla warfare which was difficult to combat. Eventually it was overcome but only by employing brutal and what some people considered barbarous tactics, burning Boer farms and rounding up the inhabitants into 'concentration camps'.[8]

The Boer War did lasting harm to Britain's reputation. It was to be seen that victory at such a cost was as damaging as a defeat. It marked the beginning of the end of the British Empire. In France and Germany particularly there were vitriolic attacks on the way the Boers had been treated, and the Queen herself was subject to scurrilous and abusive language, blighting the end of her life.

This was to come on 21 January 1901. For some months her powers had been declining and she died peacefully at Osborne surrounded by her family, including the Kaiser, in tears and visibly moved. The news of her death was received by the public with stunned disbelief. Most people had not known a time when she was not the reigning monarch. She had been thought immortal and life without her seemed unimaginable. Something irreplaceable had disappeared.

---

[8] These must be distinguished from those of Nazi Germany. Although conditions in them were dreadful and there were many deaths, there was no programme of extermination.

FURTHER READING

CLEOPATRA

Bradford, Ernie, *Cleopatra* (Hodder and Stoughton, 1971)
Chauveau, M, *Cleopatra – Beyond the Myth* (Cornell, 2002)
Hughes-Hallet, Lucy, Cleopatra – *Histories, Dreams and Distortions* (Bloomsbury, 1990)
Kleiner, D, *Cleopatra and Rome* (Belknap, Harvard, 2005)
Tyldesley, Joyce, *Cleopatra: Last Queen of Egypt* (Profile, 2008)

MARY QUEEN OF SCOTS

Fraser, Antonia, *Mary Queen of Scots* (Weidenfeld and Nicolson, 1969)
Graham, Roderick, *Life of Mary Queen of Scots – An Accidental Tragedy* (Birlinn, 2008)
Mackay, James, *In My End is My Beginning – A Life of Mary Queen of Scots* (Mainstream, 1999)

CATHERINE DE MEDICI

Frieda, Leonie, *Catherine de Medici* (Weidenfeld and Nicolson, 2003)
Heritier, Jean, *Catherine de Medici* (Allen and Unwin, 1963)
Knecht, R J, *Catherine de Medici* (Longman, 1998)

CHRISTINA QUEEN OF SWEDEN

Compton Mackenzie, Faith, *The Sibyll of the North – The Tale of Christina Queen of Sweden* (Cassell, 1931)
Masson, Georgina, *Queen Christina* (Secker and Warburg, 1968)

QUEEN ELIZABETH

Neale, J E, *Queen Elizabeth* I (Cape 1934)

Perry, M, *The Word of a Prince – Life of Elizabeth I from Contemporary Documents* (Folio Society, 1990)

Ridley, Jasper, *Elizabeth I* (Constable, 1987)

Strachey, Lyttton, *Elizabeth and Essex– A Tragic History* (Chatto and Windus, 1928)

TSARINA CATHERINE I

Anderson, M S, *Peter the Great* (Thames and Hudson, 1978)

Longworth, Philip, *The Three Empresses* (Constable, 1972)

MARIA THERESA

Moffat, M M, *Maria Theresa* (Methuen, 1911)

Morris, C L, *Maria Theresa* (Eyre and Spottiswoode, 1938)

MARIE ANTOINETTE

Erickson, Carolly, *To the Scaffold, Life of Marie Antoinette* (Robson, 1992)

Mayer, D M, *The Tragic Queen – Marie Antoinette* (Weidenfeld and Nicolson, 1968)

CATHERINE THE GREAT

Almedingen, E M, *Catherine the Great* (Hutchinson, 1963)

Anthony, Katharine, *Catherine the Great* (Jonathan Cape, 1931)

Coughlan, Robert, *Elizabeth and Catherine, Empresses of All the Russias* (MacDonald and Jane's, 1975)

Cronin, Vincent, *Catherine Empress of All the Russias* (HarperCollins, 1978)

EMPRESS JOSEPHINE

Bruce, E, *Napoleon and Josephine – An Improbable Marriage* (Weidenfeld and Nicolson, 1995)

Cole, Hubert, *Josephine* (Heinemann, 1962)

Epton, Nina, *The Empress and Her Children* (Weidenfeld and Nicolson, 1975)

Erickson, Carolly, *Josephine* (Robson, 1999)

QUEEN VICTORIA

Bolitho, Hector, *Victoria – The Widow and Her Son* (Cobden-Sanderson, 1934)

Fulford, Roger, *The Prince Consort* (Macmillan, 1949)

Longford, Elizabeth, *Victoria RI* (Weidenfeld and Nicolson, 1964)

Lytton, Strachey, *Queen Victoria* (Chatto and Windus, 1921)

INDEX

221